W9-BQY-363

DREAM JOBS

A Guide to Tomorrow's Top Careers

ROBERT W. BLY AND GARY BLAKE

A Wiley Press Book
JOHN WILEY & SONS, INC.
New York • Chichester • Brisbane • Toronto • Singapore

Library of Congress Cataloging in Publication Data:

Bly, Robert W.
  Dream jobs.

  (Wiley self-teaching guides)
  Includes index.
  1. Vocational guidance. 2. Occupations. I. Blake,
Gary. II. Title.
HF5382.B56   1983   331.7'02   83–6773

ISBN 0–471–89204–1

Printed in the United States of America

84 85 10 9 8 7 6 5 4 3 2 1

Again, for Amy
—RWB

For Dr. Stephen Aaron
—GB

Acknowledgements

We would like to thank the following people for taking the time to talk with us about what they do.

Hugh Farrell, Hammond Farrell, Inc.
Amil Gargano, Ally & Gargano, Inc.
Jane Trahey, Trahey Advertising
Stephen N. Finkel, The Direct Marketing Group
Burt Manning, J. Walter Thompson
Lisa Chu, Control Data Corporation
Thomas B. Sprecher, Professional Management Group
Richard Donovan, Rodenberg/Richardson
Ralph Windel, author of *Boardroom Ballads*
Bridgford Hunt, The Hunt Company
Jean Blake, Bon Bon Travel
Adele Gross, Bon Bon Travel
Lucyna Von Schlossberg, Lexington Travel
Richard Stern, Richard B. Stern Associates
Joan Rodenberg, Rodenberg/Richardson
William McCulloch, William McCulloch Associates
Jon Isear
John Goodfriend
Brett Caine
Michael Stephens
Gary Rubin
Gloria Michaels
Evelyn Kanter
Robin Weber
Tricia Page
Wesley Masters

Thanks also to our editor, Alicia Conklin, and to our agent, Dominick Abel.

Introduction

Most Americans define themselves by their work. It's part of the puritan work ethic that we are what we do.

Is it any wonder, then, that we spend so much of our time looking for work, getting used to our jobs, striving for promotion, planning our careers, and keeping our resumes updated? Regardless of the state of the economy, most of us realize that work can be exciting, well-paying, and fun—*if* we have the right job.

Dream Jobs is a career guide to nine glamorous, fast-growing, "in the news" industries—businesses that can offer you challenging, rewarding, lucrative careers. Some—computers, cable TV, advertising, public relations, consulting, and travel—you've probably heard of and want to know more about. Three others—training and development, telecommunications, and biotechnology—may be less familiar to you, but they're just as exciting, and they're growing just as fast.

How did we come to select these particular fields? Simple. We studied the help-wanted ads, paid attention to the news, and talked with job-hunters, executive recruiters, and career counselors. We found nine industries that were "hot" in the sense that they had more career opportunities and challenges to offer ambitious, energetic people than many other, more traditional fields. Here's a quick preview of what you'll learn about:

- **Cable TV.** Television is a glamorous industry, but it has always been tough to break into. With the recent cable explosion, the inexperienced and untrained can now get jobs involved with producing shows, packaging programs, or selling cable services.

- **Computers.** "Computers" is as much a career buzzword of the 80s as "plastics" was in the 60s. Data processing is one of the five fastest-growing industries of the decade, and we'll tell nontechnical people how they can break into this high-paying, high-tech field.

- **Training and Development.** With $30 billion a year spent on employee training, training and development is the "sleeping giant" of the corporate world. We'll show teachers, businesspeople, and students how they can apply their teaching skills to big business and earn far more than they would in academia.

- **Biotechnology.** Cloning is now science fact, not science fiction, and industry is seeking thousands of engineers, biologists, and chemists to put genetic engineering theories into full-scale production in many areas, including pollution control, medicine, agriculture, and chemical processing. More than 300 corporations are already gearing up for the coming biotechnology boom. We'll show you who they are and how to get a job with them.

- **Consulting.** If you're a self-starter with ideas and expertise to sell, consulting for big corporations can earn you $500 a day or more. We'll tell you how to go about it the right way.

- **Advertising.** A perennial favorite for young, bright, energetic people. We'll tell you how to get a foot in the door, how to move up the ladder, which agencies are hot, and which are not.

- **Public Relations.** Another communications-oriented industry open to aggressive, bright beginners. We'll tell you how to promote your own public rleations career as effectively as a PR agency promotes its clients.

- **Travel.** If prospects of self-employment and trips to faraway places sound enticing, a career as an independent travel agent may be the dream job for you. Tips from the pros will tell you how to get there in style.

- **Telecommunications.** American business wastes $3–4

billion a year on poorly managed corporate communications systems. A good telecommunications manager can cut his company's communications expenses by 15 to 20 percent or more. And that kind of performance is richly rewarded. We'll introduce management-minded readers to this fast-growing, high-paying, but under-publicized field.

With one exception—biotechnology—*you don't need a technical degree or other special training to succeed in these fields.* This book examines each industry with an eye toward how liberal arts majors and other nonspecialists can break into the business and rise to the top. In data processing, for example, we focus on careers in computer *sales*, not programming, because sales and marketing is one area within data processing where you can earn an impressive income without an in-depth technical knowledge of computer programming. Or consider our aproach to cable TV—we'll show how a background with a general consumer goods company can get you into show business quicker and easier than a knowledge of TV and film production can.

Because we have had experience in eight of these nine fields, we felt we could get to the sources of accurate, detailed, and relevant information. We interviewed top executives, recruiters, recently hired employees, students, and other people who talked candidly about the pros and cons of each industry. We combed the library for the most pertinent books, articles, and company literature in these fields. We sought out information about salaries, job descriptions, training programs, employment opportunities, trade associations, professional journals, buzzwords, and career planning. We then knit all these facts together into chapters that will give you the flavor, as well as the facts, about each industry. Where appropriate, we have also included examples of resumes, cover letters, help-wanted ads, wage formulas, slogans, and the clothing appropriate to a particular field.

If you're looking for a down-to-earth survey of nine exciting fields, you've come to the right book. We have spared you the usual "rah-rah" kind of career writing, and have tried to include only those items that will help both entry-level job-seekers and more experienced career-changers break into and make it in the industry of their choice.

Of course, no authors, no experts, and no book can provide a magic formula that gets you the job you dream of. We can only supply advice, information, and the counsel of people who have already made it to where you want to be.

How, then, do you get that dream job? First you must set your sights on the career, company, and job that you want. Then it takes patience, perseverance, hard work, and a bit of luck and timing to achieve your goal.

This book can only point the way.

The rest is up to *you*.

Contents

Advertising

IN GENERAL

There's an old joke about the high visibility of an advertising professional's work: "Lawyers file their mistakes and doctors bury them, but advertising people publish theirs."

Advertising is a highly visible, highly creative, and highly idiosyncratic industry where the idea—or, in advertising jargon, the *concept*—is king. Simple minded as some of these concepts may seem ("Coke is it," "Aren't you hungry for Burger King now?," "GE: We bring good things to life"), top advertising people are paid five- and six-figure salaries to create and execute advertising campaigns for television, radio, newspapers, and magazines.

In 1981, the major advertisers spent more than $35 billion on advertising, and they didn't run all those costly commercials just to satisfy their egos. The object of advertising is never art, entertainment, or even information, say the experts. Such things are just means to an end; the end is increased sales, and thereby higher profits, for the advertisers. As marketing expert John E. Kennedy says, advertising is "salesmanship in print."[1]

Interestingly, advertising agencies seem to suffer less from slowdowns in the economy than do their clients. *Fortune* magazine (9-6-82, p.7) reports: "Advertising shows signs of being a recession-resistant industry these days. Corporate America has turned in dismal second-quarter earnings, but most of Madison Avenue eked out at least modest profit increases." Some increases have been more than modest. At BBDO, Inc., the nation's sixth-largest agency, business was up

12 percent in 1981. Interpublic, the parent company of Mc-Cann-Erickson, Inc. and SSC&B-Cintas, showed a profit increase of 40 percent. Thus, advertising, traditionally seen as an unstable industry offering little job security, may be one of the safest places to work in the recession-plagued 80s.

Let's take a quick look at what ad agency people do and what they get paid for doing it. (The salary figures quoted here are from *Adweek* magazine's 1982 Salary Survey Report.)

Account executives are the agency's representatives to the client. The account exec's job is to understand the client's marketing problems and explain them to the agency's "creative department" so that they can come up with advertisements to solve these problems. For these services, account execs earn anywhere from $15,000 to $65,000 a year, with $27,000 the average.

It is in the *creative department* that ads and commercials are conceived and executed. *Copywriters*, the people who write the advertising, earn an average salary of $27,000 a year. Junior copywriters start in the high teens, and seasoned pros can earn well over $60,000 a year.

Art directors, who design the ads, earn $25,000 to $45,000 and average about $28,000. *Television producers*, who make the commercials, earn $25,000 to $60,000. And *creative directors*, the managers who supervise copywriters, art directors, and other creative people, earn an average yearly salary of $38,000, with top creative directors earning $80,000 and more.

The *traffic manager* keeps track of all projects going on in the agency, coordinates the flow of work, and makes sure deadlines are met. This position offers broad exposure to all departments in the agency. The traffic manager at a medium-size agency can earn between $15,000 and $20,000 a year. It's a good entry-level position for aspiring account executives or production managers.

The *print production manager* oversees the production and printing of ads, brochures, billboards, and other print promotions. He or she must be knowledgeable in printing, typography, paper stock, photoengraving, and all other facets of graphic arts production. The average salary for a production manager is $26,300, with experienced managers earning salaries in the mid- to upper-$40,000 range.

Now, back to the business side of advertising. *Media planners*, the people who decide in what programs and publications to run commercials and ads, earn average yearly salaries of $18,700. *Marketing research directors*, who design surveys and other studies to find out the characteristics of the perfect cola drinker, hamburger buyer, or what have you, earn $25,000 to $35,000 a year.

Of course, the people at the top—the president, the chairman, or the chief executive officer—carn the highest salaries. Paul C. Harper, Jr., Chairman/Chief Executive Officer of Needham, Harper, and Steers, earns $322,000. Bruce Crawford, President/Chief Executive Officer of BBDO, Inc., makes over $500,000 a year. And Grey Advertising Chairman Edward H. Meyer's annual salary is just shy of the $1 million dollar mark.

The *Adweek* survey also mentions a couple of factors that influence salaries. Generally, they increase with the size of the agency and the farther east it is located. So, a creative director at New York City's Young & Rubicam, Inc. (the United States' largest agency) may earn two or three times as much as a creative director at a small agency in the South or Midwest.

The *Standard Directory of Advertising Agencies* (also known as *The Agency Red Book*) lists more than 4,400 agencies in 50 states. These firms employ a total of 100,000 advertising professionals. The rest of this chapter will tell you how you can become advertising professional number 100,001.

WHAT IT TAKES

Unlike law, medicine, or corporate management, the road to advertising success is not well defined. There is no undergraduate course of study for aspiring copywriters and creative directors that is equivalent to prelaw or premed programs. In fact, a young copywriter recently said that one of the things she loves about the business is that no one she knows actually *planned* to become an "ad man."

What, then, is the ideal education for a career in advertising? Is it a broad course of liberal study or a firm background in business? The answers from professionals vary, but most do hold a liberal arts degree in high esteem. (The following quotes are assembled from interviews with and articles by top people in the advertising industry.)

"The best academic education for cub writers is to teach them to read books and to write Petrarchan sonnets."[2]

"A good business background is probably more beneficial than wandering through the halls of Plato."

"The large agencies with package goods accounts are looking primarily at MBA's. I'm not sure that an MBA by definition makes anybody qualified for this business because you have to be *in* the business to learn how to function effectively."

"Women should take economics, accounting. If you take stained glass windows in the early Renaissance period, you're limiting yourself. A degree in finance is much more useful. You must understand finance to be in the advertising business, to be an account executive."

"I think there's no substitute for a liberal arts education. I think that people in the advertising business who are very successful are people who can do a great many things well."

"You can bring any number of backgrounds to advertising, which makes it kind of interesting. A liberal arts degree would probably suit you more appropriately for the long term because it provides a greater understanding of the world."

"We've hired a newspaperman, a laundromat owner, a novelist, a salesman, and a secretary as copywriters. It doesn't matter what education and experience you have, as long as you're good."

"I don't think a lot of people will take chances on people without something that's all very well circumscribed—resume, credentials, references, and education all perfect is a very easy hire."

"I'm interested in people who bring an unusual background to their work—somebody who looks at the world in a way that is indeed correct, but somehow different."

"Show me what you can do for me. Show me how you translate the *features* of your resume—education, courses, extra-curricular activitives—into benefits you'll bring to the agency."

"You need a very fertile mind, a very imaginative sense, and a good sense of what is going to turn people on as far as consumers are concerned. College should teach you how to think as a creative person."

The late William Bernbach, cofounder and former Chairman of Doyle Dane Bernbach, Inc. (the agency that handles Volkswagen and Polaroid, among others), was often quoted as saying, "Rules are death in the advertising business." And while formulas are no substitute for wit, ability, and a desire for hard work, dozens of interviews with advertising professionals who have "made it" in the business seem to indicate that there *is* a best way to make it to the top. This suggested career path, a four-point plan for success, is outlined below:

1. *Get a solid background in the liberal arts.* Learn history, philosophy, psychology, science, and basic math. Study politics and sociology. Read the classics. But don't become merely a depository for facts. Use college to learn how to think and write clearly and creatively. And it helps to squeeze in some business courses— marketing, management, advertising, economics, accounting, and finance—that apply directly to an advertising career.

   Naturally, specialists need special skills. A copywriter must be a skilled writer. An illustrator must be able to draw. A television director must have a thorough knowledge of film and video production.

2. *Start at a smaller agency to gain broad experience.* "People beginning in the business should try, initially, to work for a small to medium-size agency because they'll get exposed to more people in different functions," says Hugh Farrell, President of Hammond Farrell, Inc., in New York. "And they'll get a chance to see first-hand what each department does."

   The experts agree that the more you know—about both the agency's and the client's business—the more you'll grow. Starting at a small shop will give you exposure to more agency functions, since an employee at any small company must handle a variety of tasks, whereas people at large corporations must usually specialize in one narrow discipline or department.

"I don't think anybody coming right out of school should decide exactly what it is they want to do in this business," adds Farrell. "They need to investigate the various disciplines in advertising—media, art direction, copywriting, account management, marketing research, and so on."

3. *Obtain a position where you can learn and grow.* The pivotal point in a young ad man or woman's career comes when he or she is employed by someone who can teach them the business. Your position under this mentor should be one in which you can grow within the company and be promoted into a higher position that other ad people respect.

4. *Climb up the ladder at a big agency. Or, become a high-paid specialist at a big agency. But don't end up at a small company.* There are two ladders that lead to success in advertising. One involves taking on more and more managerial responsibility and moving up in title from copywriter to group supervisor to department head to vice president to executive vice president. The second is to become so good at your specialty—writing, art, account management, or research—that you can command a top salary without sacrificing *doing* for *managing.*

But whichever path you choose, manager or specialist, do it at one of the top agencies. "Avoid ending up at an obscure little agency," warns Amil Gargano, President of Ally & Gargano, Inc., in New York. "People are affected by credentials." The experts say that you shouldn't spend too much time doing tiny print ads for unknown accounts at unknown agencies. Making the jump to a "name" agency will become more and more difficult as your age and experience increase.

So, make the move to a top shop fairly early on in your career. By having some previous experience at a smaller agency or related industry, you can join a big agency at a higher than entry-level position, thus eliminating additional years of trainee and apprentice-type positions.

GETTING STARTED

There are three things to bring with you on the interviews for your first job (and every job) in advertising: you, your resume, and, if you're a creative person, your portfolio.

The portfolio—also known as the "book"—is a sample case of the things you've written, designed, drawn, supervised, managed, or whatever it is you do. Maxine Paetro's book, *How to Put Your Book Together and Get a Job in Advertising* (Hawthorn Books), will tell you everything you want to know about the technical details of assembling the book—what kind of portfolio case to use, whether or not to put your name on the outside of the portfolio, and how to arrange your material. These details are important, to be sure, but they are not the key issue here.

What *is* essential, according to Amil Gargano, is that the portfolio reflect the best creative work you can do. "If your published ads are boring, why bother to show them?" asks Gargano, whose own agency is responsible for the entertaining commercials of Federal Express and MCI Communications.[3] "I'd like to have people show me things that *they* feel good about, not things that somebody else feels good about."

But what if the ads you designed for the school paper or local community shopper are just plain dull? Or what if you've never done any ads at all? Gargano suggests you create some ads on your own so that you'll have a portfolio that shows what you can do. One exercise he recommends is to flip through some magazines, select half a dozen ads that could stand some improvement, and rewrite or redesign them to create new ads that are better than the originals. Then put the "before" and "after" versions of each ad side-by-side in your portfolio to show to prospective employers.

Whit Hobbs, an advertising consultant and columnist for *Adweek* magazine, doesn't believe that your book has to be restricted to advertisements if you're a novice in the field. "Bring me something you've written or drawn that *you* think is good, that you're proud of, that is the best you can do," writes Hobbs in *Adweek* (3-3-80, p.12). "I'm interested in how you perform in an area where you know exactly what you're doing.

It's up to *me* to make the judgment: Will the person who wrote these pieces for the college paper, or this short story, or these lyrics, or did these sketches or these charming little spots be a good creative person in advertising?"

Writers and artists aren't the only people who can make use of a portfolio. If you're a media person, bring along some media schedules you planned, along with the results of the campaign, if available. Likewise, a market researcher can include surveys, reports, questionnaires, and other material he or she has created.

Oddly, most agency execs warn newcomers that their creativity should be limited to the samples in their portfolios. Their resumes should look like that of *any* business person. They should be organized, neat, professional, and concise; not flashy, cute, or clever.

"Don't submit a 'creative' resume," instructs Hugh Farrell, whose own agency, Hammond Farrell, Inc., produces highly effective advertising for RCA, General Electric, Research-Cottrell, and other major firms. "We don't read resumes to be entertained. The resume should be brief, and simply state the facts. The cover letter should make it clear you know the nature of the agency you're applying to and, in brief form, why you think you're right for that company. I think it can be nice to have something that's a *little* bit distinctive so that it sticks out of a pile of resumes, whether it is a buff or gray or pink-colored paper stock."

Madison Avenue's flashy image may lead some outsiders to make the false assumption that the advertising industry is less professional and businesslike than, for example, insurance or investment banking. While advertising is certainly less stuffy and mundane than many other occupations, don't make the mistake of thinking of an advertising agency as a refuge for artists or writers who hate to wear three-piece suits and can't hack it in a corporation. To try to create the image of a freewheeling, devil-may-care creative maverick is largely a mistake, especially for beginners. Agencies seek young people who are professional, businesslike, and interested in how they can use their intelligence, imagination, and talent to help the agency serve its clients better. "Be businesslike," Whit Hobbs instructs job-seekers. "Agency people are busy, they're under pressure, they don't have time for kid stuff."

As in other industries, being businesslike means sending out neatly typed, letter-perfect resumes and cover letters. *All* agency executives we spoke with lamented the declining writing skills of today's college graduates, and none will hire a candidate who shows signs of this in his or her application for a job. "The resume and cover letter should be completely devoid of any typos, misspellings, or grammar mistakes," says Farrell. "Those mistakes are the kiss of death." Farrell says he will not consider hiring a candidate if there is even a single typo in the letter or resume. Being businesslike also means being prompt and well dressed for job interviews. It means being able to articulate—both on paper and in person—who you are, what you have done, and what you can do in the job you seek in an interesting, clear fashion.

Some additional advice on job interviews:

> "I don't think anybody should dress for an effect. Your outfit should be comfortable, not jarring" —Hugh Farrell.

> "Your best shot at an interview is being yourself. If you pretend to be somebody else, it's not going to get you very far, because eventually you're going to have to revert to what you are, and if you're showing a false front and that's what got you hired, you're going to get caught" —Amil Gargano.

> "Look good. Businesslike. Serious. The fact is, people— all people—are strongly influenced by first impressions. And the first look at you will disclose that 90 percent of the real you is covered by clothes. So dress accordingly. Argue about the hypocrisy after you get a job" —Philip Karch and Thomas Hagan, Karch and Hagan Advertising, Englewood, Colorado.[4]

> "Use any connection you can to get in. Go to the space salesman, the printers. Find a resource to somehow get in the door" —Jane Trahey, Trahey Advertising, New York and Chicago.

> "Most people are their own worst enemies in getting hired. They talk too much, they don't answer the questions succinctly . . . They speak about extraneous things that

have absolutely nothing to do with the situation. They name drop when it's not necessary" —Eugene Judd, President, Judd-Falk, Inc. (the nation's largest executive search firm specializing in recruitment of marketing and advertising executives.)[5]

"Give me reasons to buy . . . Convince the interviewer that you are that rare bird—someone who will give 100 percent, 100 percent of the time. You have to sell dedication because you don't have any experience" —Charles Coffey, Jr., President, Weightman Advertising, Philadelphia.[6]

"Follow-up. I've made room in my day for you, at least take the time to drop me a note and say thanks. It's not simply a matter of courtesy (which does impress me), but it's also a way of making a good impression stick" —Paula Green, Director, Paula Green, Inc., New York.[7]

If there is a "style" that describes the ideal candidate for a career in advertising, it can be summed up in a few adjectives—creative, self-confident, enthusiastic, and above all else, businesslike and professional. Your prospective employers want you to be yourself, and they don't recommend that you put on any false fronts to impress them. But be forewarned—it *is* a mistake to set aside the conventions of proper business etiquette because you assume that advertising is more of a "creative playground" than a corporation. Advertising may be more fun than other industries, but as we have said, it is a multibillion dollar business that demands the same attitudes, dress, and proper behavior as insurance, accounting, and other more traditional areas of employment.

However, because of its highly visible nature and high regard for bright ideas, advertising is less conservative than most other industries. Hence, your tactic in an interview or cover letter should be to put your best foot forward—without having it end up in your mouth. Brashness, confidence, even a little *chutzpah*[8] are fine, as long as they're tempered with maturity and an awareness of what to bring to the job—and the job interview.

Okay. Let's say you're ready to start sending out resumes and going on interviews, but you don't know where the jobs are. Here are a few sources and suggestions you will find interesting and helpful (complete information on all directories, books, and magazines referred to in the text is provided in the box titled "To Read"):

- As we've mentioned, the *Standard Directory of Advertising Agencies* lists about 4,400 ad agencies—4,400 potential employers for you. Agencies are listed alphabetically and indexed by state. Listings include the names of key personnel, gross income, and major accounts. *The Agency Red Book* is an excellent starting place for any letter-writing campaign.
- Your local *Yellow Pages* lists most of the agencies in your area. The only disadvantage is that the *Yellow Pages* doesn't list the names of the *people* you should write to. Of course, a phone call is all it takes to get that additional information.
- Two magazines, *Advertising Age* and *Adweek*, contain weekly "help-wanted" ads. *Adweek* has a "positions-wanted" section which runs classified ads from unemployed advertising people seeking work. You, too, can take advantage of this—and the first two weeks of advertising are *free!* Both magazines also publish annual directories of the major advertising agencies.
- *The Creative Black Book* (Friendly Publications) lists thousands of advertising agencies, printers, art studios, photographers, TV production companies, and other advertising-related businesses. It's an excellent source of prospects, especially for someone considering a career outside of traditional advertising agencies (a production person might prefer to work for a print shop, for example).

To Read

We asked Burt Manning, Vice-Chairman of J. Walter Thompson, what books on advertising he recommends to young people entering the business. Mr. Manning cited the following three works (all published by Crain Books, 740 N. Rush St., Chicago, IL 60611):

Creating Effective TV Commercials by Huntley Baldwin. How commercials are made.

A Technique for Producing Ideas by James Webb Young. A step-by-step procedure by which you can produce ideas on command. A proven technique for understanding and mastering the creative process.

How to Become an Advertising Man by James Webb Young. How to succeed in advertising by being *good* at it.

We'd like to add two selections of our own to the book list:

How to Put Your Book Together and Get a Job in Advertising by Maxine Paetro, New York, NY: Hawthorn Books. How to break into the business, put together a portfolio, and get your first job in advertising. This book is mainly for creative types such as artists and copywriters.

Confessions of an Advertising Man by David Ogilvy, New York, NY: Atheneum. A highly idiosyncratic view of the advertising business by one of its most successful practitioners. Great reading.

Books provide an overview, but in advertising, as in *any* industry, trade magazines keep you up-to-date on current events and trends. Two magazines that are "must read" are:

Advertising Age, 740 N. Rush St., Chicago, IL 60611. A thick weekly news tabloid that covers, in great detail, the goings-on of the advertising industry both on and off Madison Avenue.

Adweek, 820 Second Ave., New York, NY 10017. *Adweek* is published weekly in five regional editions that focus on news concerning your own particular corner of the country. In addition, *Adweek's* smaller magazine-size pages, concise format, and lively columns make it easier to read and somehow less formidable than its ponderous competitor.

Other magazines that might interest you include:

Marketing Communications, 475 Park Ave. South, New York, NY 10016. All about retail advertising and promotion. Monthly.

Business Marketing, 220 East 42nd St., New York, NY 10017. For people involved with advertising and marketing of industrial and high-technology products and services. Monthly.

Direct Marketing, 224 7th St., Garden City, NY 11530. The magazine of direct response advertising (mail order and direct mail). Monthly.

Madison Avenue Magazine, 369 Lexington Ave., New York, NY

10017. A magazine about advertising and the ad agency business. Monthly.

Magazine Age, 6931 Van Nuys Blvd., Van Nuys, CA 91405. All about advertising in magazines. Runs a lot of good "how-to" articles. Monthly.

Marketing & Media Decisions, 342 Madison Ave., New York, NY 10017. Focuses on the "numbers" aspect of advertising—marketing, market research, media planning—rather than on the creative. Published 14 times a year.

There is also one important industry directory you should know about:

The Standard Directory of Advertising Agencies: The Agency Red Book, National Register Publishing Co., Inc., 5201 Old Orchard Rd., Skokie, Il 60077. Published and updated three times a year. Lists all important agencies and their personnel, offices, and clients. Most libraries have *The Agency Red Book* in the reference section; if you know someone in an advertising agency, he or she will surely have access to a copy.

YOUR FIRST BIG BREAK

In some businesses, the first goal to shoot for, "the first big break," is as clear as day. If you're an actor, it's getting your first speaking role on television, in the movies, or maybe on Broadway. To a writer, it's a first published article, a first book, or a first best-seller.

But what about advertising people? Is the first big break your first job? Or the first *good* job? How about the first job working at a major agency? Or is it writing your first commercial and seeing it aired on the *Tonight Show?*

"A good break is getting a job reporting to someone from who you can learn prodigiously, and from which you can get promoted to a better job at that first agency," answered Hugh Farrell when asked to define the *first big break.* Farrell also offered a second definition: "The first time you are promoted into a job that has stature in the minds of the people you hope to work for someday."

One young copywriter, now successfully freelancing for New

York advertising agencies, reports that *his* first big break came not on the agency side, but on the advertiser side. "My first job was my first big break. I was working for an electronics manufacturer, writing sales brochures," says Bob. "My boss there was a real pro, with some 20 years in the business. He gave writing seminars throughout the country and had even written a book on writing. When I went into the position, I knew nothing about sales, advertising, marketing, or even how to write persuasively, clearly, and concisely. When I left a year later, I had learned in 12 months what college or any other position couldn't give me in a decade. Life in that job was essentially a free education, 8 hours a day, 5 days a week."

Oddly, obtaining a position with a major agency is *not* always a first big break leading to bigger and better things. Nancy, just out of college, landed a job in the media department of Young & Rubicam, Inc., a $2 billion a year organization with over 6,861 employees. Initially overjoyed at making the big-time so early in the game, Nancy found that when she quickly outgrew the entry-level job she'd been hired to do, the agency was not ready to move her up. And so, she left the prestige and glory of Madison Avenue within a year to take on a position at a small, unknown agency in New Jersey. For the time being, she's happy. The new agency is giving her all the responsibility she can handle, and a great education in the process.

WHAT TO SHOOT FOR

The theme to the TV series *The Jeffersons* speaks of "moving on up" to the East Side. But George Jefferson owns a dry cleaning business. How does a young copywriter or account executive move to the better positions at the bigger agencies in the advertising world? Burt Manning, Vice-Chairman of J. Walter Thompson Company (and Chief Executive Officer of J. Walter Thompson USA), the second largest advertising agency in the country, did it in a rather unconventional way:

"Unlike a lot of people who have been successful in business, I've focused almost exclusively on the immediate assignment or project in hand," says Manning. "My mode of operation was to take whatever that assignment was and try to do it better than it had ever been done before in the history of the world. That was it. Then I'd try to do the next one the best. The projects, in my mind, were never a means to an end—they *were* the end."

Manning, who started out as an aspiring novelist and never attended college, feels that today's young advertising professionals spend too much time planning their careers and not enough time doing their jobs. At his agency, performance is rewarded, because "when you're really good and productive, what you do gets noticed." Career planning, he feels, is something one should do after hours.

Despite his high position and lofty set of titles, Manning still devotes himself to the creative rather than the administrative aspects of advertising. His agencies' current campaigns include Burger King, Pepsi, Chevron, the American Red Cross, and Oscar Mayer.

Like many top executives in advertising, Mr. Manning advises newcomers to shoot for the big agencies—J. Walter Thompson, of course, or one of the other top 10 (listed in the box titled "The Top 10 Advertising Agencies in America Today"). Simply put, these agencies do better work for better clients and pay better salaries. Working on a national account—such as Ford, Philip Morris, or Mobil Oil—gets your work into the sight of other people in the business. But no one will be likely to see or care about the 4 × 6 inch ad for ball bearings you designed for an engineering magazine.

In the advertising industry, there are first-class agencies and second-class agencies, filled with first- and second-class people. Aim to work at a first-class agency. It isn't any harder to get into a good agency than a poor one, and you'll become a better advertising professional because you'll be working with first-rate people.

This advice applies even if you don't want to move to New York or some other major hub of advertising. Jane Trahey, President of Trahey Advertising, advises young people to "seek out the best agency in your city—there are certain agencies that have clout and are well known for producing a good product. If I were a young person who wanted to work in the ad business, I would do anything to work in one. If you stick with it long enough," Trahey continued, "somebody will hire you. I've had people pursue me until finally I say, 'My God, if they want to work for me that badly, give them the job!' "

Trahey also offers five additional tips for someone who wants to succeed in advertising:

1. Do your homework.
2. Get involved as much as you can—know what is going on at the rest of the agency and what other accounts they handle.
3. Like what you're doing. *Care* about what you're doing.
4. Set your own standards and be satisfied with your own work.
5. Cultivate contacts—this will help you skip a lot of steps as you climb the ladder to success.

Commentary from other industry leaders supports Trahey's tips. For example, David Ogilvy, in his book *Confessions of an Advertising Man*, expounds on Trahey Tip Number 1, "Do Your Homework":

"Set yourself to becoming the best-informed man in the agency on the account to which you are assigned," advises Ogilvy, founder of Ogilvy & Mather, Inc., the world's third-largest advertising agency. "If it is a gasoline account, read text books on chemistry, geology . . . Read all the trade journals in the field . . . Read all the research reports and marketing plans that your agency has ever written on the product. Spend Saturday mornings in service stations, pumping gasoline . . . Visit your client's refineries and research laboratories . . . At the end of your second year, you will know more about gasoline than your boss; you will then be ready to succeed him."[9]

In the same vein, Hugh Farrell tells of an account executive in his agency who, in an effort to provide better service to his welding account, went out on his own, took a welding course, and became a certified welder—a highly skilled and well-paying profession in its own right. The message is clear: The more you know about the client's business, the more valuable you are to the account. And the more valuable you are to the account, the more valuable you are to your agency, *especially* if it's one of their better accounts.

It's also important to know all you can about your *agency's* business as well as about the client's business (Trahey Tip Number 2). Amil Gargano explains how this can help to build a successful career:

"People who advance in this business have a much larger grasp of both the advertising business and the client's business. If you're an account executive, you would want to understand the creative process very well—that makes you a better account person. Somebody who has a much larger view of things is going to be able to make a much larger contribution to a company—and you take people in terms of what their contributions are." Or, as David Ogilvy put it: "Managers promote the men who produce the most."

Trahey adds a sixth suggestion—Trahey Tip Number 6: "My slogan in life is to throw up so many balls in the air, do so many different things, that some of them will have to stick," says Trahey. "If nothing else, you'll look busy . . ."

And a seventh ingredient for success—hard work—is added to the Trahey recipe for success by Hugh Farrell:

"I think it is prudent of young people in the business who haven't 'made it' to be willing to spend an inordinate amount of time at work, because that time is the learning time and gives them a chance to do more—and by doing more, they have more of their own work to be critiqued," said Farrell.

To some, it is just this image of the industry—long hours, low pay, and a prolonged period of initiation—that scares many people away from advertising. Now, it's true that hard work is rewarded—as it is in any business. It's also true that, because of its nature as a "service business," you may be called to work long hours when your agency faces a true crisis—such as putting out a four-color brochure in 3 weeks or redoing 12 magazine ads overnight because the client wants his wife's picture in them. But Farrell and others note that, for the most part, advertising people work the same or only slightly longer hours than their peers in other industries. Indeed, hard work and long hours of overtime are rewarded, but the majority of advertising professionals can do their jobs well and satisfy their superiors in a normal, if somewhat hectic, 8- or 9-hour day.

Equally as frustrating is the feeling that you'll have to spend the first few years earning far lower wages than your classmates in medicine, manufacturing, and other professions. And, to some extent, it's true: Senior advertising people can out-earn other business professionals, but juniors do suffer low pay during a rather prolonged training period. *Adweek* columnist and advertising consultant Whit Hobbs explains why:

"Beginning salaries are low, because advertising is an art that can't be learned overnight, and you aren't worth whatever you're getting until you learn it," writes Hobbs in *Adweek* ("You're [Probably] Overpaid." 7-81, p. S.S.44). "You aren't really in a job, you're in a learning program, and you're fortunate to be there, lucky that you found someone willing to invest money in your potential ability."

Amil Gargano calls this extended training period, "the short pants syndrome," and says that to avoid wearing the "junior" label for a long period of time you should keep moving up the ladder so you can get more money, more responsibility, and more respect. This move can be made within the agency, or it can be a hop to a new company.

The Top 10 Advertising Agencies in America Today

If you're ambitious, on the move, and *willing* to move, the starting gate to advertising's fast track is likely to be found at one of the top 10 agencies listed below. (Note: Addresses give the location of each agency's headquarters, but it is quite possible that the company has a branch office in your area.)[10]

1. *Young & Rubicam, Inc.,* 285 Madison Ave., New York, NY 10017; phone (212) 210-3000. *Total 1981 billings:* $2.4 billion. *Number of employees:* 6,861. *Major accounts:* AT&T, Dr. Pepper, Kentucky Fried Chicken, 7-Eleven Food Stores, Atari, Lincoln-Mercury. *Key personnel:* Alexander Kroll, President, Young & Rubicam

USA; Mark Stroock, Senior Vice-President/Director, Corporate Relations.

2. *J. Walter Thompson Co.*, 466 Lexington Ave., New York, NY 10017; phone (212) 210-7000. *Total 1981 billings:* $2.2 billion. *Number of employees:* 7,419. *Major accounts:* Burger King, Chevron, Hewlett-Packard, Kellogg Cereals, Oscar Mayer, Pepsi-Cola. *Key personnel:* Burt Manning, Chief Executive Officer (CEO), J. Walter Thompson USA; Walter J. O'Brien, Chief Operating Officer, J. Walter Thompson USA.

3. *Ogilvy & Mather, Inc.*, 2 East 48th St., New York, NY 10017; phone (212) 688-6100. *Total 1981 billings:* $1.9 billion. *Number of employees:* 5,810. *Major accounts:* Gallo Wines, Hallmark, American Express, General Foods, Publishers Clearing House, TWA. *Key personnel:* Kenneth Roman, President; Graham Phillips, Executive Vice-President, New York.

4. *McCann-Erickson, Inc.*, 485 Lexington Ave., New York, NY 10017; phone (212) 697-6000. *Total 1981 billings:* $1.9 billion. *Number of employees:* 6,225. *Major accounts:* Coca-Cola, Del Monte, Exxon, General Motors, Gillette, Nabisco, Pabst. *Key personnel:* W. Scott Miller, Executive Vice-President/Creative Director; Francis J. Van Bortel, Executive Vice-President/Account Strategy; Eugene A. DeWitt, Executive Vice-President/Director of Media; George B. Hatch, Executive Vice-President/Finance and Administration.

5. *Ted Bates Worldwide*, 1515 Broadway, New York, NY 10036; phone (212) 869-3131. *Total 1981 billings:* $1.6 billion. *Number of employees:* 4,247. *Major accounts:* American Cyanamid, Colgate-Palmolive, HBO, Kal Kan, M&M's, Prudential Insurance. *Key personnel:* Robert A. Bruns, Executive Vice-President, Ted Bates New York.

6. *BBDO, Inc.*, 383 Madison Ave., New York, NY 10017; phone (212) 355-5800. *Total 1981 billings:* $1.4 billion. *Number of employees:* 2,996. *Major accounts:* Pillsbury, Black & Decker, *The Wall Street Journal*, Firestone, Quaker Oats, Del Monte. *Key personnel:* Jerry J. Siano, Vice-Chairman/Worldwide Creative Director; Louis T. Hagopian, Chairman/Chief Executive Officer.

7. *Leo Burnett Co., Inc.*, Prudential Plaza, Chicago, IL 60601; phone (312) 565-5959. *Total 1981 billings:* $1.3 billion. *Number of employees:* 3,236. *Major accounts:* Union Carbide, Allstate Insurance Companies, Green Giant Co., Heinz, Keebler, Maytag, Memorex. *Key personnel:* John J. Kinsella, President.

8. *Foote, Cone & Belding*, 401 N. Michigan Ave., Chicago, IL 60601; phone (312) 467-9200. *Total 1981 billings:* $1.2 billion. *Number of employees:* 3,790. *Major accounts:* Sara Lee, Pearle Vision

Centers, Lipton Tea, British Airways, Clairol, Frito-Lay. *Key personnel:* John E. O'Toole, Chairman/Chief Creative Officer; Norman W. Brown, President.

9. *Grey Advertising, 777* Third Ave., New York, NY 10017; phone (212) 546-2000. *Total 1981 billings:* $1.2 billion. *Number of employees:* 3,285. *Major accounts:* ABC, Canada Dry, Borden, Doubleday & Co., B.F. Goodrich, Kenner. *Key personnel:* Alex Gerster, Senior Vice-President, media; Richard M. Karp, Executive Vice-President, creative services; Shirley Young, Executive Vice-President, marketing, planning, and strategy development; Stephen K. Zimmerman, Executive Vice-President, account services.

10. *SSC&B, Inc.* 1 Dag Hammarskjold Plaza, New York, NY 10017; phone (212) 644-5000. *Total billings:* $1.2 billion. *Number of employees:* 3,721. *Major accounts:* Carnation, Dun & Bradstreet, Lego Systems, Inc., Mennen, Olympus Camera, and Sterling Drugs. *Key personnel:* Malcolm D. MacDougall, President/director of creative services; Lawrence E. Camattina, Executive Vice-President, media and network planning.

You can't help but notice that 8 of the top 10 agencies have their headquarters in New York. While it's true that New York City has traditionally been the hub of the advertising industry, today's trend is toward the South and West. There are now thriving advertising communities in most major metropolitan areas, including Chicago, San Francisco, Los Angeles, Detroit, Philadelphia, Washington, D.C., Baltimore, Atlanta, Seattle, Minneapolis, Pittsburgh, and Cleveland, to name a few.

JOB-HOPPING

As you spend more and more time in the advertising industry, you will become a *specialist* in a discipline (copy, media, or research) or in a client's business (automobiles, package goods, or health care). There are pros and cons to this. On the plus side, you'll be worth more to other agencies that need your special skills or experience. But the minus is that your options may become limited. If you step outside your area of expertise, it's likely that you won't be able to command the salary and position you probably deserve.

As a result, job-hopping can take place with some frequency in the early years, but by the time you hit 40, any move should be considered carefully. Judy Wald, an executive search consultant specializing in the placement of advertising people, says that the most a candidate should have changed jobs between the ages of 21 and 41 is five times. Contrary to the popular image, job-hoppers in the advertising industry are viewed with the same uncertainty and suspicion as in more conservative industries.

"The people who change and never stay in one place more than a year—forget it!" says Wald. "There's definitely something wrong with them."[11] Amil Gargano believes that people who hop from job to job every year or so would probably be happier as freelancers or running their own agencies. And Hugh Farrell says he would be "hesitant" to hire anyone who stayed at his previous positions less than two years.

WHEN YOU'VE MADE IT

Once you've made it, once you've truly arrived at the pinnacle, what then? What's the reward in it all? And what do you do next? What have you sacrificed to get to the top? Opinions from the leaders as to what defines success vary, from winning industry awards, such as Clios, to starting your own agency. (The following quotations are assembled but not invented.)

"To me, the reward is variety. Every client is different: Calvin Klein one day, computers the next."

"Recognition from my peers."

"Getting results for my clients—with every ad, every commercial, every campaign."

"I feel some remorse about not being able to do all the creative work myself."

"Open up your *own* agency. If you can open up the smallest shop in the world, you're ahead of the game from every point of view. Number one, you're the last person to be fired. Number two, you make the business what you want it to be."

"Make yourself indispensable to your agency's top client. That way you will never be fired."

"Get industry awards. Peer recognition."

"It certainly won't hurt, but it is not important to win creative awards."

"Find your own level of satisfaction. People feel successful inside knowing what they are and how they conduct themselves."

"Money. I've always made more money as a copywriter than my friends who do other kinds of writing."

What is the ultimate for an advertising professional? Money, excitement, power, and the opportunity to be creative are all a part of it. But most of the successful advertising people we interviewed pointed to inner satisfaction, a contentment with a job well done, as their main reward for a life spent on Madison Avenue. David Ogilvy emphasizes the importance of this feeling in *Confessions of an Advertising Man* when he asks us to remember the Scottish proverb:

Be happy while you're living,
For you're a long time dead.

Biotechnology

IN GENERAL

In a recent survey, more than 6,000 chemical engineers, chemists, and other technical types were asked, "What makes people accept a job?" They answered that salary was the second most important consideration. The first was *interesting work*.

If you're a scientist or an engineer looking for a specialty or planning to switch industries, consider a career in biotechnology. Also known as recombinant DNA, genetic engineering, gene splicing, cloning, and bioengineering, biotechnology is the science of modifying the genetic makeup of microorganisms for the purposes of research and commerce. Its goal is to produce new life forms that manufacture commercial products—foods, chemicals, fuels, and drugs—more efficiently and at lower cost than conventional technologies. Also, by altering the characteristics of living organisms, biotechnology can create heartier strains of wheat, self-fertilizing flowers, and plumper pigs. It is, by anyone's standards, *very* interesting work.

In June, 1980, the U.S. Supreme Court ruled that new life forms created in a laboratory could be patented under existing U.S. laws. This paved the way for the commercialization of genetic engineering. Now the rush is on among the genetic-engineering firms to recruit biochemists, molecular biologists, microbiologists, immunologists, and geneticists.

Right now, the biotechnology industry is in its infancy. Gene-splicing techniques were first developed in the 1970s. Thus, job opportunities are presently somewhat limited, although Ph.D.s entering the field can earn more than their counterparts in other industries or academia. But consultants, journalists, and scientists predict that biotechnology will be to the 1980s what microcomputers were to the 1970s and transistors were to the 1950s. Here is what some of these experts are saying:

> "The ultimate impact on the chemical and pharmaceutical industries could be similar to that which followed when an understanding of solid state physics was brought to electronics: genetic engineering is, in effect, ready to graduate from the vacuum tube to the transistor."
> —*Business Week* (August 9, 1976)

> " . . . Biotechnology holds the promise of as much, if not more, success than any recent technology. Historically, how many budding technologies were recognized as having this much potential?"
> —Irvin Schwartz, Editor
> *Industrial Chemical News* (January, 1982)

> "It's a revolutionary technology. The methods developed by the biotechnology industry are going to be of crucial importance to many other industries."
> —Zsolt Harsanyi, Vice-President
> E.F. Hutton[1]

> "Gene splicing is the most powerful and awesome skill acquired by man since the splitting of the atom."
> —*Time* magazine (March 9, 1981)

> "Biology will be to the twenty-first century what physics and chemistry were to this century."
> —John Naisbitt, *Megatrends* (Warner Books)

Biotechnology is just now moving out of the lab and into the marketplace. More than 300 companies and dozens of universities are involved in the development and commercialization of genetic-engineering techniques. And industry is working on applications of genetic engineering in many areas, including chemical processing, food processing, agriculture, animal husbandry, pharmaceutical and medical products, pollution control, mining, and petroleum recovery in oil wells. As amazing as it may seem, genetically altered microorganisms can be used in all these areas. In fact, the U.S. Patent and Trademark Office has already approved more than 3,000 biotechnology-related patents, ranging from a "bug" that eats up oil spills to a hormone for treating dwarfism in humans.

A brief survey of some recent developments in the field will give you an idea of its enormous potential:

- Today's gene-altering technology can produce steers that grow to maturity in six months and giant "supercows" the size of an elephant that are capable of giving 45,000 pounds of milk a year, three times the yield of an ordinary cow.
- Horticulturists at Kansas University have created a "pomato," a plant they hope will bear both tomatoes and potatoes.
- Genetically altered crops can produce their own fertilizers and pesticides and can live for weeks without water.
- By implanting synthetic human genes in bacteria, scientists have created a microorganism that produces human insulin. Currently, insulin for diabetics is extracted from the organs of slaughtered animals—a costly, resource-limited technique. Genetic engineering could make insulin far more plentiful and much less expensive.
- A "hybridoma," a cell created by fusing a human cancer cell with a white blood cell, acts as a "living factory" to manufacture antibodies that can be used to treat a wide variety of diseases.
- Several manufacturers are marketing "gene machines" that automatically create genes from commercially available chemicals. They can do in a week what human technicians take months to accomplish.
- Dr. Ananda Chakrabarty of the University of Illinois used gene splicing to produce one strain of bacteria that eats oil spills and another that ingests the poisonous "Agent Orange." Dr. Chakrabarty says, "Genetic engineering techniques are so powerful that we can make microorganisms to solve a lot of our problems."[2]

- A genetically engineered growth hormone has raised milk production in normal cows by 12 percent with no additional feeding. The hormone is simply injected under the skin like a measles shot.
- Recombinant DNA has resulted in bacteria that can synthesize interferon, an anticancer agent. Genetic-engineering techniques could reduce the cost of this drug from $150 to $1 a shot.
- Gene splicing has also produced bacteria that can extract petroleum from nearly exhausted oil wells, mine ores on the ocean floor, and convert garbage to chemicals and energy.

Once these gene-driven processes are commercialized, there will be a huge market for "bioengineered" products. A report by International Resources Development, Inc. estimates annual sales of $3 billion for recombinant DNA products by 1990. A less conservative study by the T.A. Sheets Company projects a $27 billion market by the end of the decade. Seventy-five percent of that market will be for existing products produced better, faster, and at less cost via genetic methods than by conventional techniques. The other 25 percent will be for new products created by gene splicing and other biotechnology techniques.

Among the best-selling, gene-produced products will be interferon, synthetic antibiotics, vaccines, insulin, and human growth hormone. By the year 2000, the annual sales of these and other bioengineered products is expected to exceed $50 billion and could go as high as $100 billion.

Corporate America plans to cash in on this coming boom. According to an article in *Industrial Chemical News*, some $200 million in private capital had been invested in the commercial future of genetic engineering as of December, 1980. Industry sources predict biotechnology could attract an additional $4 billion in investments by 1985.

This kind of growth will produce thousands of new jobs for the scientists who create new life forms in the lab, as well as for the engineers who put these processes into mass production. Where the jobs will be—and how to get them—is the subject of this chapter.

A Look at the Technology

Horror stories—all purely fiction—go hand-in-hand with the development of the new genetic technology. Grade B science fiction films and pulp novels predict the duplication of human beings through cloning or depict mad scientists manipulating DNA to create half-human, half-animal monstrosities. Meanwhile, newspaper and magazine articles warn of the danger of manmade microorganisms escaping from sealed laboratories to infect the outside world.

To be sure, cloning raises legitimate moral and ethical questions that must be answered, and lab safety is a very real issue. But, scientists are not busy creating replicas of wealthy businessmen or breeding killer plagues. Their present research uses the relatively scientific techniques described below:

Gene splicing is the basic technique of recombinant DNA. Here, a bit of genetic material from a foreign cell is spliced into a host cell. The new cell then incorporates the characteristic of the foreign gene. For example, the gene controlling the production of insulin in human cells has been spliced into a bacteria, causing the bacteria to produce human insulin. Gene fragments may be synthesized in a laboratory from substances known as *mononucleotides*. A decade ago, complex genes were synthesized by hand and the process took months. Now, automatic gene machines can do it in days. (Vega Biochemicals and Bio Logicals are two companies that sell commercial models of such machines to genetic-engineering laboratories.)

Essentially, gene splicing modifies the genetic makeup of an existing organism to control the activities of the cell. In a sense, it creates new life forms to be used as miniature chemical plants.

Cell fusion, another recombinant DNA technique, takes a more direct approach to creating new life forms. In cell fusion, two different cells are joined together to form hybridomas—long-lived hybrid cells that produce antibodies. Since cells multiply at a rapid rate, a single hybridoma can produce billions of antibodies in a relatively short period of time. Such antibodies are called *monoclonal* antibodies because they are cloned (replicated) from a single cell.

Cloning. What about cloning? Yes, it *is* a reality. Cloning cells in the laboratory is now an everyday event. It's easy to clone carrots, tadpoles, frogs, and simpler forms of life, and there have been reports of scientists cloning white mice. So, theoretically, it is possible to clone human beings and other higher mammals. This means a genetics laboratory could create a duplicate of you from a single cell of a hair, a bit of skin, a piece of a surgically removed tonsil or appendix. In the same vein, it may be possible to recreate extinct species from specimens found frozen in arctic regions. If we so choose, dinosaurs, wooly mammoths, and Neanderthal men could walk the Earth again.

WHAT IT TAKES

Since biotechnology is such a highly technical field, describing the requirements is relatively simple and straightforward.

For research, biotechnology companies need biologists, chemists, and biochemists. A Ph.D., plus a research background in a field closely related to genetic engineering (genetics, biochemistry, microbiology, molecular biology), is usually required. Starting salaries for Ph.D.s just out of school can range from $35,000 to $40,000 a year, and company stock may be included as part of the compensation package. This compares favorably with what your counterparts in more traditional industries are earning. In 1982, for example, the average Ph.D. chemist annually earned $37,500—and that was for *all* levels of experience!

As laboratory experiments are scaled-up to full-size manufacturing operations, the biotechnology industry will need fewer Ph.D. biologists, chemists, or biochemists and more engineers, particularly chemical engineers, along with plenty of technicians and operators. The technicians can get their basic education at two-year programs offered by community colleges or tech schools. Employers will then train them in the particular skills required to operate equipment in a genetics lab or biotechnology plant.

A 4-year B.S. degree is a necessity for any engineer who wishes to work in industry, but advanced degrees are not required. A chemical engineer with the ink still wet on his B.S. diploma can expect to earn between $20,000 to $30,000 a year, the median salary being $26,500. The median 1982 annual salary for chemical engineers of *all* levels of experience was $39,000, up 14.7 percent over the previous year.

In industry, the engineer is generally more sought after and better rewarded than the scientist. In basic research, the opposite is true.

"Industry places a higher premium on chemical engineers than on chemists because chemical engineers can deal with a broader range of problems that have a direct bearing on a company's profitability," says Alexis T. Bell, Chairman of the chemical engineering department at the University of California at Berkeley. As a result of industry's quest for qualified engineers, freshmen enrollment in chemical-engineering programs is increasing; there were 6,527 B.S. degrees in chemical engineering awarded in 1981 versus 3,581 in 1977; an increase of 82 percent in just 4 years![3]

This differentiation between engineers and scientists will separate the highly paid from the moderately paid, as biotechnology shifts into full-scale commercial production.

"Traditionally, it has been the job of engineers to take what scientists develop and put it to use," explains Peter Clark, President of Epstein Process Engineering, Chicago. "Engineers have already worked their way through much of the fundamental sciences—chemistry, physics, mathematics. What is left, but biology?"[4]

Epstein adds that "chemical engineering is the most relevant discipline to biotechnology." The reason: Many of the industrial operations that biotechnology plants will use—batch reactors, continuous reactors, fermentation tanks, distillation columns—are already taught in the chemical-engineering curriculum. In addition, many of the promising commercial applications of biotechnology—commodity chemicals, petrochemicals, enhanced oil well recovery, food processing, pollution control, and energy production—are traditional areas of employment for chemical engineers working in industry.

However, chemical engineers aren't the only engineers who will profit from biotechnology. Mechanical engineers are needed to design and build new types of processing equipment to be used in genetic-engineering plants. Electrical engineers will produce the sophisticated control systems and instrumentation required to regulate this equipment. Computer scientists will program computer-graphic systems used to study the intricate structures of complex biological molecules. Agricultural, mining, petroleum, and environmental and sanitation engineers may also use genetic-engineering technology in their work.

In addition to the basic engineering curricula, students considering a career in biotechnology should take as many biology electives as they can. Also, they should read technical literature in the field. Engineers don't need the same in-depth knowledge as laboratory scientists, but they *do* need to speak the researcher's language so that they can communicate and work with them effectively.

The biotechnology newsletter *Newswatch* reports that four universities—the University of Maryland (Baltimore County), the University of North Carolina, East Carolina University, and M.I.T.—plan to offer degree programs in biotechnology. "Biotechnology is coming of age," explains Anthony J. Sinskey, professor of applied microbiology at M.I.T. "Since the technology is now used to make industrial products, people trained in the basic principles of biotechnology are needed. The universities are preparing students to fill this niche."

If you're already in the work force, full-time studies in biotechnology may not be for you. But many universities, professional associations, and other groups offer continuing education courses for scientists and engineers who have already completed their graduate and undergraduate work. One such course is the seminar "Genetic Engineering for Chemists and Chemical Engineers," offered by Dr. James E. Bailey of Pasadena, California. It includes such technical topics as restriction enzymes, RNA splicing, and virus vectors.

If the truth be known, a smattering of business courses—administration, accounting, finance, and marketing—will be helpful to scientists and engineers planning careers in industry. Inspired by childhood chemistry sets or science fiction stories, many scientists- and engineers-in-training assume their days will be spent doing research in university laboratories or programming computers. But the fact is that private industry finances 70 percent of this country's research and development (R&D) work. As a result, 60 percent of U.S.

chemists are employed in business, not academia. By the end of the decade, more than 90 percent of all college and university graduates will work in the private sector.

This trend permeates all emerging sciences as they develop into mature technologies, and biotechnology is no exception. E.F. Hutton Vice-President Nelson Schreider estimates that the current genetic-engineering research load is two-thirds academic, one-third industrial. By 1985, however, he predicts that industry will handle *three-quarters* of all research, basic and applied, in recombinant DNA. So, as a "genetic engineer," you can expect that your work will be directed toward producing products for profit, and you should have some sense of how your performance affects the company's bottom line. Business courses can help.

GETTING STARTED

Whether you are just deciding on what speciality to study or have been working in industry for years, you need to begin your job search or career change in an organized, systematic fashion similar to the way you would plan an experiment or the construction of a chemical plant. In his pamphlet *How to Get the Job You Really Want*, consultant Keith Ellis outlines a six-step procedure that chemists and engineers can follow in their job searches. Ellis' six steps are:

1. *Gather the facts.* What are your capabilities, interests, accomplishments, education, experience?
2. *Analyze the facts.* Do they point toward a career in biotechnology? Or do your interests lie elsewhere? Make the move to biotechnology because it *interests* you, not simply because it looks like "a good thing to get into."
3. *Prepare the sales piece*, that is, your resume. Resumes for academics, known as *curriculum vitae*, are often long, multipage affairs listing every award, paper, and project the scientist or engineer has been connected with. Resumes aimed at industry should be concise, polished, and written to emphasize the benefits the

employer will receive by hiring you. (Interestingly, a recent survey showed that 87 percent of industrial chemists felt they needed guidance in preparing an effective resume.)

4. *Plan your selling program.* Where will you apply? How will you sell yourself to employers? What will make them want to hire *you?* Plan a coordinated campaign of letter writing and phone follow-ups. (One tip: Time your mailing so that letters arrive on Wednesday or Thursday. Midweek mail gets a better response than Monday or Friday mail.)

5. *Prepare for the interview.* Send for the company's product literature and annual report. Read up on the company, its products, and its genetic-engineering programs. Find out how your background fits in with the job being offered.

6. *Keep at it.* Persistence pays off. Years ago, *Life* magazine ran a story on a Ph.D. scientist who had wallpapered his den with the hundreds of letters of rejection he received when he applied for research positions in industry. Being a technical expert is no guarantee of instant job offers. Often, you have to work hard to get the job you want.

As a rule, the elements of a job search—getting leads, making contacts, writing cover letters and resumes, going on interviews, and so on—are pretty much the same in every industry and for every profession. The only difference is the relative importance of these elements in a particular type of business.

The crucial factor in starting your job search in genetic engineering is obtaining *leads.* Which are the companies involved? Where do you find out about them? Whom do you call? Where do you write? Many biotechnology companies are listed in standard industry sourcebooks such as *Moody's Industries, The Thomas Register, Dun & Bradstreet,* and the *Chemical Engineering Catalog.* But there's no single source—no definitive catalog, periodical, book, directory, or want-ad—that serves as a comprehensive guide to the genetic-engineering industry. Therefore, we have tried to provide much of this material in the appendices at the end of this chapter. We have included a directory that lists dozens of corporations actively involved in biotechnology. We also list trade associations and periodicals you can consult.

Still, finding out where the genetic-engineering jobs are is one of the toughest tasks you face. Contact corporate recruiters, colleagues, executive search firms, friends, family, and former professors. See if they can help. Also, check newspaper listings. A number of biotechnology jobs have been advertising in the "Business Section" of *The Sunday New York Times* over the past few months.

YOUR FIRST BIG BREAK

Your first big break in genetic engineering will come when you are employed by a firm working in one of the "hot" applications of recombinant DNA technology. For example, using gene splicing to produce insulin is hot, but cloning laboratory mice is not. Here are the areas that have the greatest potential in commercial biotechnology:

- *Pharmaceuticals*—Genetic engineering can improve the production of vaccines, hormones, enzymes, antibiotics, and vitamins; it can also synthesize insulin, interferon, human growth hormone, and other substances. The market for genetically engineered pharmaceutical and medical products could exceed $3 billion by 1990. Many of the major pharmaceutical houses—including Abbott Labs, Eli Lilly & Company, Miles Labs, and Pfizer, Inc.— have extensive genetic-engineering programs already underway.
- *Chemicals*—Biotechnology can provide cleaner, cheaper, more efficient ways of producing acetic acid, citric acid, alcohols, oxidated alkenes, glycerol, and other compounds. "The list of companies now active in genetic engineering reads like a Who's Who of the U.S. chemical industry," reports the trade publication *Chemical Engineering Progress* (November, 1982). This list includes Dow Chemical Company, DuPont, Exxon, and Koppers.

- *Agriculture/animal husbandry*—Major applications in this area include gene splicing to produce genetically superior strains of food crops and creating vaccines and hormones to ensure healthier, larger, better livestock. One much-publicized example of "agri-genetics" is the use of gene splicing to create "nitrogen-fixing" crops that produce their own fertilizer. Monsanto is the big spender in agri-genetics research. Other firms doing important work in this field include Amoco, Biogen, Calgene, and Collaborative Genetics.
- *Energy sources*—Genetically altered microorganisms are being tailor-made for a variety of applications in this area. Some of these "bugs" may produce substitutes for oil, coal, and other fossil fuels. Others may convert waste into energy, or increase the efficiency of oil rig operations.

A biologist doesn't have to be an expert in vaccines or vitamins to work in the pharmaceutical applications end of the biotechnology field. Nor does the geneticist need a thorough knowledge of pollution control to create bugs to consume oil slicks. Such highly specific application knowledge is helpful, of course; however, it is not a prerequisite, especially for newcomers to the field. "Don't underestimate your abilities, even for skills you don't have," says Kelley Harrington, a research chemist for Eli Lilly & Company. "It is a rare person who has had the opportunity to learn or experience everything involved in a certain position. The most important qualities employers look for are a willingness and ability to learn."[5]

WHAT TO SHOOT FOR

With the advent of recombinant DNA, the science of biology has become big business. "The genetic engineering firms are no longer 'science factories.' They are beginning to look like normal businesses," said Harvey S. Price, Executive Director of the Industrial Biotechnology Association (IBA), a trade group whose members are corporations involved in genetic engineering.

As with any other "normal business," people who work in biotechnology are concerned with such everyday issues as job satisfaction, potential for advancement, salary, and benefits. Though it may come as a surprise to some, scientists are basically no different from bankers, doctors, lawyers, advertising executives, and others who work for a living. Biologist Jonathan King of M.I.T. explains:

> They (scientists) are into making a living. Take the guy who is a senior vice president for Kellogg's Corn Flakes and is trying to make it up to the president. Why does he want to do this? Because he likes corn flakes? No, because he has been brought up all his life to want to succeed and to have status, to have prestige and make more money, or be more powerful . . . Is science any different? No![6]

To achieve these goals, you want to work for one of the best and brightest firms—a company that succeeds in business, makes a profit, and treats technical employees with respect. How, though, can engineers and scientists evaluate prospective employers? A recent survey[7] conducted at 17 universities asked senior engineering students what qualities they seek in companies they might work for. Here is the tally of the vote:

1. *Technical reputation.* The results showed that 88.6 percent of students surveyed responded that "technical reputation" was the number one factor in selecting an employer. Students preferred companies with advanced R&D programs, competent technical staff, and high-quality products.
2. *Progressiveness.* 68.7 percent of the engineering students surveyed responded that they want to work for a firm oriented toward professional growth and creativity.
3. *Size.* Respondents felt that larger firms offer greater opportunity and diversity than smaller companies. Most felt that only large corporations have the facilities needed to sponsor innovation.
4. *General climate.* Engineers want to work in a place that is stimulating, friendly, professionally oriented, relaxed, and informal.

5. *Standing of technical professionals.* Naturally, engineers want a company that treats its technical employees as the equals of business and administrative types.
6. *Salary.* High starting salary was seen as more important than rapid advancement or large raises.
7. *Location.* Only 5.2 percent of students surveyed considered location an important factor in choosing an employer.

In genetic engineering, the first two factors on the list—technical reputation and progressiveness—are practically givens. Any company doing research in biotechnology is, by virtue of the newness of genetic engineering, a progressive company and a technical leader in the industry. It is the third factor—size—that marks a dividing line between biotechnology companies. Basically, there are two types of companies in this field:

1. Small, entrepreneurial companies whose primary product is genetic-engineering research, development, and commercialization. Many of these firms were founded by university professors and are partially funded by venture capital. The "big four" venture firms in genetic engineering are Biogen, Cetus, Genentech, and Genex. Most genetic-engineering companies (and there are dozens of them) have anywhere from a dozen to a few hundred employees, with annual sales ranging from $100,000 to several million dollars.
2. Large, established firms—mainly chemical and pharmaceutical companies—that are entering the field through in-house research and joint-venture or co-ownership of small genetic-engineering companies. Standard Oil, for example, owns 50 percent of Cetus. Monsanto has interests in Genex, Genentech, and Biogen. Corning Glass Works has a joint venture with Genentech to develop enzymes for corn-syrup production. And Dow Chemical is building its own genetic-engineering laboratory at its Midland, Michigan, headquarters.

Large corporations offer security, high salaries, attractive benefits, extensive resources and facilities, and multiple career options. Many engineers and scientists prefer large corporations to small business, believing that only big business has the money to finance first-class R&D efforts. And, only large corporations can afford to train entry-level employees recruited from college campuses.

Still, small companies have their advantages, too. For one thing, they do away with management hierarchies and bureaucratic red tape. Decisions are made by individuals, not by committees. As a result, small companies can act more swiftly than corporate giants. Moreover, recent studies show that, contrary to the beliefs expressed by the engineering students in the survey, small businesses are responsible for most of the nation's new jobs, economic growth, productivity improvement, and innovation. In genetic engineering, the majority of technological breakthroughs have been made by researchers at small genetic-engineering firms, not in large corporate R&D labs. For example, Herbert Boyer, a cofounder of Genentech, holds the first patent ever granted in the recombinant DNA field.

Another advantage of small, entrepreneurial genetic-engineering firms is that many of them offer new recruits a piece of the company in the form of stock or other profit-sharing deals. (When *Chemical Engineering* magazine asked its readers, "What single benefit that you do not receive now is most desirable to you?," *profit-sharing* was the number one response.)

WHEN YOU'VE MADE IT

Biotechnology is the newest, least-established field covered in this book. Certainly, no science so young has ever gotten so much attention. Unfortunately, it's nearly impossible to plot a career path in genetic engineering. The oldest firms have been around for less than a decade, which means that the senior statesmen of industrial biotechnology started in the business *after* America put a man on the moon. There are no old-timers, no 20-year men, no gold watches in genetic engineering. Who is to say where you should be after a lifetime in this field? No one has had that experience yet.

Who, then, has "made it" in biotechnology? Certainly the dozens of entrepreneurs who have started successful genetic-engineering companies have made it. Most of them are self-made millionaires as a result of their ventures into this new technology. In his best-selling book *Megatrends*, John Naisbitt describes the shift from big business to entrepreneurship and small business as one of the major trends shaping the future of American society. The pioneers in genetic engineering are flowing with this trend.

Academics, too, are cashing in on recombinant DNA. University professors earn $1,000 or more a day as consultants to corporations involved in biotechnology. Indeed, many academics sit on the boards of genetic-engineering firms. Also, a significant amount of university research in genetic engineering is sponsored by the private sector.

This raises an interesting point. Basic researchers in academia traditionally share their findings by publishing research results in scientific journals. Industry, on the other hand, depends on well-kept trade secrets to maintain a competitive edge. Will the cross-fertilization between universities and corporations stifle scientific freedom? Or will it provide the financial impetus to do more and better basic research? Only time will answer that question. One thing, however, is clear: The majority of the jobs—engineering as well as research—will be in the private sector. Fewer and fewer genetic engineers will be able to opt for an academic environment. Scientists and engineers with highly specialized genetic-engineering skills will command the top salaries, especially in chemical processing, pharmaceuticals, and other industries that look to genetic engineering for cost-effective solutions to production problems.

A LOOK INTO THE FUTURE

Today, the United States is the undisputed world leader in genetic-engineering technology, which is due to our leadership in fundamental research. However, other nations, particularly Japan, are playing a quick game of catch-up. Also, the Japanese are ahead of us in fermentation technology, a crucial factor in scaling-up genetically driven reactions to full-scale production. We need engineers to develop competitive production technologies now if we are to maintain our lead in the future.

Most genetically engineered projects are still in the development stage. A few, such as insulin and interferon, have reached the market in limited quantities, but they are not in full-scale production yet. However, large biotechnology production facilities should be up and running by 1985 or so. By the 1990s, genetic engineering could dramatically alter the way we engineer chemical, petrochemical, and pharmaceutical plants. The British *Economist* claims that "biotechnology is one of the biggest industrial opportunities of the late 20th century." And Bill Dunn, publisher of *U.S. News & World Report*, writes that biotechnology is "nothing less than a biological revolution, and it promises to have the impact of the discovery of fire, invention of the printing press and splitting of the atom."

Still, at present, the bottom line is that no genetic-engineered products are in mass production. Probably, they will be by the middle of this decade. Probably, genetic engineering will create synthetic substitutes for fossil fuels, produce cures for major diseases, and significantly increase the yield of the world's food crops. *Probably.* But, until the first genetically engineered product hits the shelf—until industry sees a return in its recombinant DNA investment—the future of biotechnology is not guaranteed. As Ralph Hardy, Director of life sciences for DuPont, puts it: "Recombinant DNA research as of today can only be considered an emerging scientific success story, with many chapters yet to be written."[8]

This chapter of *Dream Jobs* can only describe the emerging potential of career opportunities in genetic engineering. The final chapters on the industry are still to come.

A Directory of Genetic-Engineering Firms

This directory lists smaller firms specializing in genetic engineering, as well as large established corporations involved in the field. It was gleaned from various articles in trade publications and the popular press. None of the companies specifically requested to be listed here. We do not guarantee that all of these firms are currently involved in recombinant DNA research.

Company	Description/comments:
Abbott Labs Abbott Park North Chicago, IL 60064 (312) 937-6100	Spends approximately $1 million/yr on genetic-engineering research for diagnostic tests used to detect such disorders as hepatitis.
Advanced Genetic Sciences, Inc. Oakland, CA (415) 547-2395	—
Agrigenetics Corp. Boulder, CO (303) 443-5900	A $70 million agricultural seed and legume company. Working on nitrogen-fixing bacteria. Member, Industrial Biotechnology Association (IBA). R.N. Drygden, President; David Padwa, Chief Executive Officer (CEO).
Allelix, Inc. Mississaugo, Ontario	Member, IBA.
Allied Corp. Columbus Rd. & Park Ave. P.O. Box 4000R Morristown, NJ 07960 (201) 455-2000	Owns 10 percent common stock in Bio Logicals of Toronto.
ALPHA Therapeutics Corp. Los Angeles, CA (213) 225-2221	Member, IBA.
Amicon Corp. Division 182 Conant St. Denver, MA 01923 (617) 777-3611	Member, IBA.
Amoco Chemicals Corp. 200 E. Randolph P.O. Box 8640-A Chicago, IL 60680 (312) 856-3200	Spends $2-3 million/yr on recombinant DNA research. Works with plants, algae, bacteria in applications for chemicals, health care, and agriproducts.

Applied Medical Devices
(805) 499-3617

—

Applied Molecular Genetics, Inc.
Newbury Park, CA

Member, IBA.

Armos Corp.
South San Francisco, CA
(415) 872-0123

Manufacturer of
gene-synthesizing devices.

Beckman Instruments, Spinco
Div.
2500 Harbor Blvd.
Fullerton, CA 92634
(714) 871-4848

Manufacturer of
gene-synthesizing devices.

Bethesda Research Laboratories,
Inc.
Gaithersburg, MD
(301) 840-8000

Producers of endonucleases,
restrictive and annealing. In 1980,
had 150 employees and sales of
$2.5 million. James Barrett,
President.

Biogen, Inc.
50 Church St.
Cambridge, MA 02138
(617) 864-8900

Pioneer in applying biotechnology
to industrial applications.
Currently developing animal
growth hormone. Participants
include International Nickel,
Monsanto, Schering-Plough.
Robert Fildes, President. Member,
IBA.

Bio Logicals
Toronto, Canada
(416) 366-4863

Manufacturer of
gene-synthesizing machines.
Participant: Allied Corp. plus
other joint ventures.

Biosearch
San Rafael, CA
(415) 459-3907

Manufacturer of
gene-synthesizing devices.

Biotechnical International, Inc.
Cambridge, MA
(617) 864-0040

Member, IBA.

Biotech Research Laboratories,
Inc.
Rockville, MD
(301) 251-0800

Thomas Li, President.

Bristol-Myers Co.
345 Park Ave.
New York, NY 10154
(212) 546-4000

Has awarded Genex a contract to
produce interferon.

Calbiochem-Behring
La Jolla, CA
(619) 450-9600

Low-volume producer of
endonucleases and annealing
enzymes.

Calgene, Inc.
Davis, CA
(916) 753-6313

Genetically altered plants. Cloned a gene to withstand herbicides, and developing nitrogen-fixing bacteria. Aldis Adamson, Vice-President.

Celanese Chemical Co., Inc.
1250 West Mockingbird Lane
Dallas, TX 75247
(214) 689-4000

Has established a joint research program with Yale.

Cetus Corp.
Berkeley, CA
(415) 949-3300

Participants include Standard Oil, Shell Oil, and National Distillers. Cetus is the oldest genetic-engineering firm—founded 1970. Will manufacture interferon at new process-development facility in Emeryville, CA. Expects to market a vaccine for colibacillosis (a diarrheal disease). Using genetically altered bugs to produce antifreeze and other chemicals. Member, IBA. Ronald E. Cape, Chairman of the Board.

Clinical Assays
Div. of Travenol Laboratories, Inc.
Cambridge, MA
(617) 492-2526

Member, IBA.

Collaborative Genetics
Waltham, MA
(617) 861-9700

Current projects include gasohol, interferon, nitrogen fixation. In 1979, had sales of $5 million. Working on manipulation of yeast via gene splicing for energy transformation and industrial applications. Orin Friedman, President.

Corning Glass Works
Corning, NY 14830
(607) 974-4126

Has active in-house work on process technology using immobilized cell reactors. Also has joint venture with Genentech.

The Dow Chemical Co.
2020 Dow Center
Midland, MI 48640
(517) 636-1000

Currently spends $2 million/yr on recombinant DNA research. Expects to spend $10 million/yr within 5 years. Has invested $5 million in part ownership of Collaborative Genetics. Exploring four basic areas: human health, agricultural products, industrial enzymes, and industrial catalysts.

The Dow Chemical Co.,
cont'd

Has new genetic-engineering
laboratory in headquarters.
Member, IBA. John Donalds,
Director, biotechnology; William
H. Reily, Director, central
research, bioproducts
laboratories.

DuPont
1007 Market St.
Wilmington, DE 19898
(302) 774-2421

Has staff of 10 scientists working
on applications in agriculture,
pharmaceuticals, chemicals.
Interested in developing industrial
catalysts to prepare acetic acid
and other chemicals from
biomass. Also does in-house
interferon research. And has
established a joint research
program with Harvard.

Eli Lilly Co.
307 East McCarty St.
Indianapolis, IN 46285
(317) 261-2000

Has invested $40 million to build
its own insulin plant. Also has
joint venture with Genentech.

Enzo Biochem
New York
(212) 741-3838

Enzyme research and hepatitis
vaccines.

Enzyme Technology Corp.

Controlled by Great Lakes
Chemical Corp.

Exxon Corp.
1251 Ave. of the Americas
New York, NY 10020
(212) 398-3000

Has an in-house bioscience
research group. Interests include
oxidation reactions from
hydrocarbons via microorganisms
whose functionality can be
improved by gene splicing.

Flow Laboratories
McLean, VA
(804) 893-5925

Cell cultures, viral reagents,
interferon. World's largest tissue
culture commercializer.

Fluor Engineers & Constructors,
Inc.
Daniel International Subsidiary
3333 Michelson Dr.
Irvine, CA 92730
(714) 975-2000

Has a technology agreement with
Genentech. Building a 72,000 sq.
ft. manufacturing facility.

G.B. Fermentation Industries, Inc.
Charlotte, NC
(704) 527-9000

Member, IBA.

G.D. Searle & Co.
4711 Gold Rd.
Skokie, IL 60076
(312) 982-7000

Biological research in
development of vaccines via
recombinant DNA. Has
announced plans to put $15

G. D. Searle & Co., cont'd

million into a pilot plant to develop products using genetic engineering. Member, IBA. Hollis G. Schoepke, Senior Vice-President.

Genentech
South San Francisco, CA
(415) 952-1000

Founded in 1976. Has staff of 200. Current projects include human growth hormone, interferon, insulin, and anticlotting blood agents. Holds over 500 biotechnology patents. Participants include Hoffmann-LaRoche, Fluor, Lubrizol, and Monsanto. Has joint venture with Corning Glass to develop enzymes for corn-syrup production. Gary Hooper, Marketing Manager.

General Electric
1 River Rd.
Schenectady, NY 12345
(518) 385-5669

Some in-house research.

Genetic Engineering, Inc.
Northglenn, CO
(303) 457-1311

Uses gene transfers to produce cows that grow faster and give more milk.

Genetic Instruments, Inc.
Denver, CO

Manufacturer of gene-synthesizing devices.

Genetics Institute
Boston, MA
(617) 232-6886

Member, IBA. Gabriel Schmengel, President.

Genex
Rockville, MD
(301) 770-0650

Founded in 1971. Manufactures enzymes and other chemicals via gene splicing. Participants include Koppers and Monsanto. Has contract with Bristol-Myers to produce interferon. Member, IBA. J. Leslie Glick, President.

Gulf Oil
Gulf Bldg.
P.O. Box 1166
Pittsburgh, PA 15230
(412) 263-5000

Has a modest program in microbiological processing of hydrocarbons and carbohydrates to convert them to chemicals.

Hem Research Corp.
Rockville, MD
(301) 770-5700

Produces fibroblast interferon.

Hoechst
Somerville, NJ
(201) 231-2000

Funding gene research at Harvard.

Hoffmann LaRoche, Inc.
Nutley, NJ 07110
(201) 235-5000

Member, IBA.

Intercontinental Econergy Assoc.
New York, NY
(212) 473-6950

Has formed a new biotechnology
process group that will evaluate
financial aspects of biotechnology
projects.

International Plant Research
   Institute
San Carlos, CA
(415) 595-5335

—

Kennecott Corp.
117 State Rd.
Avondale, PA 19311
(215) 365-3195

Biological research.

Key Energy Ventures
Tampa, FL
(813) 623-5666

Extracts interferon from human
white blood cells.

Koppers Co., Inc.
1900 Koppers Bldg.
Pittsburgh, PA 15219
(412) 227-2000

Co-owner of Genex. Interested in
alcohol production, energy, and
minerals processing.

Life Sciences
St. Petersburg, FL
(813) 345-4371

Producer of leukocyte interferon.

Lubrizol Corp.
29400 Lakeland Blvd.
Wickliffe, OH 44092
(216) 943-4200

Co-owner of Genentech.
Interested in specialty chemicals.

Miles Laboratories, Biotech Group
1127 Myrtle St.
P.O. Box 932
Elkhart, IN 46515
(219) 262-7453

Biological research.

Molecular Genetics, Inc.
Minnetonka, MN
(612) 935-7335

Member, IBA.

Monsanto Co., Inc.
800 Lindbergh Blvd.
St. Louis, MO 63166
(314) 694-1000

Has interests in Genex,
Genentech, and Biogen.
Interested in agricultural and
ethical drug applications. Building
a major new research laboratory.
Thomas Lewis, Director,
corporate research laboratory.

National Distillers
97 Park Ave.
New York, NY 10016
(212) 949-5000

Working with Cetus on alcohol production from biomass. Also interested in fatty acids and sugar fermentation.

National Patent Development
　Corp.
375 Park Ave.
New York, NY 10022
(212) 826-8500

Leukocyte interferon via recombinant DNA.

Neobionics
Boston, MA

Monoclonal antibody production.

New England Biolabs
Beverly, MA
(617) 927-5054

Restriction enzymes, endonucleases and annealers. 1979 sales of $3 million. Donald Comb, President.

Novo Laboratories, Inc.
Wilton, CT
(203) 762-2401

Member, IBA.

Occidental Petroleum
10889 Wilshire Blvd.
Los Angeles, CA 90024
(213) 879-1700

One of its companies—Zoecon—is working on gene manipulation for plant improvement.

Petrogen
Illinois

Enhanced petroleum recovery in oil wells.

Pfizer, Inc.
235 E. 42nd St.
New York, NY 10017
(212) 573-2323

In-house work in plant genetics.

Pharmacia, Inc.
800 Centennial Ave.
Piscataway, NJ 08854
(201) 526-3575

Member, IBA.

Phillips Petroleum Co.
17 D1 Phillips Bldg.
Bartesville, OK 74004
(918) 661-5164

Member, IBA. John Norell, Director, chemical research.

Rohm & Haas
Independent Mall West
Philadelphia, PA 19105
(215) 592-3000

Agri-genetics.

Schering Plough Corp.
Bloomfield, NJ
(201) 429-4000

Building $106 million interferon plant in Ireland. Has a 16 percent interest in Biogen. Member, IBA. Hugh D'Andrade, Senior Vice-President, administration.

Shell Oil
1 Shell Plaza
Houston, TX 77002
(713) 241-4083

Started biotechnology department in June, 1980. Gave contract to Cetus for interferon studies.

Smithkline Beckman Corp.
1 Franklin Plaza
Philadelphia, PA 19101
(215) 751-4000

Member, IBA. Harry Green, Vice-President.

Standard Brands (subsidiary of
  Nabisco)
9 W. 57th St.
New York, NY 10019
(212) 888-5100

Biological research.

Standard Oil of California
225 Bush St.
San Francisco, CA 94104
(415) 894-7700

Co-owner of Cetus.

Standard Oil of Indiana
200 East Randolph Dr.
Chicago, IL 60601
(312) 856-6111

Co-owner of Cetus.

University Patents
Boston, MA

—

The Upjohn Co.
7000 Portage Rd.
Kalamazoo, MI 49001
(616) 323-4000

Pharmaceutical and medical applications.

U.S. Merck & Co.

Invested $23 million in a genetic research laboratory.

Vega Biochemicals
Tuscon, AZ
(602) 746-1401

Manufactures a computerized gene synthesizer. Member, IBA.

Waters Associates, Inc.
Maple St.
Milford, MA 01757
(617) 478-2000

Manufacturer of gene-synthesizing devices.

W.R. Grace & Co.
Grace Plaza
1114 Ave. of the Americas
New York, NY 10036
(212) 819-5000

Bioengineering research division is working toward high-yield production of six amino acids.

Professional Societies with an Interest In Biotechnology

Industrial Biotechnology Association, 2115 E. Jefferson St., Rockville, MD 20852, (301) 984-9598.

Alliance for Engineering in Medicine & Biology, 4405 East-West Hwy., Suite 210, Bethesda, MD 20814, (301) 657-4142.

American Biological Society, 3615 Carson, Amarillo, TX 79109, (806) 355-9369.

American Institute of Biological Sciences, 1401 Wilson Blvd., Arlington, VA 22209, (703) 527-6776.

Society for Industrial Microbiology, 1401 Wilson Blvd., Arlington, VA 22209, (703) 256-0337.

Biomedical Engineering Society, P.O. Box 2399, Culver City, CA 90230, (213) 789-3811.

American Chemical Society, 1155 16th St. N.W., Washington, D.C. 20036, (202) 872-4600.

American Institute of Chemical Engineers, 345 E. 47th St., New York, NY 10017, (212) 705-7338.

Manufacturing Chemists Association, 1825 Connecticut Ave., N.W., Washington, D.C. 20009, (202) 887-1100.

Magazines and Newsletters Covering Biotechnology

Biotechnology Newswatch, McGraw-Hill, 1221 Ave. of the Americas, New York, NY 10020, (212) 997-4343.

Chemical Engineering, 1221 Ave. of the Americas, New York, NY 10020, (212) 997-1221.

Industrial Chemical News, 633 Third Ave., New York, NY 10017, (212) 986-4800.

Bio/technology, 15 E. 26th St., New York, NY 10010, (212) 689-9140.

Genetic Engineering Letter, 1097 National Press Building, Washington, D.C. 20045, (202) 347-3868.

Applied Genetics News, P.O. Box 2070 C, Stamford, CT 06906.

A Glossary of Genetic Engineering Terms

Bacteria. One-cell microorganisms that produce chemical substances. Bacteria come in three different shapes: spheres, rods, and spirals.

Chromosome. A DNA-containing body found in the nuclei of plant and animal cells. Chromosomes determine and transmit hereditary characteristics, such as hair color, height, and color blindness. Human cells have 46 chromosomes.

Clone. To create a genetic duplicate of an individual organism through asexual reproduction via stimulation of a single cell.

DNA. Short for deoxyribonucleic acid. DNA consists of a long chain of molecules in a double-helix configuration, and it is found in the nuclei of cells. DNA carries chemical messages of inheritance from generation to generation. DNA replicates itself and directs the assembly of protein molecules by the cell.

Express. To pass on the genetic characteristic caused by gene splicing to future generations of the cell.

Gene. Genes are units that make up chromosomes. Each gene performs a specific function.

Hybridoma. A hybrid cell made by fusing cancer cells with white blood cells. Hybridomas produce monoclonal antibodies.

Insulin. A hormone secreted by the pancreas. When the body fails to produce sufficient insulin, diabetes is the result.

Interferon. A medum-size protein that acts as an antiviral, anticancer agent. In the human body, cells form interferon as a response to virus infection. Interferon interferes with the virus, inhibiting its development.

Plasmid. Plasmids consist of three or four genes linked in a small circle and located outside the chromosomes.

Protein. Any of a group of complex organic compounds of high molecular weight. Proteins are composed of amino acids and are essential for the growth and repair of living tissue. Proteins are manufactured by the cells of all living organisms. The human body contains more than 100,000 different types of proteins.

Recombinant DNA. A lab technique for splicing together genetic material from unrelated organisms to manufacture new forms of life. Also known as *genetic engineering, biotechnology, gene splicing,* and *cloning.*

Virus. Virus molecules are composed of nucleoproteins formed from either DNA or RNA. Outside of cells, viruses are dormant crystalline chemicals. Inside a cell, they multiply like living things and take over control of the cell's protein-manufacturing operation, which they use to make more virus molecules.

Cable TV

IN GENERAL

"There's no business like show business," says the song. And for thousands of writers, actors, programmers, engineers, technicians, managers, administrators, public relations specialists, salespeople, and marketing executives, cable television is the quickest and most accessible way of getting a piece of the entertainment industry pie.

Cable TV is one of the fastest-growing industries of the decade. In 1982, it employed 40,000 people. By 1990, that number will increase to more than 100,000. Each month, the industry adds 1,000 new employees and 250,000 viewers (known as "subscribers" in cable jargon). "In many fields, hiring freezes, layoffs, and few promotions are the rule rather than the exception," reports *The New York Times*. "But not in cable television. The cable industry is growing at a rapid rate, and career opportunities are many and varied."[1]

Growth is only one aspect of cable's appeal to job-seekers and career-changers. Another is its freshness. The cable industry isn't old enough to be set in its ways; employers seek young, innovative, unspoiled talent. "There are a tremendous amount of entry-level positions in cable," says cable consultant Robin Weber. She points out that the majority of cable employees are under 35 and a significant percentage are women.

Glamour also plays a part in the cable explosion. Remember, cable TV is a special type of *television*. And television has always been an exciting, attractive industry.

Before you look for a job in cable TV, however, you should

understand the basics of the business; most people don't. They can't differentiate between a programming service, such as HBO, and a local cable system, such as Manhattan Cable. To the majority of viewers, cable is a mysterious brown box with 36 buttons on it. They don't know or care where the shows on the brown box come from. But you should, so here's a quick overview of the cable television industry:

Let's begin with a definition. According to the National Cable Television Association, *Cable television* is "a communications system that distributes broadcast television signals as well as a variety of satellite signals by means of a coaxial cable and/or optical fiber." In other words, an underground cable carries the show from the cable operator to your TV set. Conventional network TV, on the other hand, is broadcast over the air. That is why a TV set requires a special hook-up to receive cable channels.

There are basically two sides to the cable industry: *Programming services* and *cable systems*. The cable systems are, in a sense, the "retailers" of the business. They buy products—packages of programs—from the programming services and then offer these programs to their subscribers. Today, there are more than 4,700 cable systems in approximately 13,000 communities. Of American homes with TV, 29 percent now receive cable; the number is expected to increase to 50 percent by the end of the decade.

Manhattan Cable is probably the largest cable system in America. It has 300 miles of cable passing 350,000 homes. Of these, 170,000 households subscribe to the service, which currently carries over 50 programming services on 32 different channels.

If cable systems are the retailers, programming services are the "manufacturers." They supply products—movies, sports events, and other programs—to cable systems. Actually, it's inaccurate to call programming services manufacturers, since few of the shows they offer are produced in-house. Generally, they obtain programs in two ways. They either buy the rights to feature films (*Jaws, Superman II,* and *Star Wars* have recently run on cable), or they finance programs created by independent producers. Since programming services do not as a rule create their own shows, careers in cable production are almost nonexistent, unless you want to work for an independent producer. Few independents are making films and video solely for cable. However, the demand for their services is growing, and many film, commercial, and broadcast producers are producing shows for cable.

If a director's chair or producer's position are not in your cable future, you might ask, "What is?" Well, two-thirds of the positions in cable are technical, with a heavy emphasis on electronics and electrical engineering. But take heart. There are still many other jobs in cable—marketing, sales, affiliate relations, public relations, and programming, to name a few— that are waiting to be filled by bright, eager, creative, *nontechnical* people.

We will discuss specific positions later. Right now, let's find out what cable companies look for in would-be cable moguls.

WHAT IT TAKES

While the cable industry provides 1,000 new jobs every month, many large cable companies receive that many resumes *every week*. Clearly, cable is an attractive industry and competition for entry-level jobs is stiff. So what does it take to break in?

First, the basics. Wayne Tukes, Student Liaison for Minorities in Cable and New Technologies (MCNT), lists four prerequisites for cable employees[2]:

1. Communications skills—verbal and written
2. Determination
3. Creativity—the ability to have ideas
4. Social Skills—the ability to relate well to others

A desire for hard work and an aggressive, competitive personality are two more traits all television professionals must have, says Evelyn Kanter, Manager of Corporate Television for a Fortune 1,000 company and a former on-air reporter for WABC-TV's *Eyewitness News*. "Television is the hardest work you'll ever do," claims Kanter. "If you're an easygoing, noncompetitive person, it's not the place for you." She describes the ideal TV professional as enthusiastic, energetic, intelligent, sharp, and "interested."

Cable may be a young, fun, creative business, but it is a *business* just the same. Cable employers stress that job candidates must have basic business skills and know-how in addition to show business savvy. If you want a career in cable and you're still in school, take courses in business administration, finance, and marketing. A B.A. in business administration is excellent preparation for a career in cable management, marketing, or sales.

Real-life business experience is also valuable. More and more cable companies are luring employees away from advertising agencies and consumer-goods companies, because both these industries are marketing oriented. As cable puts added emphasis on marketing, an MBA will become more of an asset. Today, however, few programming services express a preference for MBA's (HBO is a notable exception). It is even less important on the systems side of the business.

Whatever your major in college is or was, be sure to take additional courses that qualify you for the position you want. "The potential cable employee needs to structure his or her education to improve career opportunities," explains Thomas E. Wheeler, President of the National Cable Television Association.[3] If you want to produce made-for-cable specials, take courses in filmmaking and video production. If you want to wheel-and-deal with high-powered corporations, come into the business as a lawyer specializing in the entertainment industry. Do you want to be in a position to decide whether your cable system operator should bid on a new franchise? Study market research and financial analysis. If you want to break in as a public relations or advertising person, English, Journalism, and Marketing are good majors.

Technical people especially need to keep up their training. What was state of the art last year is obsolete today. And you can't hide gaps in your technical knowledge for long. Evelyn Kanter remembers interviewing one candidate whose technical competence was suspect. She asked, "Did your instructor teach you how to fix the servo in this camera?" "Yes," the enthusiastic candidate replied, and was promptly disqualified for the job. The reason? The servo is part of the video recorder—there is no servo in a camera.

Ms. Kanter stresses that candidates should have a specific job in mind when they apply for employment. Here is a look at some of the positions available with cable programming services:

- *Sales*—Sales representatives sell programs to cable operators. They are responsible for sales presentations, contract negotiations, and solving customer problems. Entry-level salaries range from $12,000 to $20,000 a year, including commissions. Experienced cable salespeople earn $30,000 a year and up. There are no formal requirements, but a sales background is helpful.
- *Marketing*—The marketing staff provides marketing assistance to cable systems that carry the service's products. It does market research, develops strategy, and creates promotional campaigns. Entry-level market researchers earn $12,000 to $15,000 a year. Experienced marketing executives earn $25,000 to $35,000. The recommended education includes a college degree in business administration plus courses in statistics and data processing.
- *Affiliate relations*—Affiliate relations people provide on-going service to the cable-programming service's customers. They get involved in training, consulting, marketing, sales, billings, and distribution of materials. Entry-level salaries are in the low to upper-teens. The Director of Affiliate Relations can earn $40,000 a year and more.
- *Programming*—The programming department collects and packages programs for distribution. However, they do *not* write, direct, act in, or produce these shows themselves. Programmers screen films and features, decide whether they're right for the service, evaluate the financial considerations, and put together the program schedule that the service markets to cable systems.
- *Producers* at cable services act as liaison between independent production companies and the cable service.

Producers secure talent, plan production schedules, set budgets, and monitor the progress of the production to ensure that programs are produced correctly and delivered on time. Because there are so many people with production/programming backgrounds, this is the roughest area to break into. If you're serious about working for HBO, ESPN, Showtime, or one of the 70 other programming services in the country, you'll have a better shot in sales, marketing, or affiliate relations.

Although these are the five "hot spots" in cable programming services, don't forget that these services are large corporations. They have the same conventional functions as other large corporations. These include purchasing, engineering, accounting, human resources, legal, data processing, and personnel. While ordering paper clips or filing resumes may not be your idea of a dream job, *any* first job in cable can lead to bigger and better things. "Get in and work your way up," advises Gloria Michels in a "Careers in Television" seminar she teaches at New York's Learning Annex. "Go in as a bookkeeper and hang around the production office and let them know that's where your interest lies."

Cable programming services are one place to start. Cable systems are another; the systems side offers an even greater variety of career options. To explore these, we need to take a look at how cable systems are established.

If your town wants to get cable TV, it will issue a "request for proposal" (RFP) to several cable operators. Each operator has a team of specialists who will analyze the RFP. *Market analysts* find out what kind of audience the proposed cable system would have. *Programmers* take information provided by market analysts and specify what schedule of programs would satisfy this audience. *Financial analysts* determine the costs involved. *Public relations specialists* smooth the way by keeping the community and local media informed of all developments.

This stage of the process is known as *franchising*. After the cable operators submit their proposals and price-bids for the system, the local government awards a contract—the franchise—to the company with the best proposal and lowest price.

This company will build and operate the cable system to serve the community. The cable specialists who do this preliminary franchising work earn between $15,000 and $45,000 a year.

Next, cables are laid and the system is built. The *surveyors* and *construction workers* who do the hands-on physical labor earn $5 to $10 an hour. Incidentally, construction is one of the largest expenses in cable television; it costs $30,000 a mile to wire a cable system.

The system itself consists of a complex collection of cabling, antennas, receivers, wires, amplifiers, and other electronic gear. The *chief engineer*, who designs and implements the system, earns $35,000 to $50,000 a year and probably has a "double E" (electrical engineering) degree. The *chief technician*, charged with overall system maintenance, earns $18,000 to $28,000, while the technicians he supervises earn $13,000 to $21,000. Technicians usually receive their training at trade schools or two-year colleges having special programs in cable technology.

Once in operation, the cable system has many of the same positions available as the programming services company. *Sales staff* solicit subscribers for the cable system; they earn $12,000 to $25,000 a year, including commission. *Customer service representatives* handle customer service and complaints; their annual salary range is $11,000 to $16,000. *Marketing directors* earn $20,000 to $30,000 on the systems side. The system's *general manager* earns $18,000 to $50,000, depending on the size of the company.

GETTING STARTED

U.S. Labor Department statistics show that 48 percent of all jobs come through personal contacts. In cable TV, the percentage is probably higher. Larry Steward, a career specialist in the cable TV field, estimates that four out of five new positions are never advertised. "Competition for jobs in this industry is very, very stiff," says Steward. "One important key to your success will depend on your ability to penetrate the industry and find the openings." He added that contacts are the single-best source of vital information and direct job leads. Evelyn Kanter concurs. "It's more important than ever to network," she says.

If a career in cable is your dream job, start building a network of leads and contacts *now*. Don't wait until you're out on the street and knocking on doors. "We advise students not to wait until you are ready to graduate to begin your career search," says Claude Wells of Minorities in Cable and New Technologies. "Your career begins as you enter the doors of any institution of higher learning vis-a-vis internships, business contacts, and professional affiliates."[4]

Is your career search stymied, then, if you don't have an uncle who's "in the business"? No. Anybody can build a network of contacts. But it will take time—and perseverance.

"It ain't easy" is how Gary Rubin, a regional affiliate coordinator for The Entertainment Channel, describes networking in the cable industry. "At the beginning, follow any possible lead, because you never know who's going to know who, or who's going to help you," he says. "Think through your background— parents, friends, teachers, colleagues. Is there anybody who has any connection to the cable or entertainment industries? Then, start making phone calls. And every time you meet somebody, ask, 'Is there anybody else I can talk to?' "

Trade publications are a great source of leads. During your job search you should be a regular reader of *MultiChannel News, Variety, CableVision, Backstage, Hollywood Reporter, Broadcasting,* and *Cable Age.* Scan the news and feature stories. Is HBO planning a new division? Fire off a letter to the person in charge. Is there a new franchise in Gary, Indiana? Write to the general manager of the system operator. (In fact, excellent employment opportunities exist in areas recently franchised. Contact local government officials in areas you would relocate to and find out the status of cable in these places.) *This* is how most jobs are won—through leads, openings, and direct contacts. By all means, send your resume to employment services and respond to help-wanted ads. Every shot is worth taking. But the best shots come through direct contact with a specific person, and not by responding to "blind" ads and sending your resume to "Box Y-19."

Your local library has three reference books that will serve as an excellent source of names and addresses. These are the *Television Factbook* (with its *Cable Addenda)*, the *Cable Sourcebook*, and the *Cable Contacts Yearbook.* Here you'll find the names, titles, phone numbers, and addresses of executives at all the major cable programming services and systems as well as independent production companies.

Once you've established a list of strong leads, you need to make contact. The basic tools for this task are the resume, cover letter, and telephone.

The resume should highlight any experience you've had that somehow relates to the position you're seeking in cable TV. Think a minute: Did you sell ads for the school paper? Then note on your resume: "As Sales Representative for the *Campus Times,* I helped campus and community advertisers develop advertising programs, create copy and layouts, measure sales results, and gain editorial coverage in the paper." Did you take an introductory course in filmmaking? Then your resume might indicate your "hands-on experience with state-of-the-art 3/4-inch video equipment." Review your courses, extracurricular activities, work experience, and overall background. You're bound to find knowledge and skills that a cable company can use. The resume is your sales brochure. It should translate these skills into benefits the employer will receive by hiring you.

Each resume you send out should be accompanied by an individually typed cover letter. The letter is addressed to the specific person (usually a vice-president) in charge of the department you're applying to. You should already have this name in your lead-list. If you don't, call the company and get it. Busy executives are not likely to respond to mail addressed to "To whom it may concern." *Always find out the person's name.* And make sure you spell it right.

What about sending a resume with a general letter of introduction to the personnel department? Expert opinion varies. Gloria Michels advises candidates to send a resume to personnel, because they know where all the job openings in the company are and they'll get your resume to the right person.

Others disagree. "You do not want to go to the personnel

department—*ever*," says Evelyn Kanter. "They are very straight . . . and we are flakey." Robin Weber thinks that the personnel department "is the *last* place you want to send your resume." She urges job-seekers to send letters and resumes to the vice-presidents in charge of the departments they would like to work for.

Below, we have reprinted an example of a sharp, direct letter—the kind of letter that gets attention and interviews:

Dear Mr. Burgay:

Consistently creative ideas. Hard work. Unending devotion. Impressive organization. Superior results. As a potential member of your company, these are just a few of the qualities and assets I can offer you. Would you consider seeing a young, dynamic individual who wants to be a part of the team?

If the answer is (a) you better believe it, (b) I'd consider it, or (c) there's an outside shot, then PLEASE read on, so I may suggest how I can help you!

My last three years have been spent developing and sharpening programming and marketing skills that I believe can be of use to you. This past year was spent as a sales trainee with Sony's Consumer Products Division, an experience sure to stand me in good stead for years to come. The previous two, my final two years of college, were spent as a producer with the on-campus theater company. Choosing, developing, and promoting plays helped me develop the beginnings of a pretty keen sense of commercial programming.

Most importantly what I can offer you, Mr. Burgay, is a desire to achieve highly successful results from whatever task is assigned me, and an administrative ability that facilitates this. If I have not made myself clear yet, allow me to: I would give my LEFT ARM (I'm a lefty) to be involved with your group in a production/programming capacity! Please allow me a few minutes of your time. I believe you will be pleased at what you see.

Thank you for your consideration. I look forward to meeting with you.

Sincerely,

Matt Sokoloff

Keep in mind that the cover letter is really a direct-mail advertisement selling a product (you) to a consumer (the employer)! Like all effective advertisements, this letter must do five things:

1. *Get attention.* Note how Matt Sokoloff does this by listing the benefits of hiring him in the first few sentences. And the technique of using short sentence fragments adds to the letter's "wake up and take notice" quality.
2. *Show a need.* Tell the reader that he is looking for someone just like you, even though he may not know it. If you're responding to a help-wanted ad, say so.
3. *Satisfy the need.* Make it clear that you're the person who can fill the job.
4. *Prove your case.* Here is where you highlight the one or two most important points on your resume and include additional information that proves you're the most qualified candidate for the job.
5. *Ask for an interview.* At the reader's convenience, of course. It's also a good idea to thank the reader for taking the time to look at your material.

Once you've sent out letters and resumes, don't sit back and wait for the responses to come pouring in. If you do, you may be disappointed. Gloria Michels tells of one school that required each of its graduating students to send out 300 letters of application to cable employers. *Most students received only six or seven replies*, a response rate of about 2 percent. You can expect similar results.

To turn dead letters into interviews, you've got to pick up the phone and call. Call again and again until you get through. You've undoubtedly heard the saying, "The squeaky wheel gets the grease." Well, if a company receives 1,000 resumes a week, yours isn't going to stay on the top of the pile when next week's 1,000 come pouring in. The way to keep opportunity alive is to follow up with calls and letters.

When you do get through, you might be told, "Sorry, but we don't have any job openings and we won't for some time." Robin Weber has come up with a tactic that might change this "no" into a "maybe."

"Suggest getting together for a 'shmooz session,' " says Weber. Even if there is no position open, ask for one-half hour of the executive's time. Tell her you would like to get her advice and learn more about her company. "This way, you make contact for future openings and referrals," explains Weber.

This works more often than you would suspect, and the reason is pure ego. Imagine your response if someone asked to spend time with you simply because you are wise, successful, and knowledgeable—regardless of whether you could do anything for them. Weber says that the people in charge of cable TV are surprisingly accessible, and she calls on vice-presidents all the time.

If (hallelujah!) your persistence results in an interview, be prepared to sell yourself in person as effectively as you have in print.

"The most important thing about an interview," says Gloria Michels, "is whether the interviewer looks at you and thinks: *The two of us can work together.*" Since cable companies may interview dozens of candidates for a single opening, you've got to stand out from the crowd. "There are a lot of people out there going for the same job," observes Evelyn Kanter. "You have to make them want *you.*"

Gary Rubin offers some tips for successful interviews:

"Try to present yourself in a highly professional manner," says Rubin. "Take great care in your clothes; look your best. Personal grooming is very important. I carried in a nice briefcase, and always had the latest issues of cable trade magazines and *The New York Times* in there. Be prepared, be professional, but be yourself, and let your positive points come out."

YOUR FIRST BIG BREAK

In novels and the movies, aspiring show-biz types pack up their bags and head to Hollywood for a career in movies, or to New York, if they want to make it in network television. But for cable neophytes, the "Big Apple" may be rotten.

"Everybody wants to come to New York," notes Evelyn Kanter, "and New York is the toughest place to find a job—because everybody wants a job!"

Cable was first developed for rural areas that were not adequately served by broadcast television. And it's in rural areas—the South and the Midwest—that your first job in cable may lie.

"Anybody who can leave New York, *leave New York*," recommends Gloria Michels. "There's nothing like the experience you can get outside of New York. Start with a small company in a small town, and you can get experience that will stand you in good stead. Start in New York, and you can get frozen in your position—and that can be deadly to your career. At a smaller company, you can flip between departments . . . Those people who make up their minds to go to a small town usually do get a job."

As we have mentioned, cable TV is a rapidly growing industry. Revenues from subscribers increased at a rate of 17.3 percent over the past decade, from $490 million in 1972 to $2.4 billion in 1982. The 1983 *U.S. Industrial Outlook* predicts that by 1987 cable TV will bring in subscriber revenues of $8.3 billion. As more towns and cities grant cable TV franchises, career opportunities at the local level will continue. The National Cable Television Association reports that employment in cable TV will continue to increase about 10 percent annually. Thus, there will be a steady demand for business administrators, sales and marketing specialists, engineers, and technicians.

Don't despair if your first big break brings you paltry paychecks. Like advertising and public relations, the entertainment industry has traditionally paid low salaries to entry-level employees on the theory that people will want to work in the business because of its glamour. Cable TV has followed suit, so a beginning affiliate relations coordinator or sales specialist may have an annual income in only the low to mid teens. The good news is that once you're in the business, salaries can quickly catch up with what your counterparts are earning in retailing, manufacturing, and other, more conventional lines of work. As *Cosmopolitan* magazine reports, "Once you learn the business, your chances for advancement are excellent."

One much-publicized, entry-level program is the "video

journalist" position at CNN. CNN—Ted Turner's Cable News Network—features live, 24-hour news coverage on cable TV systems throughout the nation. CNN hires cable neophytes as trainees—video journalists—at minimum wage, and rapidly advances them to production spots. Working as a CNN employee will put you in good company; Bella Abzug, Barry Goldwater, Ralph Nader, and Phyllis Schafly have all been commentators for this all-news network.

Another way to get on cable TV is through public access. By law, cable operators are required to reserve a few channels for use by the general public. For about $50, you can buy an hour of air-time during which you can show your own production. Writing, directing, taping, producing, and starring in your own program is a great way to get experience in cable TV. And, if your show is really good, showing a tape of it to the right people might put you on the payroll of a programmer or independent producer.

For students, an internship can lead to the first big break, so a summer job could conceivably turn into full-time employment after graduation. Or, you might even volunteer your time—work for no compensation—to prove how much you want to be part of cable and that particular company.

A few people break into cable by landing a job in a cable-related industry such as venture capital firms, marketing agencies, equipment suppliers, or independent program producers. Independent producers especially will need to hire more people, as the limited supply of movies and sports events increases the demand for made-for-cable productions. However, most production companies have only a few people on-staff—a producer/director, an executive producer, a production manager, and clerical and sales staff. When they need extra help, they hire freelancers.

If you want to escape from the boredom of a dull career and you think the entertainment industry will be more exciting, you're not alone. The students in one session of Gloria Michel's "Careers in Television" seminar included a secretary, a salesman, a banking executive, a management consultant, a medical technologist, a freelance writer, a dancer, an actor, a

Yugoslavian lawyer, an archaeologist, and the manager of a firm that markets lingerie. They all wanted to break into television. And thousands of people from all walks of life have already made the switch to a career in cable TV. You can, too.

WHAT TO SHOOT FOR

"Success is half what you know and who you know," says Evelyn Kanter, "and the other half is being in the right place at the right time to use the first half."

To many job-seekers and career counselors, getting *any* job in cable in the 1980s is being in the right place at the right time. Thirty years ago, when the industry was in its infancy, only 14,000 homes were wired for cable. Today, cable TV reaches 28 million subscribers. By 1987, this number will increase to 37 million.

Still, not all cable companies are created equal, and the industry is undergoing a shakedown which only the more profitable companies will survive. Naturally, you want to be at a company that prospers, so it's important to take a close look at prospective employers.

On the cable systems side, *size* is the important factor. Because cable TV is such a highly capital-intensive industry, only the larger cable operators offer secure employment with the promise of steady promotion. Cable systems range in size from small independent operators serving communities with less than 5,000 homes to giant systems with 100,000 subscribers or more. (If you want to find out the sale price of a cable TV system, multiply the number of subscribers by $600.) The largest operators—MSO's (see Glossary)—own multiple systems; these include ATC, Warner Amex, Cox, and Teleprompter.

On the programming-service side, there are two types of companies: Ad-supported networks and pay TV channels.

As with the major networks, ad-supported cable TV stations run commercials and earn a substantial portion of their revenue by selling air-time to advertisers. The major ad-supported cable networks include CNN, WTBS, ESPN, ARTS, MTV, and USA Network. These and the other ad-supported cable companies had combined advertising revenues of only $100 million in 1981 compared with *$11 billion* for the broadcast networks.

Pay TV channels—which include HBO, Showtime, The Movie Channel, and Spotlight—charge individual subscribers about $10 a month to receive the channel's schedule of movies, sports, and specials. In general, the pay TV networks are faring better than ad-supported cable TV. (Keep that in mind when you look for a job.) Part of the reason is that movies make up the bulk of pay TV programming, and movies have proved to be by far the most popular form of cable TV entertainment. HBO, the most successful pay TV enterprise, had 1981 revenues of $310 million.

When you evaluate prospective cable employers, ask about size and profitability. Take a look at the annual report. As Michael Dann, Senior Program Adviser to ABC Video Enterprises, points out, "The companies whose services survive won't necessarily be the first ones in, but the ones who've learned the most while investing the least."[5]

Once you're in the business, you'll have an inside track on which companies are hot and which are not. If you see an opportunity, say the experts, grab it. "The nature of the business is: Everybody wants to be one step bigger than they are," says Evelyn Kanter. "It's a very incestuous business; people bounce around a lot; in TV, they *expect* you to job-hop. For every person who works hard and has a game plan and knows where she wants to go, there is someone else who gets there by a fluke."

Just because the competition is on the same fast track you are doesn't necessarily mean it is cut-throat, however. On the contrary, people in cable TV are, more often than not, ready and willing to lend a hand to those on the lower rungs of the career ladder. "Even though it's competitive, people are rather helpful," observes Ms. Kanter. And Gloria Michels offers a piece of advice: "Become friends with the people you are working with, and they'll help you go up the ladder."

WHEN YOU'VE MADE IT

"You know you've made it when _____*."* In consulting, you might complete the sentence with, "I know I've made it when I've got my own business, earn $1,000 a day, and have, as clients, half a dozen of the Fortune 500." An advertising executive might say, "I know I've made it when I'm the supervisor in charge of the Burger King account at J. Walter Thompson."

But in cable TV, it's not so easy to fill in the blank.

Today's cable executives know they've made it when they're $65,000-a-year vice-presidents at MSO's or large programming services. But the industry is changing so fast, with so many new job functions and career opportunities being created every year, that the top spot for the cable executive of the 1990s may not have even been invented yet.

To help you plan your cable TV future, here's a quick look at some of the up-and-coming new technologies and services:

- *Pay-per-view TV.* Five hundred thousand homes are now equipped with special equipment that lets them tune into championship fights, first-run films, and other specials on a pay-per-view basis, which means they pay a one-time fee for a single viewing of the event. This service could boost the overall popularity of cable TV and increase the demand for programmers and producers to put together packages of pay-per-view programs.

- *Videotext/teletext.* These technologies allow news and other information to be shown on your TV screen in a text format. If this catches on as a news medium, then writers, editors, and journalists will be needed to prepare copy for videotext/teletext channels.

- *Interactive data communications.* Thanks to videotext, in the near future you'll be able to shop at home over your TV. The TV screen will display information as text, and you'll select items or answer questions with a special key-pad plugged into the set. This type of "interactive" system allows two-way communication with the cable operator, as well as with other subscribers. Other interactive activities will include voting, "electronic mail," classroom instruction, and banking—all of which can be done from the comfort of your favorite easy chair.

• *Informmercials.* With cable-time selling at a fraction of the cost of network air-time, cable advertisers can afford to run long, leisurely "informmercials"—commercials that are 2, 5, or maybe even 10 minutes in length. Moreover, a few advertisers and their agencies are producing their own full-length programs. "One of the things that's going to save cable is corporate sponsorship of programming," says Evelyn Kanter. "An ad agency producing a commercial show for its client, rather than a commercial. *That's* the future of cable TV."

• *Video publishing.* Many newspaper and magazine publishers are considering creating cable TV shows based on their publications. This may result in additional jobs for production-types—writers, producers, directors, and "on-air" personalities.

• *More channels.* Originally, cable TV had 12 channels. But many systems today offer more than 30. And in a few years, that number could increase to 100 or more. Programming services will need to create more products to fill these new channels.

• *DBS (Direct Broadcast Satellite).* As we have mentioned, your community must be wired with underground cables to receive cable TV. DBS is a technology that bypasses cables; a small satellite dish on the individual subscriber's rooftop picks up program signals directly from the communications satellite. DBS will create a new market for programming services while it competes with cable operators.

• *STV (Subscription Television).* STV is a technique for broadcasting pay TV programs over the air. Program signals sent over the air are scrambled electronically; the scrambled signals are then decoded by a special receiver in the subscriber's TV set. This technology may allow broadcasters to compete with cable TV in the pay TV arena.

At present, the future of the cable TV industry is uncertain, as new technologies and business opportunities continue to proliferate. "Predicting cable is like trying to make predictions about politics, the economy, and the weather—all at the same time," says William Donnelly, a Senior Vice-President at Young & Rubicam, Inc. But for some, that's part of the pleasure of being an entertainment industry pioneer. Says Rodney Erickson, Co-chairman of Time Buying Services, "This is more fun than the beginning of (broadcast) television because it is more confusing."[6] The communications professionals who can create order out of this cable TV chaos will be richly rewarded in the years to come.

Cable TV in a Nutshell

Cable technology isn't all that complicated. Here is a 60-second guide to how cable programs get from the programmer's studio to your TV set:

A *programming service* ("A" on the diagram) broadcasts "live" shows produced in its studios as well as feature films and other prerecorded material.

These signals are transmitted over either a *cable* or a *microwave line* (B) to an *uplink transmitter* (C). In just 1/10th of a second, an antenna sitting atop this transmitter beams the signal to a *satellite* (D) orbiting 22,300 miles above the equator.

The satellite is powered by solar panels that resemble wings; hence, satellites are known as "birds" in cable TV jargon. Modern communications satellites have 24 channels ("transponders") capable of transmitting and receiving signals. A satellite programming service must have access to a transponder in order to operate.

The satellite accepts the uplink signal, reamplifies it, and beams the signal down to a receiving antenna system known as an *earth station* (E). From the earth station, the signal is transmitted to a *head end* (F). This is the electronic control center of the cable TV system. The head end transmits the program signal over *cables* (G) to the *television sets* of individual viewers (H). The local cable TV operator owns and controls the earth station, the head end, and the cabling that runs from the control center to individual homes and apartment buildings.

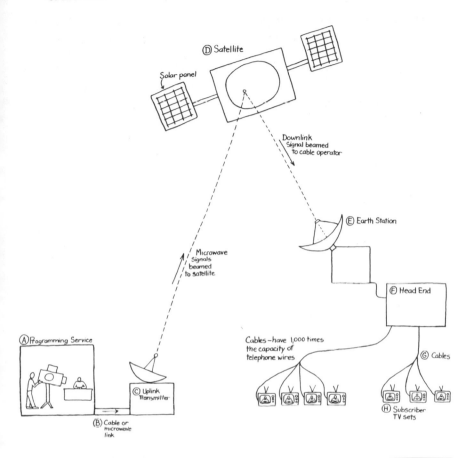

A Glossary of Cable Television Terms

Broadcasting. Transmitting signals over the air to TV sets and radios. The conventional TV networks—ABC, NBC, and CBS—are broadcasters. Also known as "over-the-air" television.

Cable operator. A company that operates a "cable system" over which cable signals are sent to viewers.

Cable television. A system that distributes broadcast television signals and satellite signals through "coaxial cables." These cables consist of copper wire surrounded by insulation and encased in aluminum.

CATV (Community Antenna Television). A term now used interchangeably with cable TV, CATV was originally a community antenna service used in areas that didn't have clear broadcast reception.

DBS (Direct Broadcast Satellite). A proposed system approved by the F.C.C. in which signals would be transmitted directly from a satellite to individual homes equipped with receiving antennas.

Franchise. A contract between a cable operator and a local municipality. The franchise is the cable operator's license to operate his system in the area.

HBO (Home Box Office). The first pay TV network of movies and special programs.

Independent. A cable operator not affiliated with an MSO (multiple system operator).

Interactive television. A cable TV system that allows two-way communication between viewers and the system operator.

MDS (Multi-point Distribution Service). A pay TV service using microwaves to transmit a television signal to individual homes, apartment buildings, and condominiums.

MSO (Multiple System Operator). A company that owns and operates more than one cable TV system. Warner Amex, Cox, and Teleprompter are multiple system operators.

Narrowcasting. Programs of a highly specific nature directed toward smaller audiences.

Pay TV. Movies, sports, and other specials available to cable TV subscribers for a monthly charge in addition to the basic cable fee.

Public access. Cable TV channels available for public use at low cost. Public access channels allow individuals to produce their own programs.

Subscriber. A person who pays a fee for cable TV service.

STV (Subscription Television). Pay TV programs delivered via MDS or over-the-air. Signals are scrambled, and must be decoded by a special receiver in the subscriber's TV set.

Case History: How the Charmin Salesman Switched to Cable

Gary Rubin, 23, changed careers when he moved from a sales job with Procter & Gamble to the position of Regional Affiliate Coordinator for The Entertainment Channel, a cable TV programming service. Here's how he did it:

Q: Briefly describe your job.

A: The Entertainment Channel markets programming services to cable systems. I handle affiliate relations, which is basically providing service to our customers. My major task is giving a training presentation that teaches everybody in the cable system about our channel—how to understand it, suggestions on how to sell it to subscribers. Second, I coordinate details for the system, such as preparing numerical reports. I also help develop individually tailored marketing plans for each cable system and each market.

Q: Where did you go to school and what was your major?
A: I graduated from the University of Michigan in 1981. My degree is a Bachelor of General Studies, with dual concentrations in business-economics-marketing and theater-film-entertainment.

Q: And what was your first job out of college?
A: I went to work for Procter & Gamble (P&G) as a sales representative. I had the very distinguished honor of selling Charmin, White Cloud, Bounty, and—ready for these two?—Pampers and Luvs.

Q: Why did you decide to move to cable?
A: Since I was 16, I've had an affinity for theater, and that grew into a love of the entire entertainment industry. Cable—I hate to say it—was the trendy and hot thing. It caught my attention, and when I started reading cable trade magazines, I became enamored of it.

Q: Did your dual degree—a blend of business and theater—make you an especially attractive candidate to cable companies?
A: I think so. But the thing that helped me get the job in the end was my experience with P&G. Hiring from consumer-products companies is a big trend in the cable industry.

Q: Why?
A: The cable business has just, in the last year, woken up to the concept of marketing. *Just.* And nobody had done cable marketing before, at least as a science. Now they're trying to bring in people that have marketing backgrounds with large package-good companies . . . like P&G.

Q: How did you begin your job search?
A: Well, I was a little spoiled about the whole thing, I admit. I just became very unhappy at P&G knowing more and more that I had to follow my inkling to be in the entertainment industry. I left P&G cold with the confidence that I *would* get a job in the entertainment industry and probably in cable. It didn't work out as easily as I thought it would—it took me 6 months to get the right job!

Q: How many resumes did you send out in that time?

A: I'll qualify this answer and say I don't think that the resume is the effective tool in getting a job in today's cable industry.

Q: What is?

A: I found that a personal letter, followed by a series of phone calls, was most effective. Also, connections—there's no better way to do it than mentioning names, so you have to build a network of contacts. I also used a technique that was extremely successful in the later months. After I got in to see somebody, I would send them a mailgram. They all commented to me how impressed they were with this. The key thing is: *You've got to be different.*

Q: How many letters did you send out?

A: I ended up sending out 300 letters and going on 50 interviews.

Q: Any tips on writing the cover letter?

A: Write a letter that will stand out. A letter that's different. Be creative. Put it on a very fine stationery—pay to have a letterhead done professionally. Because they've got to look great. Put "personal and confidential" on the envelope. Nine times out of ten they ignore it, but the tenth time it works! And the opening few sentences have to catch the person's attention.

Q: What are some of the "guerilla tactics" you used to get your foot in the door?

A: Befriend everybody in the company. When that secretary picks up the phone, you better make her your friend—and fast. The secretaries are right arms to their bosses, and you must work through them to get to the person you want to see. Treat secretaries well, because they can be your best friends; they can go in and pitch you to their boss. And that gives you a real edge going into the interview.

Q: What are the traits of the ideal candidate in cable TV?

A: Aggressiveness and creativity are both very important. They're looking for conceptual people, hard workers. *Very* hard workers. You put in long hours in this business. I travel a lot, and the nights I travel I may not get back until 10 or 11 o'clock. It helps if you can bring a useful skill to the job, such as programming or selling. Cable is too new and not enough money is being made to set up extensive training programs.

Q: Do you have a career game plan?

A: The cable business is so young, I don't know if there's a strict pattern to follow, such as there would be at P&G. I plan to move fairly quickly and I do have every intention of reaching a very high point in the entertainment industry.

Note: As this book went to press, The Entertainment Channel went out of business and Gary Rubin took another position.

To Read: Periodicals

On Cable, 25 Van Zant St., Norwalk, CT 06855, (203) 866-6256. Cable TV's version of *TV Guide.* Monthly.

Broadcasting, 1735 DeSales St., N.W., Washington, D.C. 20036, (202) 638-1022. A weekly news magazine covering the television industry.

CableVision, Titsch Publishing, Inc., 2500 Curtis St., Denver, CO 80205, (303) 295-0900. A weekly magazine covering cable TV programming, marketing, trends, and products.

MultiChannel News, Fairchild Industries, 1762 Emerson St., Denver, CO 80218. The newspaper of the cable TV industry.

TVC, Cardiff Publishing Company, 3900 S. Wadsworth Blvd., Denver, CO 80235, (303) 694-1522. The business magazine for cable TV operators.

Variety, 154 W. 45th St., New York, NY 10036, (212) 582-2700. Weekly magazine of the entertainment industry. Covers theater, film, radio, and TV.

View: The Magazine of Cable TV Programming, Marco Communications, 150 E. 58th St., New York, NY 10022, (212) 826-4360. A magazine for cable TV operators and programmers.

Cable Age, 1270 Ave. of the Americas, New York, NY 10020, (212) 757-8400. For executives in the cable TV industry. Twice monthly.

Cable Communications Magazine, 4 Smetana Dr., Kitchener, Ontario, N2B 3B8, (519) 744-4111. Magazine covering Canada's cable TV industry. Monthly.

Cable Marketing, 352 Park Ave. South, New York, NY 10010. Monthly tabloid for cable TV executives involved in marketing and management.

The Pay TV Newsletter, Paul Kagan Associates, Inc., 26356 Carmel

Rancho Blvd., Carmel, CA 93923, (408) 624-1536. Semimonthly newsletter on investments and regulations in the cable TV industry.

Books

Television Factbook, Services Volume and *Cable Addenda to Television Factbook,* 1836 Jefferson Place, N.W., Washington, D.C. 20036, (202) 872-9200. Comprehensive reference books listing cable TV systems, programmers, manufacturers, and associations.

Cable Sourcebook, Broadcasting Publications, Inc., 1735 DeSales St., N.W., Washington, D.C. 20036, (202) 638-0888. Lists all U.S. cable systems, multiple systems operators, and programmers.

Cable Contacts Yearbook, Larimi Communications Associates, Ltd., 151 E. 50th St., New York, NY 10022, (212) 935-9262. Lists the names of the people in charge of cable TV networks, news services, local programs, multiple systems operators, and independent producers.

The Community Medium, edited by Nancy Jesuale and Ralph Lee Smith, The Cable Television Information Center, 1800 North Kent St., Suite 1007, Arlington, VA 22209. An overview of various cable TV services, including local programming, data communications, satellite services, and interactive systems.

Handbook for Producing Educational and Public-Access Programs for Cable Television by Rudy Bretz, Englewood Cliffs, NJ: Educational Technology Publications, 1976, 132 pp.

Cable Television: Developing Community Services by Polly Carpenter-Huffman, Richard C. Kletter, and Robert K. Yin, New York, NY: Crane-Russak, 1975, 275 pp.

Cablecasting Production Handbook by J.L. Efrein, Blue Ridge Summit, PA: TAB Books, 1975, 210 pp.

On the Cable: The Television of Abundance, Report of the Sloan Commission on Cable Communications, New York, NY: McGraw-Hill, 1971.

Cable Television, 2d ed. by J.E. Cunningham, Indianapolis, IN: H.W. Sams, 1980, 392 pp.

Television in Transition by James Watson, Crain Books, 740 N. Rush St., Chicago, IL 60611.

TV Trade Associations

Minorities in Cable and New Technologies, 624 S. Michigan Ave., Suite 616A, Chicago, IL 60605, (312) 922-9043.

Cable and Consumer Electronics Council, Institute of Electrical and Electronics Engineers (IEEE), 345 E. 47th St., New York, NY 10017, (212) 705-7900.

National Federation of Local Cable Programmers, 3700 Far Hills Ave., Suite 109, Kettering, OH 45429.

Cable Television Information Center, 1800 N. Kent St., Suite 1007, Arlington, VA 22209, (703) 528-6836.

National Cable Television Institute, P.O. Box 27277, Denver, CO 80227, (303) 761-8554.

National Cable Television Association, 1724 Massachusetts Ave., N.W., Washington, D.C. 20036, (202) 775-3550.

Women in Cable, 2063 M St., N.W., Suite 703, Washington, D.C. 20036, (202) 296-4218.

Placement Firms Specializing in Cable TV

Communications Marketing, Inc., 2323 Tampa Ave., El Cajon, CA 92020, (800) 854-2837.

Baker Scott & Co., 1259 Route 46, Parsippany, NJ 07054, (201) 263-3355.

Key Systems, 0106 Naw Bridge Center, Kingston, PA 18704, (717) 287-9635.

National Technical Careers, 1701 W. Euless Blvd., Suite 120, Euless, TX 76039, (817) 571-2455.

Career Marketing Associates, 5031 South Ulster, Suite 430, Denver, CO 80237, (303) 779-8890.

Jim Young & Associates, Inc., 1 Young Plaza, 1235 Ranger Hwy., Weatherford, TX 76086, (800) 433-2160.

Pro/File Associates, 90 Madison St., Suite 100, Denver, CO 80206, (303) 399-1718.

Donald G. Nelson and Associates, 1651 E. 4th St., Suite 215, Santa Ana, CA 92701, (714) 973-1722.

Steward Communications Group, 420 E. 55th St., Suite 11A, New York, NY 10022, (212) 752-4299.

Top 50 Cable TV System Operators

1. *Tele-Communications, Inc.*
   54 Denver Technological Center
   P.O. Box 22595
   Denver, CO 80222
   (303) 771-8200

2. *American TV and
   Communications Corp.*
   160 Inverness Dr. West
   Englewood, CO 80112
   (303) 773-3411

3. *Group W Cable*
   888 7th Ave.
   New York, NY 10016
   (212) 247-8700

4. *Cox Cable Communications,
   Inc.*
   53 Perimeter Center Pkwy.
   Suite 300
   Atlanta, GA 30346
   (404) 393-0480

5. *Storer Cable Communications*
   P.O. Box 4605
   Miami, FL 33169
   (305) 866-0211

6. *Warner Amex Cable
   Communications*
   75 Rockefeller Plaza
   New York, NY 10019
   (212) 484-8000

7. *Times Mirror Cablevision, Inc.*
   P.O. Box 19398
   2381 Morse Ave.
   Irvine, CA 92713
   (714) 549-2173

8. *New House/Metrovision Inc.*
   211 Perimeter Center Pkwy.
   Atlanta, GA 30346
   (404) 394-8837

9. *Rogers/UA Cablesystems*
   315 Post Rd. West
   Westport, CT 06880
   (203) 227-9581

10. *Viacom Communications, Inc.*
    1211 Ave. of the Americas
    New York, NY 10036
    (212) 575-5175

11. *Continential Cablevision, Inc.*
    54 Lewis Wharf
    Boston, MA 02110
    (617) 742-9500

12. *United Cable TV Corporation*
    4700 S. Syracuse Pkwy.
    Denver, CO 80237
    (303) 779-5999

13. *Sammons Communications, Inc.*
    P.O. Box 225728
    Dallas, TX 75265
    (214) 742-9828

14. *TeleCable Corporation*
    740 Duke St.
    P.O. Box 720
    Norfolk, VA 23510
    (804) 446-2000

15. *Capital Cities Communications*
    710 N. Woodward Ave.
    Bloomfield Hills, MI 48013
    (313) 646-6631

16. *General Electric Cablevision,
    Inc.*
    257 Riverside Ave.
    Westport, CT 06880
    (203) 226-2710

17. *Heritage Communications, Inc.*
    2195 Ingersoll Ave.
    Des Moines, Iowa 50312
    (515) 245-7587

18. *Cablevision Systems
    Development Co.*
    1 Media Crossways
    Woodbury, NY 11797
    (516) 364-8450

19. *Comcast Corporation*
    1 Belmont Ave.
    Bala Cynwyd, PA 19004
    (215) 667-4200

20. *Liberty Communications, Inc.*
    2225 Coburg Rd.
    Eugene, OR 97401
    (503) 485-5611

21. *Service Electric Cable TV, Inc.*
    Main and Pine Sts.
    Mahanoy City, PA 17948
    (717) 773-2585

22. *Wometco Communications, Inc.*
    306 N. Miami Ave.
    Miami, FL 33128
    (305) 374-6262

23. *Tele-Media Corporation*
    1331 Park Hills Ave.
    State College, PA 16801
    (814) 237-1512

24. *Texas Community Antennas
    Group*
    3027 S.E. Loop 323
    Tyler, TX 75701
    (214) 595-3701

25. *McLean Hunter*
    27 Fasken Dr.
    Rexdale, Ontario, M9W 1K7
    (416) 675-5930

26. *Century Communications Corp.*
    51 Locust Ave.
    New Canaan, CT 06840
    (203) 966-8746

27. *Multimedia Cablevision, Inc.*
    P.O. Box 3027
    Wichita, KS 67201
    (316) 262-4270

28. *Daniels and Associates, Inc.*
    2930 E. Third Ave.
    Denver, CO 80206
    (303) 321-7550

29. *Western Communications, Inc.*
    2855 Mitchell Dr.
    Suite 225
    Walnut Creek, CA 94596
    (415) 935-3055

30. *Colony Communications, Inc.*
    75 Fountain St.
    Providence, RI 02902
    (401) 277-7444

31. *Communications Services, Inc.*
    140 W. 8th St.
    Box 829
    Junction City, KS 66441
    (913) 762-2570

32. *Jones Intercable, Inc.*
    5275 DTC Pkwy.
    Englewood, CO 80111
    (303) 740-9700

33. *Harron Communications Corp.*
    1460 Russell Rd.
    Paoli, PA 19301
    (215) 644-7500

34. *Prime Cable Corporation*
    1515 First City National Bank
    Building
    Austin, TX 78701
    (512) 476-7888

35. *Centel Communications Corp.*
    1030 North Ave.
    Des Plaines, IL 60016
    (312) 635-5500

36. *Midwest Video Corporation*
    860 Tower Building
    Little Rock, AR 72201
    (501) 375-8885

37. *Harris Cable Corporation*
    10889 Wilshire Blvd.
    Suite 1240
    Los Angeles, CA 90024
    (213) 208-6118

38. *Tribune Cable Corporation*
    Box D, Colonial Offices
    Whitney Rd.
    Mahwah, NJ 07430
    (201) 891-7988

39. *Rollins Cablevision, Inc.*
    2170 Piedmont Road, N.E.
    Atlanta, GA 30301
    (404) 873-2355

40. *Cablevision Industries, Inc.*
    P.O. Box 311
    Wierk Ave.
    Liberty, NY 12754
    (914) 292-7550

41. *Gill Cable,Inc.*
    1302 N. 4th St.
    San Jose, CA 95112
    (408) 998-7333

42. *New York Times Cable*
    120 W. Merchant St.
    Audubon, NJ 08106
    (609) 547-4400

43. *Toledo Blade Company*
    541 Superior St.
    Toledo, OH 43660
    (419) 289-6000

44. *Armstrong Utilities, Inc.*
    1 Armstrong Pl.
    Butler, PA 16001
    (412) 283-0925

45. *Sutton Capital Group*
    366 Madison Ave.
    New York, NY 10017
    (212) 697-0988

46. *Communications Systems*
    700 W. Airport Fwy.
    Irving, TX 75062
    (214) 438-9450

47. *Multi-Channel TV Cable Co.*
    5533 Canal Rd.
    Valley View, OH 44125
    (216) 524-0900

48. *Cablentertainment*
    295 Madison Ave.
    New York, NY 10017
    (212) 683-2900

49. *Televents, Inc.*
    2855 Mitchell Dr.
    Suite 250
    Walnut Creek, CA 94598
    (415) 935-8610

50. *McDonald Group*
    1 Office Park Dr.
    Birmingham, AL 35223
    (205) 879-0456

Prepared by The Cable Television Information Center, 1982.

The Major Satellite-Delivered Cable Programming Services

American Educational Television Network (AETN), 2172 Dupont Dr., Suite 7, Irvine, CA 92715, (800) 854-7387. Continuing education programs for licensed professionals.

Appalachian Community Service Network (ACSN), 1200 New Hampshire Ave., N.W., Suite 240, Washington, D.C. 20036, (202) 331-8100. Continuing education programming.

ARTS, Warner Amex Satellite Entertainment Corp., 1211 Ave. of the Americas, 15th floor, New York, NY 10036, (212) 661-4500. Music, drama, dance. Personnel: Curtis Davis, Director of programming; Marc Sheldon, Vice-President of production.

Black Entertainment Network (BET), USA Network, Prospect Pl., 3222 N St., N.W., Suite 300, Washington, D.C. 20007, (202) 337-5260. For black audiences. Personnel: Robert Weissburg, Director of programming; Jean O'Grady, Acquisitions.

BRAVO, Rainbow Programming Service, 100 Crossways Park West, Suite 200, Woodbury, NY 11797, (516) 364-2222. Film, dance, and music. Personnel: Doug Vect, Manager of promotion.

Cable Health Network, 1211 Ave. of the Americas, New York, NY 10036, (212) 719-7230. Programs on physical and mental health, dieting, and sex.

Cable News Network (CNN), Southern Satellite Systems, 1050 Techwood Dr., Atlanta, GA 30318, (404) 898-8500. News.

CableText, Southern Satellite Systems, P.O. Box 45684, Tulsa, OK 74145, (918) 481-0881. News.

Christian Broadcasting Network (CBN), CBN Center, 1000 Centerville Tpe., Virginia Beach, VA 23463, (804) 424-7777. Religious programming.

Christian Media Network, P.O. Box 20121, Bloomington, MN 55420, (612) 884-4540. Religious programming.

Cinemax, HBO, Time & Life Building, Rockefeller Center, New York, NY 10020, (212) 484-1184. Pay TV service offered by HBO as a second tier of programming. Movies.

Continental Radio, Christian Broadcasting Network, 1318 Spratley St., Portsmouth, VA 23704, (804) 424-7777. News, pop, and Christian music.

C-SPAN, USA Network, 3800 N. Fairfax Dr., Arlington, VA 22203, (703) 525-3030. Coverage of the House of Representative sessions, plus special features.

Dow Jones Cable News, P.O. Box 300, Princeton, NJ 08540, (609) 452-2000, ext. 2680. Financial news in a text format.

Entertainment & Sports Programming Network (ESPN), ESPN Plaza, Bristol, CT 06010, (203) 584-8477. Sports. Personnel: Barry Black, Director of human resources.

Episcopal Television Network, P.O. Box 2060, New York, NY 10163, (212) 888-0591. Religious programming.

Escapade, Rainbow Programming Service, 100 Crossways Park West, Woodbury, NY 11797, (516) 364-2222. Adult films.

Eternal Word Television Network, 5817 Old Leeds Rd., Birmingham, AL 35210, (205) 956-9537. Nondenominational Christian programming.

GalaVision, Spanish International Network (SIN), 250 Park Ave., New York, NY 10017, (212) 953-7550. Movies, sports, and specials for Spanish-speaking viewers.

HBO (Home Box Office), Time & Life Building, Rockefeller Center, New York, NY 10020, (212) 484-1000. Movies, sports, and specials. Cable TV's first pay service.

Home Theater Network, Southern Satellite Systems, 465 Congress St., Portland, ME 04101, (207) 774-0300. Movies rated P and PG.

Lifestyle, United Video, 5200 South Harvard, Suite 215, Tulsa, OK 74135, (800) 331-4806. Background music.

Modern Satellite Network (MSN), Modern Talking Picture Service, 45 Rockefeller Plaza, New York, NY 10111, (212) 765-3100. Educational and consumer-interest programs. Personnel: Bob Feinhout, Director of programming.

The Movie Channel, Warner Amex Satellite Entertainment Corp., 1211 Ave. of the Americas, 15th floor, New York, NY 10036, (212) 944-4223. Pay service showing movies. Personnel: John Sykes, Program Director.

MTV (Music Television), Warner Amex Satellite Corp., 1221 Ave. of the Americas, New York, NY 10036, (212) 944-4257. "New wave" music plus regular rock-and-roll.

National Christian Network (NCN), P.O. Box 493, Cocoa, FL 39222, (305) 632-1510. Nondenominational religious programming.

National Jewish Television, 2621 Palisades Ave., Riverdale, NY 10463, (212) 549-4160. Programming for the Jewish community.

Nickelodeon, Warner Amex Satellite Entertainment Corp., 1211 Ave. of the Americas, 15th floor, New York, NY 10036, (212) 944-5233. Programming for youngsters. Personnel: Eileen Opatut, Programming Development.

North American Newstime, 1800 Peachtree Rd., Suite 512, Atlanta, GA 30309, (404) 351-9103. News.

Private Screenings (PS), Satori Productions, Inc., 330 W. 42nd St., Penthouse Suite, New York, NY 10036, (212) 563-2323. Adult films. Personnel: Jeff Sass, Director of acquisitions; Janice Di Madonna, Vice-President in charge of personnel.

PTL, 7224 Park Rd., Charlotte, NC 28279, (704) 527-5350. Religious programming.

Reuters Monitor Service/News-Service, Southern Satellite Systems, 1221 Ave. of the Americas, 16th floor, New York, NY 10036, (212) 730-2716. News in a text format.

Satellite Music Network, P.O. Box 31542, Dallas, TX 75231, (800) 527-4892. Country and pop music.

Satellite Program Network (SPN), Southern Satellite Systems, P.O. Box 45684, Tulsa, OK 74145, (918) 481-0881. Programming for families and women.

Showtime, 1633 Broadway, New York, NY 10019, (212) 880-6633. Pay service offering movies and specials.

Spanish International Network (SIN), 250 Park Ave., New York, NY 10017, (212) 953-7507. Spanish-language series, specials, and news.

Spotlight, Times Mirror Satellite Programming, 2951 28th St., #2000, Santa Monica, CA 90405, (213) 450-6488. Pay service.

Trinity Broadcasting Network (TBN), P.O. Box A, Santa Ana, CA 92711, (714) 832-2950. Religious programming.

UPI Cablenews Wire, Southern Satellite Systems, 220 E. 42nd St., New York, NY 10017, (212) 682-0400. News in a text format.

USA Network, Route 208, Harristown Rd., Glen Rock, NJ 07452, (201) 445-8550. Sports, music, specials.

WFMT, United Video, 5200 South Harvard, Suite 215, Tulsa, OK 74135, (800) 331-4806. Classical music.

WGN, United Video, 5200 South Harvard, Suite 215, Tulsa, OK 74135, (800) 331-4806. Movies, sports, news, and programming for women and children.

WOR, Eastern Microwave, 3 Northern Concourse, P.O. Box 4872, Syracuse, NY 13321, (315) 455-5955. Movies, syndicated programming, and sports.

WTBS, Southern Satellite Systems, 1050 Techwood Dr., Atlanta, GA

30318, (404) 898-8500. Movies, sports, syndicated programs, and news.

Source: *Careers in Cable,* published by the National Cable Television Association, Washington, D.C..

Schools That Offer Technical Training in Cable Television

Maricopa County Skill Center, 4118 E. Wood St., Phoenix, AZ 85040, (602) 243-4141. Contact: Louis E. Dale.

Cox Cable Communications, 1331 N. Cuyamuaca, Suite P, El Cajon, CA 92020, (714) 562-0742. Contact: Richard Johnson.

East Bay Skills Center, 1100 67th St., Oakland, CA 94608, (415) 658-7356. Contact: Isaac Lassister.

San Diego Community College, 12th & B Sts., Administrative Office, San Diego, CA 92101, (714) 562-1150. Contact: Paul R. Workman.

ATC National Training Center, 2100 South Hudson, Denver, CO 80222, (303) 773-3411. Contact: Robert Odland.

National Cable Television Institute, P.O. Box 27277, Denver, CO 80227, (303) 697-4967. Contact: Lowell Williams.

RETS Electronic Schools, 7346 S. Alton Way, Suite A, Englewood, CO 80112, (303) 741-5873. Contact: Glenn Kriegel.

Middlesex Community College, 100 Training Hill Rd., Middleton, CT 06457, (203) 344-3052. Contact: Virginia Pettiross.

McGraw-Hill Continuing Education Center, 3939 Wisconsin Ave., N.W., Washington, D.C. 20016, (202) 244-1600.

Omega School of Communications, 548 N. Lake Shore Dr., Chicago, IL 60611, (312) 321-9400. Contact: Jim Ehrhart or Robbin Rutherford.

Dakota County Area Vocational Technical Institute, Student Services Office, 145th St. East & Akron Rd., P.O. Drawer K, Rosemount, MN 55068, (612) 423-2281.

Wadena Area Vocational Technical Institute, P.O. Box 267, 405 S.W. Colfax Ave., Wadena, MN 56482, (218) 631-3530. Contact: Jon P. Kosidowski.

Chillicothe Area Vocational Technical School, 1200 Fair St., Chillicothe, MO 64601, (816) 646-3414. Contact: Bob Chenoweth.

Cablevision Training Center, Inc., A Teleprompter Institute, 4150 Old Mill Pkwy., St. Charles, MO 63301, (314) 441-7490. Contact: Marie Veal.

Essex County College, 303 University Ave., Newark, NJ 07102, (201) 877-3274. Contact: Spencer Freund.

Mercer County Community College, 1200 Old Trenton Rd., Trenton, NJ 08690, (609) 586-4800. Contact: George Schwartz.

BOCES Electronics Cable Technician, BOCES Nike Center, Shawnee Rd., Sanborn, NY 14132, (716) 731-9620. Contact: Frank Raising.

University College, University of Cincinnati, M.L. 47, Cincinnati, OH 45221, (513) 475-3551. Contact: Dr. William Frase.

Cleveland Institute of Electronics, 1776 E. 17th St., Cleveland, OH 44114.

Garfield Skills Center, 2013 W. 3rd St., Dayton, OH 45417, (513) 268-6702. Contact: Lloyd Lewis.

South Oklahoma City Junior College, 7777 S. May Ave., Oklahoma City, OK 73159, (405) 682-1611. Contact: Bill J. Grough.

Pittsburgh Opportunities Industrialization Center, Cable Television School, 1901 5th Ave., Pittsburgh, PA 15219, (412) 255-6480. Contact: Lorette Kemp or Eugene G. Casanova.

International Correspondence Schools, Oak St., Scranton, PA 18515, (717) 342-7701. Contact: Robert Donovan.

Texas Engineering Extension Service, Electronics Training Division, The Texas A&M University System, F.E. Drawer K, College Station, TX 77843, (713) 779-3880, ext. 244. Contact: Lloyd E. Fite.

Western Wisconsin Technical Institute, 6th & Vine Sts., La Crosse, WI 54601, (608) 785-9178. Contact: William G. Welch.

Wisconsin Indianhead Technical Institute, Rice Lake Campus, 1900 College Dr., Rice Lake, WI 54868, (715) 234-7082. Contact: John Graf.

Source: *NCTA Directory of Cable Training Schools,* National Cable Television Association, Washington, D.C.

Computers

IN GENERAL

In 1981, United States computer manufacturers sold 1.4 million home computers for $3 billion. There are 5 million computer terminals in use today, and that number will double by the end of 1986. By the end of the century, 80 million Americans will own their own computers.

These figures prove what you probably already know—computers are *hot*. If the movie *The Graduate* was being filmed today, that well-meaning business executive would advise Dustin Hoffman to forget about plastics and go into data processing (DP).

Most large organizations have their own computer. According to a study by the International Data Corporation, there are 730,000 commercial-size ("mainframe") computer systems currently in operation at industrial, commercial, academic, and government installations. And this number is expected to double by the end of 1985.

All this adds up to plenty of new jobs: *The New York Times* reports that 1.4 million people now work in data processing, and that 685,000 new jobs will be added by the end of the decade. This chapter is written to help you get one of those jobs.

First, we'll give you a quick rundown of some of the positions available, along with their starting salaries. As you scan the list, you'll notice that some jobs are technical (systems analyst, programmer, EDP auditor) while others are not (documentation writer, marketing support, sales). Although few people outside the field realize it, there are many positions in data processing that do *not* require a technical background or even an aptitude for math or science. In this chapter, we'll focus on how the nontechnical person can break into and succeed in data processing without becoming a computer programmer or technician. (Of course, we'll provide career guidance for technical DP people as well.)

Here, then, is a sampling of where you might work in data processing (Salary figures, which are typical of what you would get at a large company, are taken from *Starting Salaries 1983* [a survey published by Robert Half], the *1983 Computer Salary Survey and Career Planning Guide* [published by Source Edp], the Bureau of Labor Statistics, and the *Hansen Data Processing Survey.*):

- *Marketing representative*—computer salespeople for computer manufacturers and software (program) vendors. Probably the best-paying position for nontechnical DP professionals. Starting compensation, with commissions, can be as high as the low $40,000 a year range.
- *Marketing support representative*—provides technical support in the sale of hardware and software. Marketing support reps help with customer liaison, sales presentations, and feasibility studies. This position is a stepping-stone to a sales job. Average yearly starting salary for a marketing support rep is $23,900.
- *Documentation technical writer*—documents programs and writes instruction manuals for computer users. Starting salary range: $18,000 to $27,000 a year.
- *Applications programmer*—writes programs in a "high-level" language such as COBOL, RPG-II, or FORTRAN. These programs tell the computer how to solve specific problems for business or scientific applications. Starting yearly salary range: $18,000 to $24,000.
- *Systems programmer*—writes programs to maintain the internal operating system of the computer. Starting yearly salary: $26,000 to $36,000.
- *EDP auditor*—computer "efficiency experts" that monitor computer operations. An EDP (electronic data proc-

essing) audit is similar to an accounting audit, except you go over the data processing department instead of the books. Starting yearly salary: $25,000 to $34,000.

- *Data base administrator*—A "data base" is a set of files (of computer information) logically structured and linked to each other. The data base administrator designs, develops, and administers the use of information within the data base. Starting yearly salary: $26,000 to $36,000.
- *EDP instructor*—trains company employees in the use of the system. An excellent entry into data processing for ex-teachers. Starting yearly salary: $20,000 to $28,000.
- *Systems analyst*—responsible for the design and implementation of data processing systems. The systems analyst puts together hardware and software packages to solve specific problems, and acts as liaison between programmers and end-users. Starting yearly salary: $29,500 to $36,000.
- *Computer operator*—runs programs on the computer and retrieves the results. Starting yearly salary: $15,000 to $19,400.
- *Technician*—installs and repairs computer systems. Salary range: $12,600 to $17,900 a year.
- *Data entry*—operates CRT terminals and keypunch machines. Enters information into computer via magnetic tape, disks, or cards. Salary range: $10,400 to $13,200 a year.
- *Vice-President of data processing*—also known as MIS Director. Head of the company's data processing department. Responsible for day-to-day operations and long-range planning. This is the top position at a company with a data processing department. Salary range: $49,000 to $70,000 a year and up.

Naturally, some of these positions are hotter than others. There will be more sales and marketing positions with vendors of microcomputers because of the boom in selling small computers to small businesses. In addition, the trend toward factory automation will generate 50,000 new jobs for technicians who can repair robots over the next 15 years. On the negative side, there will be a 13.5 percent decline in the number of data entry positions, because the new terminals make it easy for users to enter their own data into the system.

WHAT IT TAKES

There are two myths concerning breaking into data processing. The first says you must be a math whiz to understand computers. The second is that a B.S. degree in computer science is required.

Neither myth is true.

"You don't have to be good at math to be good at computers," says Ronnie Colfin, a Product Manager with the American Management Association.[1] "What you need to be is a very logical kind of person, somebody who thinks something through step-by-step, somebody who's very systematic. But you certainly don't have to be good at math." Colfin and other experts have pointed out that computer programming languages such as BASIC and FORTRAN resemble a human language more closely than they do a set of mathematical equations. So, if you enjoyed English or foreign languages in high school, chances are you'll be able to master the basics of computer programming.

As for training, a college degree isn't the only way to learn about computers. Many large companies—computer manufacturers, banks, insurance companies, and the Fortune 500—have training programs for entry-level data processing people. These programs often have a sharp focus on the company's own systems and languages, but an introductory computer course or two at a local tech school or evening college can round out your computer know-how nicely. Your employer will probably pay the tuition.

If you didn't major in computer science, and want to get formal training *before* you apply for a job, we recommend a program for a Certificate in Data Processing. Many accredited colleges offer such intensive training, and virtually every prospective employer recognizes the value of these Certificates. A typical Certificate curriculum includes these courses:

- VAL assembly language.
- IBM assembly language.
- Between two to four courses in high-level languages. The most important languages are COBOL, RPG-II, and FORTRAN.
- Introduction to computers—architecture, history, and terminology.
- JCL—Job Control Language.
- Flow-charting—the logic of writing computer programs.

This course of study takes 6 months to complete if you're a full-time student and 1 year if you attend school at night.

However, knowing how to program is only necessary for systems analysts, programmers, and other technical positions. People in sales, marketing, administration, training, and documentation don't have to be accomplished programmers. They just need to know the basics: What computers are, how they work, and what they can and cannot do. You can learn a great deal by reading computer books written for laypeople, and we have compiled a list of good introductory books you might want to take a look at (see the box titled, "A Short Home-Study Course in Computers"). Or, just take an introductory course at a community college or adult-education center.

As in any field, being able to speak the lingo is a sign of your expertise. We have listed a few dictionaries of computer terms in the reading list. But, for a quick introduction to the jargon, take a look at our short glossary of computer terms (see box).

A Short Home-Study Course in Computers

Many sales-oriented jobs in data processing don't require an extensive knowledge of programming and computer technology. But if you're serious about working in the computer industry, it's a good idea to learn the jargon and understand the basics of how a computer works. Below is a list of suggested books that will give you a layman's view of computers. By reading them, you can gain the computer expertise you need without stepping foot in a classroom.

First, get yourself an easy-to-read dictionary of computer terms and learn the jargon. We recommend:

A Dictionary of Computer Words by Robert W. Bly, Wayne, PA: Banbury Books.

Glossary of Computer Terms by John Prenis, Philadelphia, PA: Running Press.

International Microcomputer Dictionary (Sybex).

Next, read one or more of these books on how computers work:

Home Computers: A Simple and Informative Guide by Scott Corbett, Boston, MA: Little, Brown and Company/An Atlantic Monthly Press Book.

A 60-Minute Guide to Microcomputers: A Quick Course in Personal & Business Computing by Lew Hollerbach, Englewood Cliffs, NJ: Prentice-Hall.

A New True Book: Computers by Karen Jacobsen, Chicago, IL: Childrens Press. This is a children's book, but it's easy to read and informative to computer neophytes.

Easy-to-Understand Guide to Home Computers by Forrest M. Mims III and the editors of *Consumer Guide,* New York, NY: Beekman House.

If you would like to know more about the origins of the computer, read:

The Making of the Micro: A History of the Computer by Christopher Evans, New York, NY: Van Nostrand Reinhold Company.

It's also possible to teach yourself computer language, even if you don't have a computer to practice on. Three excellent guides to BASIC, the beginner's programming language, are:

Understanding BASIC, Sherman Oaks, CA: Alfred Publishing Company.

Problem-Solving With the Computer by Edwin R. Sage, Newburyport, MA: Entelek.

It's BASIC: The ABC's of Computer Programming by Shelley Lipson, New York, NY: Holt, Rinehart and Winston.

A Glossary of Computer Terms

To work in data processing, you need to know the latest jargon and buzzwords. Here's a quick guide to the language of computer professionals, users, and hobbyists:

Applications programs. Computer instructions written to perform a specific task, such as calculating payrolls or keeping inventory.

BASIC (Beginner's All-purpose Symbolic Instruction Code). The beginner's computer language. BASIC is standard on most home computers.

Bit. The smallest unit of data. A bit (short for *binary digit)* may be either 0 or 1.

Bit twiddler. A computer buff, a fanatic. Also known as a "hacker."

Byte. A group of eight bits. One byte can indicate a number or letter in a computer word.

COBOL (COmmon Business-Oriented Language). A computer language designed for business applications. Used primarily on large computers.

Computer. A high-speed machine that processes information according to a set of instructions stored within the machine.

Data. Any kind of information put into, processed by, or taken out of a computer.

Debug. To eliminate errors from a computer program or system.

EDP (Electronic Data Processing). The manipulation of data by the computer. Also refers to the computer industry as a whole.

Floppy disk. A type of computer memory made from a plastic disk coated with a magnetic material. Used with personal computers and other small systems.

FORTRAN (FORmula TRANslation). A computer language for engineering and scientific applications.

Hardware. The physical components of the computer. Hardware includes chips, circuit boards, tape drives, keyboards, and printers.

JCL (Job Control Language). A language to instruct the computer on how to manipulate the applications programs currently in production. Used primarily on large computers.

Mainframe. A large commercial computer. Mainframes are fast, expensive, take up an entire room, and require full-time operators to keep them running.

Microcomputer. A small desk-top computer used by one person at a time. Home computers are microcomputers.

Microprocessor. A miniature silicon chip containing the circuitry that serves as the "brains" of the microcomputer.

Minicomputer. Smaller than a mainframe and larger than a micro, the mini can be used by several people at one time and is about the size of a filing cabinet.

Operating system. The fundamental programming of the computer. The operating system coordinates the operations of the hardware.

Peripherals. All the accessories that can be hooked up to the computer. Peripheral devices include tape drives, printers, video terminals, and disk drives.

Program. The instructions written to make the computer work.

RPG-II (Report Program Generator). A simple language for commercial computer applications.

Silicon Valley. An area in the Santa Clara Valley of California where many computer companies are located.

Software. Programs, user manuals, and other documentation associated with the operation of a computer.

Time sharing. A method of computer operations allowing two or more people to use the same computer at the same time.

User-friendly. Anybody who uses a computer is a *user.* User-friendly means that the computer system is easy to use.

BUSINESS EXPERIENCE VS. COMPUTER EXPERIENCE

In an article for *The New York Times,* Ari L. Goldman reports: "Analysts in the field predict that even with an upswing in the economy, more and more people entering the computer field will be swept into the vortex of no experience, no job—no job, no experience."

In one sense, Mr. Goldman is correct: Companies hiring DP employees want experience. But—and this is a key point—*the experience doesn't have to be in data processing!* Years of work experience in a given industry are far more valuable to an employer than a technical knowledge of computers, which can always be acquired through training.

A case in point. Andy, 25, had an undergraduate degree in geology, several years of experience doing field work, and some advanced courses in gemology. He was hired by a top New York museum to catalog their vast gem collection on the museum's computer system. Andy had no programming knowledge or computer industry experience, but he was hired over many who did because of his gem and geology know-how.

So, if you've worked in textiles for 20 years and want to move into computers, apply for a position with the DP department of a large textile firm. Your knowledge of the textile industry is far more valuable to them than a whiz kid's ability to manipulate bits and bytes and RAMs and ROMs. As Jack French explains in his book *Up the EDP Pyramid* (John Wiley & Sons), "Your knowledge of an industry is valuable to any employer in that industry because your judgments in your day-to-day work will be more beneficial to the business. Without industry knowledge, you may never get a chance for a top DP position." Some industries where the data processing department plays an important role within the organization include banking, insurance, retailing, manufacturing, utilities, transportation, distribution, engineering, food processing, printing, mail-order marketing, and electronics.

Your *profession* may also make you valuable to a DP employer. A science writer, for example, could make an easy transition to writing technical manuals for a software vendor. And skilled typists are trading in their secretarial positions for jobs in data entry and word processing.

"The gamut of computer jobs is wide," write Joyce Lain Kennedy and Connie Winkler in their pamphlet *Computer Careers* (Sun Features). "The secret is to match your personal skills to the technology. If you can repair a television, for example, you can easily learn to repair a video display terminal. If you can sell industrial equipment, you probably can sell office systems. If you can teach, you can probably teach data processing."

In many ways, data processing is the same as any other industry. There are jobs for people in sales, marketing, management, and administration, as well as in technical areas. The difference, of course, is that data processing is growing so fast—two and one-half times as fast as the economy as a whole and the salaries are excellent.

In 15 years, the children learning computers in school today will be entering the job market. Because they have grown up with computers, programming is practically their native language, and many junior high school kids can out-program seasoned professionals. But even when these computer geniuses become part of the work force, *they won't have your business experience,* and that's your advantage. There's a void in data processing that needs to be filled by adults who can use computers as a business tool. And that's where you come in.

GETTING STARTED

Okay. Let's say you want to explore the idea of a career in computers. Here are some tips on getting started (taken from the brochure *A Look Into Computer Careers*, published by the American Federation of Information Processing Societies):

1. *Read at least one introductory book on computers.* You will need to do this to learn what computers are all about.
2. *Identify and learn about companies and other organizations in your area that have computer installations.* If you don't want to relocate, this will serve as a contact list of potential employers. In general, the types of companies that hire DP professionals fall into four categories:

   - Companies that use computers as part of their business—banks, insurance companies, and other service and manufacturing corporations.
   - Companies that manufacture hardware or standard software packages. These include Burroughs, Honeywell, IBM, Hewlett-Packard, and dozens of other familiar names.
   - Service bureaus—companies that sell time on their computers and offer DP-related services. These include Control Data, NCR, TRW, and Bank of America.
   - Firms that market DP-related services such as training, leasing, or recruitment.

3. *Visit computer installations. Visit a local computer store and ask for a demonstration.*
4. *Contact colleges in your area.* Their career guidance counsclors can put you on to companies who hire DP employees.

5. *Contact your local state employment agency office.*
6. *Take a course in computer programming.*
7. *Learn to use your school computer.*
8. *Contact computer manufacturers and request literature on their products, services, and career opportunities.*
9. *Write to one or more of the professional societies for information on careers in computers* (see box).
10. *Read the want ads in your local newspaper and in computer trade publications* (see box).

Professional Societies and Organizations in Data Processing and Related Fields

American Federation of Information Processing Societies, Suite 800, 1815 N. Lynn St., Arlington, VA 22209. Sponsors an annual national computer conference.

Association for Computing Machinery, 11 W. 42nd St., New York, NY 10036. Focuses on the development and application of hardware and software.

Association for Women in Computing, c/o Linda Taylor, 3752 Greenfield Ave., Los Angeles, CA 90034. For women in data processing.

Association of Computer Programmers and Analysts, c/o Linda Miller, P.O. Box 428, Greenbelt, MD 20770. For the technical side of the business—programmers and systems analysts.

Black Data Processing Associates, P.O. Box 7466, Philadelphia, PA 19101. A group for blacks in data processing.

Data Processing Management Associates, 505 Busse Hwy., Park Ridge, IL 60068. Serves managers of data processing.

Independent Computer Consultants Association, P.O. Box 27412, St. Louis, MO 63141. Support organization for independent EDP consultants.

Institute for Certification of Computer Professionals, 35 E. Wacker Dr., Chicago, IL 60601. Independent group that administers certification tests in data processing.

IEEE Computer Society, Suite 300, 1109 Spring St., Silver Springs, MD 20910. Computer engineering group of the Institute of Electrical and Electronics Engineers (IEEE).

Women in Data Processing, P.O. Box 8117, San Diego, CA 92102. For women in data processing.

Computer Periodicals

The computer industry is changing every week, and you've got to read trade journals to keep up. The major ones are:

Byte, BYTE Publications, Inc., 70 Main St., Peterborough, NH 03458. Fairly technical magazine for computer hobbyists.

Computer Decisions, 50 Essex St., Rochelle Park, NJ 07662. Monthly magazine on data processing management and technology.

Computerworld, P.O. Box 880, Framingham, MA 01701. Weekly newspaper for computer users.

Data Communications, 1221 Ave. of the Americas, New York, NY 10020. Monthly.

Datamation, 875 Third Ave., New York, NY 10022. Provides the best overall coverage of the data processing industry. Monthly.

InfoSystems, Hitchcock Building, Wheaton, IL 60187. Monthly magazine on data processing industry. Focus is on management and people.

Other Publications

Business Week. Check the information-processing section for the latest on new companies and products in the computer industry.

The New York Times. The Sunday Business Section advertises hundreds of jobs for EDP professionals.

YOUR FIRST BIG BREAK

To the computer neophyte, *any* first job in data processing can be considered a first big break. One way to achieve this is to get a job with a company in your area of interest (publishing, advertising, chemical processing, or whatever you've specialized in) and then move into the firm's data processing department. Or, you might prefer to get into a training program at

IBM or one of the other major computer manufacturers. Either way, getting that first job—and experience in the computer field—is the first step in climbing up the DP ladder.

Some successful DP professionals broke into the field in less traditional ways. Steve, 28, had an M.B.A. in finance and economics, but no computer training. Instead of going to work as a trainee with Wang or Sperry, he took a low-paying job with a computer store. Steve quickly learned all about computers and their application in business and became the store's resident expert in programs written for accounting, bookkeeping, and other financial functions. Within a year, he was offered a position with the data processing department of a large insurance company—at double his salesman's salary.

Of course, you should be somewhat selective in the choice of your first DP employer. If sales is your goal, then naturally you want to work for a computer manufacturer whose products are popular and known for their quality. If your career goals are not clear-cut, and you want to try your hand at a number of different tasks, opt for a smaller company where you can get exposure to many areas within the DP department. Here are some more questions to ask yourself when selecting potential employers:

- Is the company in a "hot" industry, such as cable TV, telecommunications, or software development? Or is it a declining, slow-growth field, such as pollution control or manufacturing?
- Is the data processing operation vital to the success of this company? Or are data processing people considered second-class citizens here?
- How large is the company? Is the company growing? By how much each year?
- Is the company a subsidiary or division of a larger corporation? Is there opportunity to move to the parent company?
- What are the company's future plans for data processing?
- Is training available? What kind?
- What is the typical career path for someone in my area?

- What is the job title? What kind of work will I be doing?
- What are the opportunities for promotion? Does the company get its senior DP employees from inside or outside the firm?

WHAT TO SHOOT FOR

If there's a super dream job in data processing, that job is in sales. In all other DP jobs, you're limited by salary. But most salespeople earn at least part of their compensation from commissions based on a percentage of the hardware and software they sell. The top computer salespeople have annual incomes in six figures. And a few have gone as high as seven!

Sales is also the career most accessible to liberal arts majors and other nontechnical types. In fact, they often make better computer salespeople than programmers or technicians. Says *Up the EDP Pyramid* author Jack French: "Marketing skills are frequently diametrically opposed to technical skills. Since selling is more emotional and psychological, the best technicians are frequently the poorest salesmen, and vice versa." For the story of how a one-time French major became a top computer saleswoman, see the box titled "Case History: The French Major Sells Computers."

Just how much do computer salespeople get paid? It depends on whom you work for and how good you are. Compensation ranges from a high salary plus 0.05 percent commission to a straight commission of 3 to 6 percent (and sometimes as high as 10 percent). As a rule, entry-level sales people earn $16,000 to $25,000 a year in salary plus a 2 to 4 percent commission.

Case History:
The French Major Sells Computers

Lisa Chu, 25, says her first love has always been language, especially French. She has never had any real interest in math or science. But today, Lisa is a Marketing Representative with Control Data Corporation in New York, and she spends her days selling software to businesspeople. Here she tells how a nontechnical person can succeed in a technical industry:

Q: Describe the jobs you've held at Control Data.

A: I started in May, 1980, as a Systems Marketing Representative, which is the technical end of a marketing team. I was responsible for selling new business in existing accounts and installing any applications that might come up, as well as supporting and educating the customers. I had a training period of 9 months, and then I went on quota.

In January, 1983, I switched from a Systems Marketing Representative to a Marketing Representative, so my responsibility now is to sell brand new accounts as well as assist in the technical end of it.

Q: What was your major in college? Your favorite subjects in high school?

A: When I first went to college I wanted to be a French major. Then I talked to someone who asked, "What do you want to do with your major?" I realized I didn't want to teach; I didn't know exactly what I wanted to do. I took economics my second year and majored in that; I have a minor in French. In high school, I didn't have any inclinations towards math or science; I liked my language courses.

Q: How did the opportunity to get into data processing come about?

A: At Bankers Trust—my first job out of college—a friend told me her husband got a very good job at Control Data in sales . . . although she didn't exactly know *what* he was selling. I wanted to get into sales, so I came to Control Data for an interview. After two interviews, I got hired.

Q: Were you nervous about getting involved with computers?

A: I wouldn't say I was nervous. I was really interested in it; I thought the computer industry would be something good to get into. I didn't know if I could handle it, because from my understanding I thought it was heavy programming. Turns out it isn't a lot of programming, and all my training was on the job.

Q: Can nontechnical people succeed in data processing, a highly technical field?

A: Absolutely. There are very few people here with a formal data processing background. Most of us have either a business or economics background and have been involved a little bit with computers. But hardly anyone is a "DP heavy." The people with real computer backgrounds go more towards the real technical jobs. If you're not a programmer, you probably want to go into sales and marketing.

Q: How can someone just getting into data processing evaluate potential employers? Should she stick to the big-name companies?

A: Not necessarily. There are a lot of smaller companies that aren't well known that can really move up in this industry. There are a lot of Apple-type firms popping up all over. If it's your first job, go for a good training program in a big company. As you become more familiar with the industry and with what you're doing, you might get a little riskier and go for a smaller company. But they have to have good products, and they should be progressive, because this industry changes so fast.

Q: What's the best preparation for a marketing career in data processing?

A: A general business background. You can get that in school or learn it on the job, as I did at Bankers Trust. Become familiar with computers through an intro course. But there's no need to become a computer expert—you don't have to love computers like a "bit twiddler" loves computers. You *do* have to keep up with what's going on in the industry.

Q: Anything else to add?

A: Just that I think I'm doing all right here. You got me on a good day—I just signed my first account!

Aside from sales, all other DP professionals are compensated on straight salary plus employee benefits (and, at some firms, a bonus based on performance). The question is whether you can earn more at a large, small, or medium-size firm.

In their seminar on "Career Opportunities in Computers" (sponsored by New York City's Learning Annex Adult Education Center), computer consultants John Goodfriend and Brett Caine advise their students that the greatest need for DP professionals is in new and growing small businesses. "A $5 million company—and there are thousands of them—might hire a DP manager plus two or three programmers plus an operator," says Caine, "and their salaries can exceed what a Fortune 500 corporation would pay, because the small company really *needs* them. On the other hand, a big company can train you and has places you can go, while a job at a little company becomes a dead-end after a few years."

As with most industries, it's the large corporations that offer the best training and opportunity for career advancement in data processing, especially for entry-level people. However, large companies have many layers of management and technical staff, which means most of their employees work in narrow disciplines on small portions of large projects. At the smaller companies, with their less structured work environments and need for more productivity per employee, an entry-level programmer or marketing support rep will probably get more "hands-on" experience in more disciplines and departments more quickly than he or she would at Perkin-Elmer or Data General.

People who opt for the large corporation should be aware of the danger of getting stuck in a narrow job function within the data processing department. In *Up the EDP Pyramid,* Jack French warns DP pros not to stay in any one job for too long. "You won't be any more qualified after 4 years in accounts payable than at the end of 2 years," says French. "Your career may end because you have become the resident expert in a single business application." He advises technical people to change job classes and levels every couple of years or so if they want to continue to climb the corporate ladder.

Because competition is so keen, most DP career counselors stress that careful career planning is vital to achieving your goals. In their *1983 Computer Salary and Career Planning Guide,* Source Edp, a professional recruiting firm devoted exclusively to the computer field, recommends that both entry-level and seasoned DP pros use a "career-planning cycle" to focus on their careers and plan for advancement. Here is the seven-step strategy they recommend:

Step 1—Understand the structure. In other words, know what the DP industry is like and what positions are available.

Step 2—Establish goals. Know where you want to be 20 years from now. And have short-term objectives, too.

Step 3—Assess current position. Is your current job meeting your goals in terms of experience gained, responsibility level, and salary?

Step 4—Assess needed exposure. Where should you go to get the experience and know-how you need to round you out, make you promotable, and get you to the top?

Step 5—Develop a plan of action that will provide you with this exposure. This action plan might call for a change of employment, a redirection of career goals, or additional education. Once the plan is set, act on it as soon as you can.

Step 6—Evaluate the results. Did your plan give you the exposure you needed to achieve your career goals?

Step 7—Take corrective action. If you didn't achieve your goal, go back to Step 1.

WHEN YOU'VE MADE IT

Because computer careers are so diverse, there's no standard measure of success.

For the computer salesperson, success is bigger clients, more sales, and increased commissions. As we have said, computer salespeople can and do earn six-figure incomes, and some have made millions.

If management is your goal, you know you've made it when you're Vice-President of Data Processing at a large corporation. This is the top spot in the DP field and the career objective of thousands of DP professionals.

Many technical people feel that to take on more management responsibility is to give up their beloved technical specialty. For a programmer, success and happiness may be writing elegant programs that solve complex scientific problems, make businesses run more efficiently, or challenge video buffs at the arcades.

For a growing number of data processing professionals, the dream job is to be found outside of corporate life. "There seems to be an entrepreneurial streak that runs through a DPer's soul," writes DP recruiter Laura Sessions in *How to Break Into Data Processing* (Prentice-Hall). "Many people leave DP to open up their own businesses—from bowling alleys to bagel shops."

Computer programming is one area particularly receptive to entrepreneurs. For instance, *Time* magazine recently reported that a few freelance software writers have become rich by creating programs that play computer games, solve puzzles, or handle business and household applications. According to programmer Jeff Garbers, "The potential gain in this industry is more substantial than any other I can think of. If you are successful, you can make a comfortable living. If you have something that really makes a big splash, you can make a great deal of money."[2] Both Apple and IBM encourage freelance software writers. These computer-for-hire programmers can make between $25,000 to $1 million or more on the sale of a single program, *if* it becomes a bestseller. VisiCalc®, a financial system for business, is one example of a program written by independents.

Publishing computer journals is another entrepreneur's dream job that's far from the mainstream of corporate computer life. *Newsweek* reports that dozens of computer journals have been launched over the past few years—many of them by individuals who saw gold in the growing legions of computer users who hunger for the latest information on products and programming. These magazines and newsletters boast a readership of about 5 million.[3] With the computer industry growing as fast as it is, there's always room for one more.

Whether you're a technician, a programmer, a salesperson, a manager, a writer, or a teacher, there's a chance at a dream job for *you* in data processing. And if you enjoy your career in the computer field, that's the truest test of having "made it." As the Chinese proverb says:

If you would be happy for a life, love your work.

Selected Computer Companies

Atari, Inc., 1265 Borregas Ave., Sunnyvale, CA 94086. Produces video games.

Burroughs Corp., Burroughs Pl., Detroit, MI 48232. Manufactures computers and other products for information management.

Control Data Corp., P.O. Box 0, Department C.P.A., Minneapolis, MN 55440. Markets computer hardware, software, and services.

Data General Corp., Westboro, MA 01581. Designs and manufactures small- and medium-size computer systems.

Dataproducts Corp., 6219 DeSoto Ave., Woodland Hills, CA 91365. Manufactures printers and other peripherals.

Digital Equipment Corp., 146 Main St., Maynard, MA 01754. Manufactures and markets computers and other systems using digital equipment.

Electronic Data Systems Corp., 7171 Forest Lane, Dallas, TX 75230. Provides commercial data processing systems for large organizations.

Formation, Inc., 823 E. Gate Dr., Mt. Laurel, NJ 08057. Manufactures and services data processing equipment.

Harris Corp., P.O. Box 37, Melbourne, FL 32901. Manufactures computers and other information-handling equipment.

Hewlett-Packard Co., 1501 Page Mill Rd., Palo Alto, CA 94304. Manufactures computers and peripherals and other electronic equipment.

Honeywell, Inc., Honeywell Plaza, Minneapolis, MN 55408. Manufactures computer hardware and software.

IBM Corp., Old Orchard Rd., Armonk, NY 10504. Manufactures computers and related products.

Intel Corp., 3065 Bowers Ave., Santa Clara, CA 95051. Manufactures memory systems and microcomputers.

National Semiconductor Corp., 2900 Semiconductor Dr., Santa Clara, CA 95051. Manufactures microprocessors and microcomputers as well as larger systems.

NCR Corp., Dayton, OH 45479. Manufactures computer systems for business and industry.

Nixdorf Computer Corp., 168 Middlesex Tpke., Burlington, MA 01803. Manufactures computers and peripherals.

The Perkin-Elmer Corp., Main Ave., Norwalk, CT 06856. Manufactures data systems and other electronics equipment.

Sperry Univac, P.O. Box 500, Blue Bell, PA 19424. Manufactures electronic computer systems for commercial and government applications.

Tektronic, Inc., P.O. Box 500, Beaverton, OR 97077. Manufactures graphic computing systems.

Texas Instruments, P.O. Box 5474, M.S. 67, Dallas, TX 75222. Manufactures calculators, minicomputers, and microcomputers.

VisiCorp., 289 Zanker Rd., San Jose, CA 95134. Produces software for IBM computers.

Consulting

THE PREYING MANTIS

Of all the businesses, by far
Consultancy's the most bizarre.
For, to the penetrating eye,
There's no apparent reason why,
With no more assets than a pen,
This group of personable men
Can sell to clients more than twice
The same ridiculous advice,
Or find, in such a rich profusion,
Problems to fit their own solution.

The strategy that they pursue—
To give advice instead of do—
Keeps their fingers on the pulses
Without recourse to stomach ulcers,
And brings them monetary gain,
Without a modicum of pain,
The wretched object of their quest,
Reduced to cardiac arrest,
Is left alone to implement
The asinine report they've sent.
Meanwhile the analysts have gone
Back to client number one,
Who desperately needs their aid
To tidy up the mess they've made.
And on and on—ad infinitum—
The masochistic clients invite 'em.
Until the merciful reliever
Invokes the company's receiver.

No one really seems to know
The rate at which consultants grow.
By some amoeba-like division?
Or chemo-biologic fission?
They clone themselves without an end
Along their exponential trend.

The paradox is each adviser
If he makes his client wiser
Inadvertantly destroys
The basis of his future joys.
So does anybody know
Where latter-day consultants go?[1]

IN GENERAL

"Don't let your son grow up to be a consultant," is the refrain of a ditty written and sung by humorist Mark Russell. Russell's song satirizes the dubious role of consultants in the government's bureaucracy.

Washington, D.C. isn't the only haven for consultants. These modern day medicine men and women advise managers at thousands of America's leading organizations, showing them new and better ways to manage time and resources, to communicate effectively, to manage money, to plan strategically, and to work efficiently and effectively.

Although few people aim at becoming consultants, many businesspeople soon recognize the field's allure. Consulting offers many rewards that self-starters value: The potential for high pay, an opportunity to see the effect of one's actions, the opportunity to work with top decision makers, and a great deal of autonomy.

A consultant gives advice or related services in any skill area of at least a quasi-professional nature for some fee or on a contractual basis.

If consultants are effective, they can save an organization a great deal of money; sometimes they can even save the whole organization. If a consultant is ineffective, he can reinforce a negative stereotype, the type embodied in this cynical definition: A consultant is someone who borrows your watch and then tells you what time it is.

This section of *Dream Jobs* discusses the two basic types of consultants: independents, and those who work for a consulting firm. The emphasis of the chapter is on becoming an independent consultant, since it is becoming easier to set up your own shop than to find work with a large consulting firm.

The topic of consulting seems to be popular, since seminars on "How to Build and Maintain Your Own Consulting Practice" are springing up all across the country. Consulting, after all, has several appealing advantages:

- *Complete autonomy*—you are able to set your own fees and schedule.
- *Specialization*—you can concentrate in those areas you enjoy most.
- *The opportunity to make a lot of money*—you can take on as much work as you want and can hustle harder when you want even more.

While working for a large consulting firm allows you to gain experience, meet contacts, and earn a weekly paycheck, you are enlarging the firm's reputation rather than establishing your own. When you do go independent, you'll find that you willingly work harder and longer, that you accept the menial tasks more willingly, and that you tap a special energy when you know that you're working for yourself. When you hear your phone ring, you get a charge out of knowing that a client is calling *you*, and not just a consulting firm.

Consulting is a $32 billion dollar a year industry and growing. *Venture* reports that there are now between 35,000 and 50,000 full-time consultants, with 2,000 new consultants entering the field each year. *Business Week* reports that the number of full-time consultants has tripled since the mid-1960s. No one can even guess at the number of part-time consultants there are in the United States.

A series of articles in the New York *Daily News* reported that over the last 5 years, New York State agencies have awarded more than 10,000 contracts, amounting to at least $600 million, to private consultants. And that doesn't include the state's long list of semi-independent public authorities that spend untold millions for outside advice.

John Naisbitt, in his best-selling book *Megatrends*, says, ". . . with the schools turning out an increasingly inferior product, corporations have reluctantly entered the education business . . . There will be a huge demand for teachers to tutor "students" with jobs in private business. Former teachers with an entrepreneurial bent will find a growing market for educational-consulting services in the new information society. (This is one answer to the problem of what to do with the surplus of teachers generated by the baby-boom kids.)"

There's even a consultant underground, which can be seen in the rows of business cards and flyers that are stapled, tacked, and taped to bulletin boards at launderettes supermarkets, banks, and photocopy stores throughout the country. These neighborhood professionals will advise you about everything from writing a persuasive love letter to choosing the right prep school for Junior. Other bulletin board advertisers will consult with you about taxes, real estate, catering, wrinkles, facial hair, exercise, meeting singles, and having hair transplants.

In the regular economy, some of the most common areas of specialization for consultants are:

- Engineering
- Accounting
- Management
- Office Design
- Personnel
- Graphics Design
- Restaurant Operation
- Health Care
- Real Estate
- Executive Search
- Communications
- Stress Management
- Computers/Data Processing
- Marketing
- Aerospace

Consultants in any of these areas share certain characteristics if they are to be successful. A study by the Association of Management Consultants developed a list of some of the important personal qualifications of management consultants. They include:

- Understanding of people
- Integrity
- Courage
- Objectivity
- Ambition
- Problem-solving ability
- Judgment
- Ability to communicate
- Psychological maturity
- Good physical and mental health
- Professional etiquette and courtesy
- Stability of behavior
- Self-confidence
- Intellectual competence
- Creative imagination

That's quite a tall order. But then, some consultants charge as much as $2,000 a day for their services! Howard Shenson, originator of a course on building a consulting practice, as well as author of numerous books on the subject, says that the average fee charged by consultants is $535 per day.

But, before you start calculating the untold millions you'll make as a consultant, remember that this figure only comes in for the days that you're working!

One-person shops account for more than one-half of all consulting operations. It is not necessary for you to be alone, waiting with bated breath for every $500 day. You could join a large consulting firm (those employing more than 50 consultants) where you will probably be kept busy every day. Your life may consist of airplane flights, long hours, and a dizzying succession of Ramada Inns, but the money is good (usually $20,000 to $25,000 a year to start), and the experience is excellent.

Medium-size firms (those employing between 10 and 50 consultants) are another option, as are small firms (which usually employ 2 to 10 consultants). Add to these the possibility of being an internal consultant, where your work is limited to a single company's divisions or subsidiaries.

As with any other small business, a consulting firm must understand the nature of its market as well as its size. Consulting firms, like advertising agencies, can start their life by meeting the need of a single, lucrative client. But they can end life just as quickly, unless they determine that there are other potential clients, and that those clients can give them repeat business. It is only through repeat business that consulting becomes profitable; without repeat business, you are always starting each month at "zero."

In this chapter, we will outline the specific types of problems that confront consultants and discuss how they can be overcome. Certainly, the opportunities are there. According to Howard Shenson, the average full-time consultant makes $50,000 a year. He also claims that a person who leaves an organization to consult can equal his or her previous salary within 65 days and increase it by half again within 137 days. "Statistics," says Shenson, "show that a full-time consultant bills an average of between 12 and 13 days a month."

Just what does it take to bill that much work? How do you get the telephone ringing? Where do you start? Let's begin with the preparation needed to enter the consulting field.

WHAT IT TAKES

Although there are few formal college courses in consulting, there are many continuing education courses that help people break into the field. "How to Succeed As a Consultant" is a highly popular course at several of New York City's adult education centers.

You need a specialty, of course, to be a consultant, but you also need a solid educational background. Most consultants have graduated from a four-year college, and a surprising number have entered the field after taking majors in the liberal arts. Perhaps that's because consulting offers the unstructured environment that many liberal arts types seek.

There are a number of courses that will serve you well in a

career as a consultant. Writing and communications courses will help you articulate problems and solutions and, in addition, will give you the polish necessary to impress high-level executives. Strong business-writing skills will help when writing a proposal or letter as well as when you write a brochure or press release for your business.

Speech skills are vital. You never know when you'll have to make presentations to groups or people who'll judge you on both the verbal and nonverbal messages you send out. A polished speaker is one who keeps eye contact and who controls his stage fright. All successful consultants must radiate confidence.

It's also wise to take courses in business math, accounting, management, marketing, and computer studies.

In addition to these undergraduate courses, you might want to look into the courses offered at a local continuing education center. There, you can take courses given by consultants themselves. You may wish to learn time management from a consultant in the area. Not only will you learn the course's content, but you will also see how the teacher handles himself in class. If you do take a class with a consultant instructor, note how the consultant uses the class—or doesn't—to promote his own firm. He may say nothing about his company, but, more than likely, he'll hand out business cards, brochures, or flyers at the end of the course. For a consultant, teaching adult education classes is a valuable way of honing presentation skills while meeting potential clients for his business.

According to Howard Shenson, the higher income consultants who rely heavily on referrals use this type of public relations and marketing. If a consultant is impressive at the local college, a student who happens to be a business executive may put in a good word for the consultant at his place of business. Consultants who are not in the upper reaches of the profession tend to rely more on telephone calls and mass mailings to find their clients.

As any consultant will tell you, quick-wittedness is as important an asset as your college degree. Teaching an adult education course is just one way of finding new prospects. You can also find prospects by reading. For example, a New York University alumni magazine recently published a list of more than 900 companies that were contributing to a particular college fund. Such a list could form the basis of a strong mailing list for any consultant interested in finding new organizations to send information to. The business section of *The New York Times* is another place where a consultant can pick up the names of executives at top companies without buying a mailing list or even going to the library.

Now, let's discuss how you can put your mental, psychological and educational tools to work as an independent consultant.

A Look at Consulting Companies

Not everyone is able to—or even wants to—be an independent consultant. Recent college graduates usually prefer to learn their craft and make their mistakes while on the payroll of an organization. The following is a selected list of large consulting firms that employ numerous consultants.

McKinsey & Company, Inc.
245 Park Ave.
New York, NY 10017
(212) 692-6000

Other locations: Chicago, Cleveland, Dallas, Los Angeles, San Francisco, Washington, D.C., and 15 overseas offices.

McKinsey serves a wide variety of businesses, including manufacturing, banking, insurance, retailing, utilities, government agencies, and nonprofit institutions. They have traditionally worked with Fortune 500 companies, but are also developing competence in helping smaller, fast-growing companies to capitalize more fully on their potential. They concentrate on management issues, working with CEO's and other senior officers. Sixty percent of their work deals with strategic management issues, and 10 to 15 percent with overall organization.

Boston Consulting Group, Inc.
1 Boston Pl.
Boston, MA 02106
(617) 722-7800

Other locations: London, Munich, San Francisco, Paris, Tokyo, Chicago.

Specializes in competitive strategy decisions requiring major commitments of a firm's resources. Their practice is focused on critical, far-reaching management decisions.

They have ongoing relationships with many large, successful corporations; their practice is divided evenly between foreign and domestic clients, with one-half of their staff based abroad. Originally, BCG worked primarily with manufacturing organizations, but they have now expanded into consumer products and financial and service industries.

The Forum Corp. 84 State St. Boston, MA 02109 (617) 723-8070	Other locations: New York, Chicago, Dallas, Pittsburgh, Philadelphia, San Francisco, Los Angeles, Houston, Vancouver, and Toronto.

Offers training programs in sales improvement, organizational development, and personal development. Their clients are drawn from the Fortune 1,000 as well as from government agencies. In the past year, they've grown from a $1.4 million organization to a $5 million firm.

The Hay Group 229 S. 18th St. Rittenhouse Square Philadelphia, PA 19103 (215) 875-2300	Other locations: Boston, New York, Chicago, Los Angeles, London, and 60 other offices worldwide.

The Hay Group is the largest human resources consulting firm in the world. It has offices in 22 countries around the world serving over 5,000 clients. It serves 40 percent of the Fortune 500 as current clients. Their mission is to help clients manage change through improving the effectiveness of their people. Specific areas include business strategy, management and education training, research in human resources technology.

Booz, Allen & Hamilton, Inc. 245 Park Ave. New York, NY 10017 (212) 697-1900	Other locations: Atlanta, Chicago, San Francisco, Houston, Dallas, Washington, D.C., and 7 overseas locations.

Offers highly diversified services, focusing on commercial and public enterprises. Concentration is on large companies, although more and more of their practice involves medium-size, rapidly growing companies. Client industries include many leading industrial companies, commercial banks, and insurance companies, as well as leading retailers, utilities, and transportation companies. They emphasize top management strategic questions.

Sources of Information About Consulting

AAPC—American Association of Political Consultants
Suite 1406
1101 N. Calvert St.
Baltimore, MD 21202

ACCCE—Association of Consulting Chemists and Chemical
   Engineers, Inc.
50 E. 41st St.
New York, NY 10017

ACEC—American Consulting Engineers Council
Suite 802
1015 15th St., N.W.
Washington, D.C. 20005

ACME—Association of Consulting Management Engineers
230 Park Ave.
New York, NY 10017

AERC—Association of Executive Recruiting Consultants, Inc.
30 Rockefeller Plaza
New York, NY 10020

AIMC—Association of International Management Consultants
Box 472
Glastonbury, CT 06033

AMC—Association of Management Consultants
811 E. Wisconsin Ave.
Milwaukee, WI 53202

IMC—Institute of Management Consultants
19 W. 44th St.
Room 810
New York, NY 10036

SPBC—Society of Professional Business Consultants
221 N. La Salle St.
Chicago, IL 60601

SPMC—Society of Professional Management Consultants, Inc.
205 W. 89th St.
New York, NY 10024

GETTING STARTED

Let's assume that you have a special area of expertise, and you're ready to establish your own consulting business. How do you start?

One of the first decisions you'll have to make is whether to work out of your home or out of an office. There are advantages and disadvantages to each. A home office offers a comfortable, low-overhead environment with access to your family, your library, and your favorite chair. However, it can also mean interruptions. It is also a rather informal place to bring a client, and the atmosphere is often conducive to goofing off. The great advantage of working from your home is the savings. But remember that while you may save the cost of renting office space, your home is not without expenses. You will still be using heat, electricity, stationery, equipment, and the telephone.

If you do use your home as your office, you are entitled to deduct a percentage of your rent or mortgage payment from your taxes. The amount of the deduction is calculated by determining the percentage of the floor space of your home that is used exclusively for business. For example, if you use 10 percent of your home for your office, you can deduct 10 percent of your rent or mortgage payment.

The obvious advantages of taking office space are its professional image and its proximity to clients. The office need not be grand. In fact, you may want to start out by sharing a suite of offices with other professionals. There are a number of office buildings that rent space to one-person businesses. They provide a single room for each person and a common lobby for all of the offices.

For consultants who never have occasion to invite clients to their place of business, a home office will suffice. Those consultants who require office space must keep the office in excellent shape. That means a neat desk, a carefully kept library, and files that are accessible and orderly. Consultants are not only selling specialized knowledge, they are selling their demeanor, their organizational skills, and their ability to control their own personal and work lives.

Regardless of where you work, you're going to need some supplies, so you had better set aside some money for start-up expenses. You'll probably need stationery and business cards, and you can't stint on their expense. Get a good graphic designer to design your stationery and cards. Make sure that they are a color that's easy on the eye; a handsome cream or off-white is usually best. The business cards should be simple, clean, and professional. They should have your name, address, telephone number, and if you wish, the type of consulting you do.

Your desk, like your cards and stationery, is an indicator about your consulting practice. If you have a metal desk, you should realize that many people feel this type of desk says "worker," not "manager." A large wooden desk creates an aura of importance. So does a fine briefcase in a deep brown or black leather. As a consultant, you can't afford to overlook "image."

What else should you have? Well, you need a lamp, file drawers, a bookshelf, and a telephone. You may want to get a "call waiting" service from the phone company. This service gives you the advantage of two telephone lines without the expense. If you are talking to someone and receive another call, you will hear a beep. By momentarily depressing the button on your phone, you will be connected to the caller. This prevents those trying to reach you from getting a busy signal. You then have the option of ending one conversation and continuing with the other. Or, you can take a message and call either or both parties back at your convenience. Other services offered by the phone company allow you to hold conference calls and to dial frequently used numbers instantly. Neither of these services is inordinately expensive.

Now, let's consider the pleasant topic of fees. How much do you charge and *how* do you charge for your services?

There is no single, universally accepted type of fee structure, and all of the possibilities have advantages and disadvantages for both the consultant and the client. The only rule of thumb is that the fee should be structured in a way that is familiar to your client. If the client is used to working with consultants on a retainer basis, use that method. If the client is used to an hourly arrangement or per diem fee structure, be ready to quote the appropriate figures for those methods. Here are some of the most common types of fee structures in consulting:

- *Hourly, daily rate*—This common method is easy enough to figure. Simply multiply your own billing rate times the number of hours (or days) you work. If your *per diem* billing rate is $500, and you work 4 days, your fee will obviously be $2,000. Don't forget to charge your client for preparation time or else this fee structure will leave you at a disadvantage.
- *Project fee*—A total price that covers all elements of a particular project.
- *Contingent fees*—In the film *The Verdict*, a lawyer takes on a medical negligence suit on a contingency basis. In other words, he receives one-third of any settlement. While this is common practice for lawyers, most consultants do not ask for payment contingent on their success.
- *Percentage fees*—When you receive a percentage fee, you are accepting payment in the form of a percentage of whatever the total project yields. For example, a consultant working on a piece of software might charge 10 percent of the software's eventual value. The consultant would be owed $10,000 if the software were eventually to yield $100,000.
- *Value of assignment fees*—Some projects have a value that exceeds the number of hours or days consumed in completing them. Usually, this type of fee structure is appropriate for risky projects. Writing a major advertising brochure or booklet, for example, may be priced to include a premium for the numerous uses and possible spin-offs that may result from the initial project.
- *Retainer fees*—When you receive a "retainer," you are guaranteeing your availability for a certain period of time in exchange for a guaranteed amount of money, sometimes paid in advance. A consultant may ask a company to agree that, during the course of 1 year, they will use his services a minimum of 10 days, billable at $500 per day. Naturally, a consultant should specify the

definition of a "day," and should make clear the number of days to be used in connection with a particular project.

- *Equity fees*—Sometimes a consultant agrees to no cash payment for his services, but asks instead for a percentage of the business; hence, the term "equity." For example, if a company is on the verge of bankruptcy, it may ask a consultant to use his skills to turn the business around. Since the firm may be cash poor, it may offer stock in the company in exchange for the consultant's services.
- *Deferred fees*—As the name implies, deferred fees are fees that are spread out over the future. It may help a client who is currently cash poor, but it may also help the consultant if he or she would rather have the income during the next tax year.

In many cases, a handshake is all that's needed to seal an agreement. But, to be safe, it is usually a good idea to spell out any consulting agreement on paper. However, there need not be a contract full with legalese. All you really need is a letter of agreement stating the services you will provide, the fee that your client will pay, and if appropriate, schedules for paying the fee and delivering the service.

In the following letter, the terms of the agreement have been woven into an informal letter to the client:

Dear Phyllis:

I'm delighted with the prospect of working with you on the Effective Business Writing/Telephone Technique seminar. I've enclosed 15 copies of my needs assessment, which the participants can fill out and return to me with several writing samples each.

The next few paragraphs spell out our agreement:

I agree to provide a 4-session, 12-hour training program in Effective Business Writing and Telephone Technique. The program will be given on February 3, 8, 15, and 22 of this year, from 2 p.m. to 5 p.m. I agree to distribute and review my needs assessment in advance of the course. Also, I will collect and review writing samples in advance of the first session.

Friendly Insurance Company, Inc. agrees to pay a fee of $3,000 for the training of a maximum of 15 people. This fee includes all expenses as well as all handout material, the needs assessment, and copies of a writing textbook for each participant.

If this is agreeable, please sign and return a copy of this letter. I'll give you a call after receiving the completed needed assessments and samples.

Again, Phyllis, I appreciate your encouragement and cooperation, and I look forward to giving this program my best effort.

A letter such as this clarifies the sequence of events in the project, puts the fee in writing, and reassures the client that the logistics have been worked out. No schedule of payment has been named, because the consultant is content to bill for his services following the completion of the program. However, if he wished to bill for part of his services prior to the end of the assignment for some reason, that would have to be spelled out.

Books on Consulting

Behavior in Organizations by L.W. Porter, E.E. Lawler, and J.R. Hackman, New York, NY: McGraw-Hill, 1975.

Organizational Diagnosis by H. Levinson, Cambridge, MA: Harvard University Press, 1972.

Managing Your Accounting and Consulting Practice by M.A. Altman and R.I. Weil, New York, NY: Matthew Bender & Co., 1978.

How To Organize and Operate A Small Business by C. Baumback, K. Lawyer, and P. Kelley, Englewood Cliffs, NJ: Prentice-Hall, 1973.

Making The Most of Management Consulting Services by J.H. Fuchs, New York, NY: Amacom, 1975.

Consulting For Change by F. Steele, Amherst, MA: University of Massachusetts Press, 1975.

The Consulting Process in Action by G. Lippitt and R. Lippitt, La Jolla, CA: University Associates Press, 1978.

Contact: The First Four Minutes by L. Zunin and N. Zunin, New York, NY: Ballantine Books, 1973.

How To Control The Quality of a Management Consulting Engagement, New York, NY: Association of Consulting Management Engineers, 1972.

Publications About Consulting

Consultants' News. Kennedy and Kennedy, Inc. Templeton Rd., Fitzwilliam, NH 03447. Monthly.

Commerce Business Daily. Government Printing Office, Washington, D.C. 20402. Published 5 days a week. Lists federal needs with information on how to get bids or proposal solicitations.

Consulting Opportunities Journal. 1629 K Street, N.W., Suite 520, Washington, D.C. 20006.

NAFCO Letter. Ivy Publishing Co., P.O. Box 7, Ischua, NY 14746. Designed for financial consultants. Monthly.

Sharing Ideas! Among Professional Speakers. Dottie Walters, 600 W. Foothill Blvd., Glendora, CA 91740. Bi-monthly.

YOUR FIRST BIG BREAK

Your first big break in consulting is usually your first assignment, or your first important assignment. Not all assignments are equally meaningful. Assignments in the private sector usually carry more weight—and more money—than those in the public sector. Fortune 500 companies have their own prestige, and working for a Fortune 500 client means that some of their gloss will rub off on you.

Although we have touched on the importance of marketing your services, the topic deserves more attention. You can't hope to create your break by simply calling contacts or friends. You need to continually and systematically market your services to a wide range of potential clients through direct mail, advertising, telephone, talk shows, adult education classes, symposiums, and luncheon or speaking engagements.

Considering the importance of marketing, it's amazing how few consultants do it well. The first thing you need is a plan based on an objective look at the people who are in the market for services such as yours. In your planning, determine the geographical area that can feasibly be served. Analyze unexplored markets. Give some thought to your competitors. How many are there? What makes you different? How do your fees compare with theirs? Will your business be seasonal? Are there weeks or months when you will not be able to contact your prospects?

As we have said, marketing must be a continuing process. It can't stop when you get busy or when you decide to reduce expenses. In fact, marketing should never be cut back, even when times are very bad. Ideally, you should earmark 15 to 20 percent of your fees from each assignment for marketing.

Let's take a brief look at some of the ways in which consultants market their services:

- *Telephone.* Nothing beats the personal touch of a telephone conversation. For a low price, you can introduce yourself and your services to a prospect. In the first few seconds, you should be able to discern whether the person at the other end of the phone is eager to know more about you or is basically disinterested. You can also probably find out if you have many competitors for the prospect's business and if the person you've called is able to purchase your service. This "pigeonholing" of a person into a "possible buyer" or not is called "qualifying." Consultants are always on the lookout for qualified prospects: People who buy consulting services and who are in a position to make the decision about whether or not to buy yours.
- *Direct mail.* A snappy "pitch" letter, a brochure, and a return postcard, if well designed and well aimed, can provide enough response to launch you. You will need a mailing list of good prospects and some luck. If your prospects don't need your services immediately, they can always file your brochure for future reference.
- *Trade publication ads.* The response will, of course, depend upon the quality of your ad, its size, and the frequency with which it runs. You'll be hitting a wide audience, so don't expect every response to be a hot prospect. To gain advertising information, simply ask a

publication for its rate card, which will tell advertising charges as well as space and deadline requirements. It may also give other important information, such as whether or not there will be any "theme issues" of the magazine. If the theme of an issue coincides with your particular consulting specialty, you might want to save your ad for that particular issue. Classified ads in large-circulation magazines can be as effective as ads in trade magazines. You should also try ads in regional newsletters, which cater to prospects in your locale.

- *Speaking engagements.* Gore Vidal, the novelist, once said that "People should never turn down sex or the opportunity to appear on television." In the case of consulting, TV will probably help your business more than sex; so will any other exposure to possible prospects. This includes speaking engagements at local clubs, organizations, professional societies, church groups, and chamber of commerce meetings.

- *Referrals.* This is the best way of getting business. It allows you "to walk in the front door" of a potential client because you have a direct endorsement from a current client. Referrals are the best marketing that can happen. Because they depend on word of mouth, there's not much you can do to get them except be good at what you do. When the situation warrants it, though, you can let satisfied clients know that you're available to help their colleagues.

Establishing yourself as an expert isn't easy. It's a slow, time-consuming process. One way is to gain a reputation as a good teacher. Another is to develop a track record at a corporation. It always helps to be visible. Write reviews, articles, or anything else that will tell people that you are a thinker and a leader. Let people know that you've done a lot of work in a particular field and that you're available for consulting.

Establishing yourself as an expert also means building credentials. Obtain references from those you've worked for, keep copies of everything you write, and take advantage of every opportunity to address a professional organization or society.

It may seem a long way off, but you might even take notes for a book you would like to write. Just having a book out is often enough to give you visibility in your field. A book reminds people of your accomplishments every time they see your name on the cover. Ken Blanchard of *The One-Minute Manager* fame will probably not have to work very hard from now on to obtain new clients—he's made a splash.

You may not yet be ready for best-sellerdom, but it is surprising how quickly a successful publication can establish a reputation. To write a book, you begin by doing what you always do—conduct research and talk to people about something that interests them. Then, write about your findings in a lively, interesting way. That's what Thomas J. Peters and Robert H. Waterman, Jr. did. These two management consultants put what they knew about "excellent" corporations into a book, *In Search of Excellence: Lessons From America's Best Run Companies.* Waterman is a Director of McKinsey and Company, a prominent consulting company. Peters was formerly with McKinsey, but now he runs his own consulting firm.

Although their book is a scholarly study of what factors make certain businesses successful over the long run, it is worth its weight in gold from a promotional point of view. Chief executive officers all around the country will buy the book. Some of the more imaginative of them will probably call in Peters and Waterman to find out what recommendations they might have for improving the profits of their company. This advice will not come cheap.

Before you write your best-selling treatise, gain some experience in publishing articles in trade and general interest magazines. Also, don't turn down the opportunity to review books in your field. Your goal should be to keep your name out in front of the public, to get exposure as a member of your industry's community, and to gain a reputation for having good ideas and expressing yourself well.

The First Client

The first client is the toughest to get. Most consultants, when starting out, establish a consulting relationship with their previous employer or with a firm in which he or she has had "hands-on" experience.

One young man, an advertising manager at an engineering firm, wanted to set up his own advertising firm. When he left his company, he continued to work for them on a freelance basis. That helped the company make a transition, and helped the consultant bring in money while starting his business.

A middle-aged editor at a large New York City newspaper syndicate decided to set up her own editorial consulting firm. Before leaving, she negotiated a 1-year contract to provide editorial consulting to her former employer. The single assignment provided her with enough money to pay the rent on her new office.

A business writing consultant, looking to break into the field of technical writing seminars, gave a low fee to a firm that asked him to teach business writing to their data processing managers. The consultant was eager to work with technical people, and would gladly have done the assignment for little or no money. The assignment helped him get his feet wet. He worked with software documentation and technical proposals instead of just with memos, letters, and reports. With that experience behind him, he was able to refer to the assignment and use it as a stepping-stone to positioning himself as a technical writing specialist.

Bridg Hunt on Consulting

"The intellectual will find his real home in consulting."

Bridgford Hunt, President of The Hunt Group, has been a management consultant for more than 20 years. He is one of the pioneers of the executive search field, and he has retained an enviable zest for his business.

Q: Bridg, what do you need to be a successful consultant?

A: You need five things. First, you need the ability to attract new clients and to get repeat business. That, by the way, also happens to be numbers 2, 3, 4, and 5 on my list as well!

Q: You have a suite of offices in midtown Manhattan. Have you ever thought of running your business from your home and saving on rent?

A: No, it wouldn't work for me. In executive search, you can't work "out of your hat." You need a physical presence in the business world. If I worked out of my home, I might be able to retain a few small clients, but it would be very hard to attract new business.

Q: Some people feel that a big, impressive wooden desk is required by consultants who are . . .
A: Skip the fancy desk. I've had glamorous offices with white walls, white file cabinets, and teak furniture. What happens is that the good furniture acquires the usual scuff marks and burn holes, and is very hard to replace. I'd rather have sturdy, less-impressive furniture, and know that if it starts looking bad, it can be scrubbed down or replaced.

Q: What personal qualities do you need to succeed as a consultant?
A: You need an analytical mind, a multi-interest mind. You need to be able to listen well, ask questions, and bring out the real problems that need to be solved. Always remember that, in consulting, there are three ways of looking at a problem. There's the problem the client sees, there's the problem he tells you about, and there's the problem that you see. The great challenge in consulting is to get the client to see the real problem and articulate it.

Q: Why did you choose consulting over a position in business? Are there things in the corporate life you miss?
A: Well, let me start by saying that the possibilities for failure in consulting are great, but I believe that consulting is ideally suited to my personality—part loner, part group oriented.

Also, I love the mix of assignments that consulting offers me. No two jobs are ever the same. I'm never bored. I enjoy meeting a variety of people, and holding discussions about different subjects with each one of them.

Q: But what do you miss in the corporate life? Is there anything a consultant never gets used to about his line of work?
A: I miss not having a material product to point to and say, "I did that," or "I made that." My product is advice, and, of course, executives. But I still sometimes wonder what I've really added to the gross national product.

As far as what consultants never get used to, that's simple: We never get used to the fear of not eating. Like an actor, every Monday morning I look for work. You must accept this if you are to succeed as a consultant.

Q: Is there a future in consulting, and if so, where is it?
A: Sure there is—in communications . . . computers . . . genetics . . . robotics. We're on the threshold of the high-technology society. Everyone who isn't yet 60 years old will probably have to know how to use a computer. Everyone. Teachers will find them-

selves being judged by their computer talents, and by the productivity they can inspire as they become handmaidens to the computer. Many teachers won't stand for this; they'll look to consulting to truly vent their intellectual powers. We're solving real-life problems in a real world, and I can see how teachers—good ones—will see consulting as the true home of intellectual activity. We help solve problems, and try to make the world a bit better. I like that.

A Few Tips on Surviving as a Consultant

1. *Keep your perspective.* Don't assume that a week without new business means that you're on your way to insolvency. Try to look at your business's progress over a quarterly or yearly period. Asking yourself how productive you've been each day is as frustrating as asking yourself how much weight you've lost each day that you diet.
2. *Don't stop marketing.* You never outgrow your need to market your services. Don't think that, because you currently have more work than you can handle, tomorrow will also be fine. Tomorrow will be fine if you plan for it by keeping your name in front of your prospects.
3. *Keep up with the times.* Don't think that any one sales pitch, direct mail scheme, or advertising strategy will last forever. Your market is constantly changing, constantly adapting to new circumstances. You must listen to what your prospects are saying, and be ready to accommodate their new needs.
4. *Know your priorities.* As in all businesses, there are parts of the job that you like and parts that you don't like. Make sure that you reserve your best energy for the important tasks. Delegate all routine matters to assistants, typists, temps, or part-time help.
5. *Keep accurate records.* Consultants are in touch with so many different people at once that they must always be ready to switch conversations, thought patterns, and frameworks instantly. The only way to do that is to keep organized notes, and keep them in a place that gives you easy access to them.
6. *Don't turn down work.* Work will rarely come in at an even pace. When it does come in, take it—even if it means long hours and missing your vacation time. There's always dead-time in which to catch up with yourself.
7. *Keep your mind and body fit.* In consulting, as in other small businesses, there's a tendency to forget that you have a private

life. Keep your private life alive by leaving time for reading, hobbies, and relaxation. Don't ignore exercise either; after all, consulting can be a rather sedentary life.

8. *Reaffirm the value and importance of what you do.* As a consultant, you're on your own. You will have no health plan, few (or no) coworkers, a lot of rejection. There may be a tendency toward depression as you ask yourself, "What have I done recently? Why am I putting up with this insecurity? The rejection?" At moments like these, it's best to think about the value of what you do, realize that you're doing what you choose to do, and that the only real security in life comes from believing in yourself.

9. *Open up new profit centers.* Consultants, like other businesspeople, must think about diversifying their offerings. Diversification, in addition to being a form of growth, can help be a hedge against a weak economy.

10. *Don't be pushy.* Being a consultant means constantly waiting to see if you have the assignment. The tendency is to call prospects to find out. Be cool. You don't want to appear overly eager, even if you are.

How to Charge for Your Consulting Services

It isn't easy to determine your per diem rate. It will probably depend upon what others are charging, your own experience, and your own self-confidence.

Here's how one consultant analyzes the costs involved with his consultancy and how much he must charge to generate an income comparable to a reasonable salary.

First, it's important to remember that with weekends eliminated there are only about 260 work-days in the year. At most, you can probably bill 140 of these days, with 120 days for which clients cannot be billed. These nonbillable days may be spent writing reports, marketing, being sick, on vacation, or observing holidays.

To arrive at and compare the per diem fees of two consultants, start with the salaries that one might reasonably expect to earn in the business world. Then add in fringe benefits and annual expenses.

The total gross needed is then divided by the 140 days for which billing can be made to arrive at each consultant's per diem fee.

Annual Expenses for Consultant

Office	$2,500
Secretary	6,000
Supplies,	
Postage	400
Telephone	1,000
Nonreimbursed; Books; Memberships; Accounting services	5,000
	$14,900

Computation of Daily Fee

Potential Salary	$35,000	$50,000
Fringe Benefits		
Pension (15 percent)	5,250	7,500
Hospitalization	900	1,000
Major Medical	1,000	1,000
Salary Insurance	500	500
Expenses	14,900	14,900
Gross for 140 days	$57,550	$74,900
Daily Fee	$403	$535

Public Relations

"With public sentiment, nothing can fail.
Without it, nothing can succeed."
—Abraham Lincoln

IN GENERAL

We have bad news and good news about the field of public relations. Briefly, the bad news first:

- Ever since the days of P.T. Barnum, publicity, also known as "public relations," has had a seedy connotation. Public relations (PR) people are derogatorily called "flacks," and have been portrayed in countless books and films as fawning, exploitive, and insensitive.
- The field of public relations is not for applause-seekers. The best PR is invisible, and the best PR people stay behind the scenes.
- Public relations is a detail-oriented, high-pressure career. It is known as a thankless profession. If you don't produce results, you're fired; if you do produce results, you don't always get full credit.

Now, the good news:

- The field of public relations is growing rapidly, and there are numerous opportunities to find entry-level positions.

- The field is exciting because you are dealing with the media as well as the public. There's often an opportunity to travel, earn a respectable salary, and use your mind in a variety of ways.
- Public relations is a challenge to people with liberal arts backgrounds. It appreciates skills in speaking, writing, and keeping up with current events.

Just what is "public relations," and how does it differ from advertising?

Public relations works toward gaining public awareness of a product or service via the editorial[1] side of the media to achieve specific goals.

While advertising people create advertisements and commercials that are paid for by sponsors, public relations people attempt to help people or organizations reach their publics in a more indirect way. A film star's publicist, for example, might suggest that the star appear as a guest on a talk show. The resulting interview would almost surely mention the star's upcoming projects.

If all of the public relations agencies of the United States were to shut their doors tomorrow, most radio and talk shows, as well as many newspapers and magazines, would soon have to follow suit. Why? Because the American media—including WNBC's *The Tonight Show*, *The Wall Street Journal*, and the major magazines—depend upon publicity releases to keep them abreast of what is going on. True, these organizations have their own staffs to help assemble material for their shows and publications, but public relations firms form a surprisingly large information lobby. In fact, they provide many of the "news" stories we see and read every day.

There are more than 3,000 *bona fide* public relations firms in the United States, and there are countless other "vest-pocket" firms that are run from the homes of individuals.

The opportunities in public relations are vast, because virtually every store, company, restaurant, and celebrity can use publicity to help gain public awareness, and, by so doing, make more money for themselves. A restaurant that puts its name on matches and ashtrays is engaging in a form of promotion; so is a consultant who sends Christmas cards to his prospects. So is an art gallery dealer or party-goods store owner who puts out a newsletter. All of these are examples of publicity or promotion, not advertising.

On a grander scale, companies and public organizations (e.g., The National Rifle Association, The Dairy Association) often spend millions of dollars to gain public acceptance, to introduce new products, and to gain media coverage. Political candidates must weigh the public-relations impact of practically every stand they take, every group they address, and every place they visit. Doctors, dentists, and dieticians often leave brochures about health scattered about their lobbies because it's good promotion.

Public relations can increase sales either directly or indirectly. An example of public relations' direct impact is the sending of press releases for a new product or a new use for an old product. An example of indirect public relations would be a food company's sending of recipes that include its product as an ingredient to food editors. These recipes may even end up in feature stories that mention the company's product. This indirectness gives public relations its reputation for nebulousness. The amount of good will or sales generated by a promotional campaign is often difficult, if not impossible, to measure.

Sometimes the best public relations involves checking or limiting the damage of negative media exposure. When a few Extra-Strength Tylenol capsules in Chicago were found to contain cyanide, the Johnson & Johnson Company limited the damage done to the product's image by acting with admirable speed, forthrightness, and savvy. They instantly acknowledged the problem and initiated a recall of the product long before the Food and Drug Administration could even suggest it. They were also accessible to the press, and they helped in the investigation. The recall cost Johnson & Johnson more than $100 million, but it upheld the company's reputation. A great deal of credit goes to the Johnson & Johnson public relations people who, through quick thinking and a respect for the intelligence of the American public, managed to avert what could have been a publicity disaster.

The public relations effort was internal as well as external.

Employees of McNeil Consumer Products Company, the Johnson & Johnson unit responsible for Tylenol, began sporting buttons with a thumbs-up design and the words "We're Coming Back."

Public relations is an exciting field, because it challenges people to think of ways in which products and services can gain media attention. If, however, public relations people fall into the habit of lying, playing down the negative, or avoiding painful issues, they can create bad publicity. When Rely Tampons were shown to be associated with Toxic Shock Syndrome, the manufacturer of Rely was reluctant to acknowledge the problem. That reluctance alone practically destroyed the brand because it destroyed the product's credibility. To be good at public relations, you must fight the human tendency to deny responsibility.

Enjoying public relations and promotion requires accepting the fact that your job is to seize opportunities to help the public see a product or service the way you see it or the way your client sees it. The field is not for shy people; it's for assertive people who are not troubled by rejection. It may involve using everything from press releases, interviews, press conferences, direct mail, and flyers to T-shirts, buttons, pens, toys, and telephone calls to help influence people to take notice of your service or product.

There are approximately 120,000 people in the public relations field, one-quarter of them women. One-half of all people in public relations work in New York City, Washington, D.C., Chicago, and Los Angeles.

In 1980, college graduates beginning in public relations started at between $10,000 and $13,000 a year, not a very high salary. However, in 1981, the average salary for top PR people was $38,000 a year. One survey quotes the 1980 median yearly salary at $35,000—up $4,000 from 1979. Salaries are highest in the Northeast ($38,000 yearly median) and lowest in the South ($31,000).

Those entering the field of public relations have never had such a wide variety of opportunities. Many veer toward consumer public relations, where they publicize products and services used by consumers: books, plays, food, health and beauty aids, travel, appliances, and restaurants. Less known, but equally important, are trade and industrial public relations, which involves publicity aimed at businesspeople, including store owners, doctors, distributors, and other middlemen.

The rapidly expanding health field offers public relations opportunities in hospitals, pharmaceutical companies, and medical associations. Another growth area, according to one vice-president of public relations for a major corporation, is human resources planning, which used to be employee communications. Another growing area, public policy planning, requires some type of government experience. There are also emerging public relations opportunities in the fields of ecology, finance, economic education, and government regulation.

In addition to these choices, the person entering public relations must decide whether to work in a corporate communications office or in a public relations agency. Public relations professionals can prosper within an agency, or they can make a home for themselves in nonprofit organizations, hospitals, or foundations, as well as governmental public interest groups (e.g. Common Cause), corporations, and trade associations. A bright newcomer with top writing and presentation skills can succeed in any of these areas.

Three Major Public Relations Organizations

Public Affairs Council (PAC). 1220 16th St., N.W., Washington, D.C. 20036, (202) 872-1790. Its members are corporate public affairs executives who want to encourage the business community to be active in public affairs. The Council provides public-affairs training seminars, workshops, and counseling for corporations beginning public affairs programs. Meets semiannually. Founded: 1954. Publications: Materials on public affairs. *Directory of Public Affairs Officers,* annual.

Public Relations Society of America (PRSA). 845 Third Ave., New York, NY 10022, (212) 826-1750. A professional society for people in public relations in business, industry, government, trade and professional groups, and nonprofit organizations. Offers continuing education programs and an executive referral service. Founded: 1948. Publications: *Channels,* monthly. *Public Relations Journal,* monthly. *Public Relations Register,* annual.

The Professional Development Institute for Public Relations/Communications Professionalism. Pace University, 331 Madison Ave., Room 603, New York, NY 10017, (212) 490-3895. Offers training resources in a wide variety of public relations areas.

WHAT IT TAKES

We have mentioned that public relations, while exciting, is also detail oriented. Although it attracts many liberal arts types, it often requires the meticulousness of an engineer. Here is a rundown of the most important skills and abilities you'll need to succeed in public relations:

1. *Define problems.* The ability to understand a problem and find ways of solving it is a key to success in public relations. Sometimes, the problem can't be solved, but it can be alleviated. For example, when the telephone company's installers went on strike, there was a lot of negative publicity about all of the inconvenience being caused. A smart PR person was hired and the negative publicity soon eased up. Why? Because the PR person made sure that important media figures were able to get their phones installed and serviced. Similarly, during the Vietnam War, campus unrest over the draft was alleviated by the development of a lottery system—a brilliant public relations feat. The war went on, but the campuses became much quieter.

2. *Think logically.* Just as computer programmers think logically when they create "flow charts," a PR person must plan projects, such as press parties, interviews, exhibits, and direct-mail programs, by thinking of each step of the project. Once a project has been conceived, the nuts-and-bolts work begins; that

means "working backwards"—deciding what has to be done by when, so that you can meet deadlines. An experienced PR professional knows that unforeseen delays are likely to slow down any project, and therefore plans must be made that allow for human frailty.

3. *Writing and editing.* These allied skills are crucial to anyone who works in public relations. Sensitivity to good writing and an ability to recognize and edit bad writing will make your written work stand out. These skills will allow you to progress from writing one-page press releases to elaborate brochures, booklets, feature stories, and press kits.

4. *Creativity.* This often overused word refers to the ability to view an old problem with fresh eyes. It's knowing the rules plus seeing beyond them.

5. *A mind for detail.* There are dozens of details involved in the simplest public relations project. Even the distribution of a press release requires writing, re-writing, editing, printing, stapling, folding, inserting, and mailing. You must buy or create a mailing list, keep it updated constantly, and purchase envelopes. You need to know procedures for getting a bulk mail permit, and you have to buy postage and address the envelopes. By the time you get to planning a press party for 500 people, the details become almost an endless stream, right up to checking to see if the microphones are working and whether or not the bartender has enough club soda.

6. *Presentation and interpersonal skills.* Your skills should involve a wide range of communication talents that cover everything from selling your ideas at a meeting or over cocktails to giving a formal speech at a press conference, trade show, or press party.

7. *Tenacity.* Publicists who are trying to place stories in the media must be tenacious or they will quickly become discouraged. One placement may require weeks of effort. Dozens of newspapers or radio stations say No before one says Yes. You must recognize that; by sticking to it, you will probably make the

placement. In short, you must have the optimism of a salesperson and the persistence of a freelance writer.

8. *Ability to work with the press and with management.* Working with managers is different from working with the press, and you must be able to switch "languages" with ease. Managers care about the bottom line; editors and reporters care about news. Each sees the publicist through different eyes, and you must be what they see.

9. *Knowledge of the media.* By understanding the media, you can learn how to best shape your communications. If you know that a particular magazine has a 3-month lead-time, you can immediately determine whether a story that's "hot" is even worth sending over. Perhaps that item should go to a daily newspaper. A knowledge of deadlines will also help you determine which media may be right for which press releases. By dealing with journalists, and by taking courses in journalism, you'll soon become accustomed to seeing your stories as an editor sees them. You'll know how a release should look, and you'll learn to phrase them to rivet the editor's attention. When dealing with TV, you'll automatically think of your client's story in visual terms. Certain topics— exercise, cooking, games, fashion—are "naturals" for TV, while others—books, restaurants, and music—are ideal for radio.

10. *Integrity.* There is no substitute for integrity and reliability. You can't afford to lie to the press—they'll never forgive you. If you try to create a smokescreen, or simply make up facts as you go along, you'll lose your credibility and never regain it. When a reporter asks you if the president of your company just awarded himself a $100,000 bonus, and you know he did, you'd better admit the truth or at least say that you'll look into it. Denying the truth or making puffed-up claims about your product will almost always come back to haunt you.

11. *A knowledge of what you know and what you don't*

know. A good manager knows when and how to delegate authority. If you're weak on the graphics end of the business, learn how to communicate with designers and then trust them to be competent in their area. You should gain enough knowledge to know just how far a printer, designer, or copywriter should be trusted. But, once you decide to trust them, don't let your ego get in the way of their creativity.

These skills and abilities can be acquired through a blend of college studies and real-world experience.

In 1980, about 90 colleges and 25 graduate schools offered degree programs or special accreditation in public relations, which is usually administered by the journalism or communications department. In addition, about 200 colleges offered at least one course in the field. Some typical courses included organizational communication, public relations management, and public relations theory and techniques.[2]

Taking college-level courses in public relations is important, but so is a general liberal arts background. Get a course or two in nonfiction writing under your belt and then major in a discipline such as economics, psychology, nutrition, or computer sciences. A degree in journalism is helpful, but only if it doesn't preclude your taking other enriching courses in a variety of fields. College is a place to learn how to think. Later, you can apply these skills to public relations through an internship program or on your first job in the field.

A college education is only the beginning. To do well in public relations takes an assertive, out-going person. It takes a knowledge of business and a knowledge of important issues. And, it takes reliability and loyalty. Don't worry about not understanding all the minutiae of printing or design. You'll have your whole career to pick up the thousands of details you'll need to round out your public relations education.

Public Relations: A Few Terms of the Trade

Backgrounder. Information supplied to the press that gives the background of a product, service, person, or organization.

"Comp." This term is used in two different ways—as short for "complimentary" or free, as when applied to tickets for public events such as films, plays, or concerts; or as short for "comprehensive," which is a rough layout of a printed piece that allows for further input before more detailed work is begun.

Contact. The person identified in promotional material as being a source of further information.

Demographics. Specific information about groups of people—age, sex, location, education—that may form a market for your product or service.

Designer/Art Director. A person involved in giving direction and shape to graphics. Includes the choosing of artistic elements involved in a promotion (e.g., logo, type size and style, paper, ink).

Dog and Pony Show. A public relations and advertising term referring to an elaborate presentation made to impress a potential client. Originally a circus expression, the phrase connotes a presentation filled with impressive visuals; one that pulls out all the stops.

Fact Sheet. A part of a press kit that lists key facts, such as who founded the company, when it was founded, or the number of employees. It is used to supplement a press release and other elements of a press kit.

Flack. A derogatory reference to a publicist.

Pitch Letter. A letter asking for a particular response. It can be used to "pitch" a product or service by placing features, arranging interviews, or requesting participation in a press conference or special event.

Point-of-Purchase Display. A method of displaying a product at the location where it is sold.

Portfolio. A notebook or carrying case filled with samples of your work, such as articles for the school paper, sample press releases, sample designs, or anything else relevant to your work in public relations. It is also known as a "book."

Sales Promotion. Any endeavor that is meant to increase sales or awareness of a particular product or service, but is neither advertising (paid space) nor public relations (editorial influence). Included in sales promotion are sales contests for retailers or distributors, brochures, and flyers.

Tip Sheet. A press release aimed at the broadcast media, showing how a client offers valuable tips to a listening or viewing audience. A book publisher might send a tip sheet about a new book to a program director or producer, to encourage him or her to "book" the author as a guest on the talk show.

Two-, Three-, Four-, or Five-Color. The number of different colors applied to a printed piece.

GETTING STARTED

Since the essence of public relations is communication, your resume, cover letter, and interpersonal style must display the crispness, clarity, and conciseness of the promotional material you write.

There is no room in this field for hackneyed cover letters, all-purpose resumes, or insubstantial portfolios. Everything you show to a potential employer must be oriented to that employer's specific needs. This may mean that you won't be able to send out resumes and cover letters *en masse*, but it also means that you'll probably get more serious consideration at those organizations that receive your material.

The ideal public relations resume describes what you've done—direct mail, press releases, photography, art direction, media contact—and it also zeros in on the results. For example, if you've written and distributed a release about a product or service, tell the reader how many media pick-ups the release received. If you were responsible for a direct-mail campaign, give your response rate. In other words, write a resume that is a functional summary of what you've done and the positive results your work produced.

If you are coming straight from college, the same principle still holds true. Did you work on the school paper? If so, how did you leave your mark? Perhaps you were responsible for instituting a column on restaurants. Perhaps you helped create a direct-mail campaign that increased circulation by 25 percent. In short, be specific, and show a potential employer that your influence was felt. Furthermore, be brief. Use bullets to summarize technical information and to focus on your accomplishments. Whatever you do, don't go overboard and say that you did things when, in fact, you didn't.

Prepare a draft of your resume and then show it to people who are used to looking at and evaluating resumes. You might, for instance, show it to people in the college placement office. You might also take a copy by the school's public affairs office. After all, they are public relations professionals, and they can give you insight into how PR people will view what you've written.

After finishing writing and rewriting your resume, get it professionally typed and offset. In public relations, more than any other field, neatness counts. No typos, strike-overs, or narrow margins are allowed.

The cover letter should be individualized. Address it to the needs of a specific employer. Form letters are out; they'll make you look foolish. Here's an example of a cover letter written to a small public relations company in New York:

> Dear Mr. _____,
>
> I am interested in interviewing for a position with your company.
>
> My career focus is primarily in 35-mm slide presentations, although I have a varied graphics background. My greatest strength lies in my ability to communicate with coworkers and clients.
>
> I have a solid audiovisual foundation. At this time, my goal is to pursue this rapidly expanding communications field.
>
> Your consideration is greatly appreciated. I would welcome the opportunity of an interview with you to tell you more about myself and will take the liberty of calling you in a week or so.
>
> Sincerely yours,

At first glance, this cover letter seems to do the job, but a closer inspection shows that it lacks care. The most important problem is that this letter was written to a one-man public relations company, hardly the type that would do this type of specialized hiring. It is obviously a form letter and was probably sent to dozens of public relations agencies simultaneously.

The letter is writer oriented, not reader oriented. Good letters focus on the needs of the reader, not the writer. Try to imagine what the reader needs to know, rather than simply parading a list of your skills in front of him. Cover letters, as with almost every other element of selling, require that you take what you have to say and put it into a format that conforms to what your reader wishes to read.

Finally, the letter exhibits blandness and tendency towards cliché. The sentence, "My greatest strength lies in my ability to communicate with coworkers and clients" is too weak to have any impact. The phrase, "Your consideration is greatly appreciated" is also weak, thanking the reader for something he has yet to do.

Another cover letter, which was sent after a brief conversation with the head of another one-man public relations shop, reads:

> Dear Charles,
>
> I have enclosed my resume as we discussed a while ago. I hope we will be able to work with eachother in the near future.
> Thank you for your consideration.

This letter presents several problems. The salutation, "Dear Charles," is overly informal. The first sentence is awkward and imprecise (enclosing a resume was probably not the subject of the discussion). The next sentence contains a typo ("eachother") and is so vague as to have no meaning. The last sentence is also too indefinite. Exactly what does the writer want? Does he want an interview? Will he call? Does he want full- or part-time work? Or does he want to be kept in mind for freelance projects?

By the way, this letter was followed up with a phone call 2 months after it was sent. Such a delay is simply foolish. By that time, the reader has forgotten the letter. The writer of a letter should follow up within 1 or 2 weeks, not when the mood strikes him or when he discovers that he is desperate for work.

Now, let's take a look at two very-focused cover letters. The first is from a freelancer looking for occasional work, and the second is from a professional who is looking for full-time employment:

> Dear _____,
>
> In every public relations agency there are times when the workload builds until the services of a freelancer who

can step in and "do" are desperately needed. When those times occur at your firm, I can help.

I have had a broad base of public relations experience, including: promotion, media placement, fund raising, program development, special events, and community programs.

I have taken ideas from their inception, coordinated the various aspects to bring the ideas into being, and produced the desired programs. This background provides me with unique experience which can be useful to your agency.

Enclosed is a flyer which outlines my experience and accomplishments, I would appreciate the opportunity to show you samples of my work, and discuss how I could be of service to your firm.

Sincerely,

This actual letter is not perfect—but it is pretty good. It has a "you" orientation that puts the emphasis on the reader's needs. Paragraph three is a bit vague, and paragraph four is one, long-run-on sentence, but basically the letter works. The next letter works even better, because it is specific and functional, thus highlighting the resume enclosed with it:

Dear _____,

As vice president of an audio-visual production company, I expanded the Acme, Incorporated account from $5,000 to $65,000 per year. I also brought in Procter and Gamble, New York Telephone, Prime Computers and Dean Witter.

. . . If you are looking for someone with strong communications sales experience, you just found him. Let me mention some specific accomplishments:

- Developed 17 new accounts which generated $425,000 in total income
- Increased my total billing 40% each year for three years
- Initiated an aggressive marketing campaign to three trade shows per year, generating at least one new client for each show. . . .

With eight years of experience in all aspects of sales and production, I believe I can generate sales and profits for your company.

If the timing is right, I would be happy to meet with you at your convenience.

Sincerely,

This is a good letter, but ultimately unsuccessful because it was sent to a one-person shop that could never be in the position of hiring this type of specialist. It is specific and clear, although it has not been individualized; therefore, it comes off as a form letter.

Let's summarize a few key points about the writing of cover letters:

1. Decide what the employer is looking for before you write a letter. Don't waste time and postage on shops that would not be in the market for what you do.
2. Be honest about your experience. Don't be afraid to admit that your background isn't a perfect match for a particular job. Stress other work you've done that might compensate for it.
3. Keep copies of all your cover letters and the ads you respond to. This helps you keep track of the salary range you've quoted and the particular job requirements of each organization. You may get a response to your cover letter months after you've sent it.
4. Name a salary range. The low side should be compatible with the salary being offered. By doing this, you'll be able to negotiate upwards if you're called in for an interview. You won't be rejected if you ask for $1,500 or $2,000 more than was mentioned in the job announcement or ad.
5. Keep the cover letter informal and conversational. The best business writing *is* conversational. Never use a phrase such as "enclosed please find," "under separate cover," or "thanking you in advance."
6. Don't use a form letter unless responding to a job advertised by an employment agency. If you have a portfolio of samples, say so, but avoid sending samples and never send your portfolio. By holding back your portfolio, you are sure of something to talk about when you eventually do get an interview.
7. Reorganize your portfolio for each interview according to the nature of each potential employer. If a place is looking for someone who primarily writes press releases, put all your press releases up front.

Now, a word about references:

1. Avoid putting the names of references on your resume or cover letter. Supply them when you are close to getting the job. That way, your references won't be bothered by personnel people who are checking references just to fill up their time.
2. Alert your references as to when they may be getting a call. Tell them about the job you've applied for so that they will be prepared to discuss your experience in light of the job you are seeking.

One final note: Collect and keep samples of every promotional piece you write, design, or edit. Keep all materials relating to elaborate direct-mail campaigns or press parties. It's more impressive to show an employer a direct-mail package when it is accompanied by a budget, a media list, and other bits of documentation that show you truly carried the project through to completion.

The 15 Largest Public Relations Agencies in the United States

1. Hill and Knowlton
   420 Lexington Ave.
   New York, NY 10017
   (212) 697-5600
   Offices around the world.

2. Burson-Marsteller
   866 Third Ave.
   New York, NY 10022
   (212) 986-8610

3. Carl Byoir & Associates
   380 Madison Ave.
   New York, NY 10017
   (212) 986-6100
   Offices around the world.

4. Ruder Finn & Rotman
   110 E. 59th St.
   New York, NY 10022
   (212) 593-6400
   Offices around the world.

5. Daniel J. Edelman
   221 N. LaSalle St.
   Chicago, IL 60601
   (312) 368-0400
   Offices in New York, Washington, D.C., Los Angeles, London, and Frankfort.

6. The Rowland Company
   415 Madison Ave.
   New York, NY 10017
   (212) 688-1200

7. Manning, Selvage & Lee
   99 Park Ave.
   New York, NY 10016
   (212) 599-6900

8. Ketchum Communications
   4 Gateway Center
   Pittsburgh, PA 15222
   (412) 456-3500

9. Doremus & Company
   120 Broadway
   New York, NY 10271
   (212) 964-0700

10. Rogers & Cowan
    9665 Wilshire Blvd.
    Beverly Hills, CA 90212
    (213) 275-4581

11. Ogilvy & Mather Public Relations
    964 Third Ave.
    New York, NY 10022
    (212) 751-8080

12. Booke Communications
    Incorporated Group
    355 Lexington Ave.
    New York, NY
    (212) 490-9095

13. Creamer Dickson Basford
    1633 Broadway
    New York, NY
    (212) 887-8010

14. Bozell & Jacobs Public Relations
    1 Dag Hammarskjöld Plaza
    New York, NY
    (212) 705-6000

15. Robert Marston & Associates
    485 Madison Ave.
    New York, NY
    (212) 371-2200

YOUR FIRST BIG BREAK

Your first break in public relations may be your first job or it may be your first client. It will give you the opportunity to discover whether or not you are cut out for the field.

In all probability, your first job will involve what engineers commonly refer to as "grunt work": Answering letters, answering telephones, writing copy for mundane products or services, or simply compiling media lists. You may find yourself in press or consumer relations, political campaigning, fund raising, or employee recruitment. Whatever you're doing, take good mental notes.

If you are at a small public relations agency, your break may come when you land your first substantial client. Suddenly, instead of writing the occasional release or fiddling with mailing lists, you'll be involved with such things as arranging press parties, placing feature articles, designing a direct-mail campaign, and working with designers and illustrators in creating brochures, logos, letterheads, and envelopes. This is your chance to fly. You'll see how much responsibility you can handle and how well you can do a number of tasks.

A neighborhood gourmet store gave one small, two-man agency the opportunity to get actively involved with the New York City food press. Their job was to launch a new $1 million gourmet store on the Upper East Side. The assignment called for a wide range of skills and the two young men did everything from naming the store to organizing the opening day press party. They both gained 20 pounds as they sampled the food so that they could write about it with conviction!

They wrote a three-page press release and a fact sheet describing some of the food that would be featured. Later on, they designed and implemented a direct-mail program that offered the store's catering services to food managers at New York's top corporations.

The account gave these young PR men a variety of clips and other samples of their work that they were able to parlay into gaining more food accounts. They could point to the stories they had placed in *The New York Times*, *The Daily News*, and *The Post*. They even managed to get *The Wall Street Journal* to mention the store on page one. Because the store owner gave full rein to the public relations specialists, they were able to create a logo, cover letters, brochures, and flyers that were well produced in addition to being well written. Most importantly, they gained rapport with the cream of the New York food press, which became a saleable commodity when they "pitched" their services to other food accounts.

Clients require you to stretch yourself as a writer. The challenge is to make a press release so interesting and inviting that an editor will use it as the basis of a story. When you've placed a story, you've made everyone happy: Yourself, the editor, and your client. You've also gained a "clip" that you can use to demonstrate to other clients or employers that you have a track record.

Similarly, when you write your first brochure, you've gained a showcase for the quality of your writing. People will instinctively react to your work with the thought: if they've done this well in the past, they'll be able to help me in the future. So, your clips—brochures, media placements, flyers, and pamphlets—are your best selling tools. Public relations professionals are intensely interested in knowing who is responsible for a successful campaign. Although you may never get to sign your name to your feature stories or brochures, your reputation as a good publicist will spread.

To make yourself special, always take a special view of every task you perform. A simple press release can be transformed into something very unusual if you care enough to make your work first-rate. One young publicist, eager to find a hook for a release being written about an acupuncturist, did some investigative work and discovered that it had been 10 years since Nixon's trip to China. He used the anniversary as the inspiration for the release's headline, "Ten Years After Nixon's Visit to China, Acupuncture Comes of Age." The release, which went on to focus on the work of a single New York acupuncturist, was widely picked up.

WHAT TO SHOOT FOR

There is no single goal for people entering public relations, because the field is so diverse. Some people want to start their own public relations company. They want the autonomy and the potential for profit that come with running their own business. They also enjoy the diverse activities that await them as head of their own agency, such as bringing in new clients, designing public relations programs, writing, designing graphics, and setting the fees for their services.

Other people want to climb the corporate communications ladder. Usually, that means becoming the communications director of a company, an association, or a government agency. The directorship may bring a high salary, an expense account, and other "perks," but it can require distancing yourself from the communication skills that brought you pleasure as you were coming up through the ranks.

When you get to be the boss, you may spend many afternoons taking care of administrative details, attending meetings, manipulating budgets, and writing memos, while your helpers write the releases, run the junkets, place the stories, and attend the photo sessions and press parties. While they're doing, you may be planning policy and setting goals for others to reach.

Your *goal* should be the development of your own skills through increasing the diversity and depth of your experience in both print and broadcast media, making new contacts and maintaining old ones, and keeping abreast of new technologies and methods of printing, mailing, and placing promotions. Some of the larger public relations firms recognize the value of diverse experience and make mobility a part of their training programs.

Some people aim at becoming the head of a large public relations department or agency, whereas others prefer the challenge of a small department. In general, the larger the agency, the more it is specialized. You may spend several years doing work that is reported on time-sheets so that the clients can be billed accordingly. For those who rebel against the notion of time-sheets, there are less regimented, more congenial shops. And, of course, there is always the option of opening your own business. A number of new public relations firms start up when a person who has been working closely on one account woos that account into becoming the first client of his or her newly formed public relations firm.

WHEN YOU'VE MADE IT

You've made it when you're doing what you want to be doing and are being paid well for it. If you're a writer, you may be content to go from high-priced project to high-priced project. A designer may wish to have his choice of assignments, taking only those that are interesting or particularly lucrative.

If you want to go into administration, you can aim at moving up the corporate ladder. But most creative people don't believe that more is necessarily better. A photographer doesn't usually want to supervise other photographers, even if it means a larger salary.

Many public relations people, however, relish the idea of implementing increasingly larger promotional projects. For instance, Herb Schmertz, director of corporate communications at Mobil Oil, has played a leading role in creating Mobil's image as a civic-minded corporation. Perhaps his boldest public-relations gambit was actually an advertising *coup*. By placing low-key, issues-oriented advertisements on the Op-Ed page of *The New York Times*, Schmertz persuaded the public to see Mobil as being concerned about the fight against industrial pollution, the high price of oil, and the search for alternative energy sources.

In the world of film and TV public relations, John Springer of John Springer Associates has handled key moments in the careers of many top entertainers. He has been a quiet, effective buffer between clients and the press on numerous occasions, including some involving Elizabeth Taylor and Richard Burton.

In a recent issue of *East Side TV Shopper*,[3] a Manhattan magazine, Springer was asked why high-powered celebrities love him:

> They trust me. Twenty years ago I started this business, and set firm rules. Always work with people you admire. Never deal in scandal, or betray a client's confidence. I've been offered huge amounts of money to write a "tell-all" book but even after a client is long dead, it's contemptible to violate a special bond.

> ". . . I know the publicist stereotype. He is supposed to be this seedy stogy-smoking man who races to the nearest pay phone, dials a scandal sheet and purrs: 'Have I got a scoop for you.' But to survive, the publicist must be responsible and respectable.

Today, John Springer Associates publicizes numerous films, plays, books, the RKO Nederlander theaters, and Strawberry Shortcake, a popular character created by the American Greeting Corporation.

The firm of Rogers & Cowan has handled personal publicity,

as well as corporate publicity, for many notables. Henry Rogers personally handled public relations during Prince Philip's extensive visit to the United States.

There have always been "kingmakers," people who stand behind political candidates and handle interpersonal, as well as public relations, functions. David Garth has achieved recognition for designing some of the cleverest public relations strategies for successful political candidates. For example, it was Garth who positioned Mayor John Lindsay in his successful bid for reelection with a campaign built around the candid admission, "I've made some mistakes."

We'll conclude this section by quoting from the Public Relations Society of America's booklet on *Careers in Public Relations:*

> Basic to all public relations ... is communicating. Well-thought-out, effectively handled communications are increasingly seen as essential to the success and even existence of organizations and causes in today's complex, fast-changing world. Every organization—governmental, business, labor, professional and membership, health, cultural, educational, and public service—depends on people. Their attitudes, attention, understanding and motivation can be critical factors in whether an organization or an idea succeeds or fails.

Selected Reference Books
in Public Relations

O'Dwyer's Directory of Public Relations Firms. 1983 Edition. $50. Published by J.R. O'Dwyer and Co., Inc., 271 Madison Ave., New York, NY 10010, (212) 679-2471. Lists more than 1,200 individual firms. Gives addresses, phone numbers, principles, numbers of employees, and areas of specialization.

O'Dwyer's Directory of Corporate Communications. Annual. $70. A guide to 2,400 companies and 300 trade associations that are public-relations intensive. Entries include company name, address, telephone, sales and business activities, as well as names and duties of principal public relations personnel. Also gives names and addresses of outside public relations counsel, if any.

Burrelle Annuals: New York State, $30; New Jersey, $25; Pennsylvania, $28; Connecticut, $19; Maryland-Delaware, $29; New England, $26; Greater Boston, $17.50; Special Groups (Minority, Ethnic), $50. Burrelle Co., 75 E. Northfield, Livingston, NJ 07039. Excellent local references.

TV Publicity Outlets—Nationwide. $89.50. P.O. Box 327, Washington Depot, CT 06794. Covers 2,500 TV program contracts. Includes three completely up-dated and reprinted editions, one every 4 months.

The Encyclopedia of Associations (3 volumes). $95. Gale Research Company, Book Tower, Detroit, MI 48226. A comprehensive and definitive listing of 13,300 trade associations, professional societies, labor unions, fraternal and patriotic organizations, and other voluntary member groups. Entries include association, location, membership, size, objectives, activities and publications.

The TV News Handbook by William B. Becker. $15.95. Insider's Guides, P.O. Box 2424, Southfield, MI 48037. Tells who to contact, what they're looking for and how to slant stories to the decision makers.

Syndicated Columnists by Richard Weiver. $30. Public Relations Publishing Company, 888 Seventh Ave., New York, NY 10006. Organizes columnists by subject matter.

Bacon's Publicity Checker (2 volumes). Annual. $99 plus postage and handling for both. Bacon Publishing Co., 14 E. Jackson Blvd., Chicago, IL 60604. Includes supplements; volumes not sold separately. The periodical volume is classified by subject or industry, with an alphabetical listing as well. The newspaper volume is in two parts—dailies and weeklies with a geographical index. Both give detailed information about each publication (i.e., its location, circulation, publication, issue dates, kinds of release used, and members of executive staff).

1982 All-In-One PR Directory. $58.00. Gebbie Press, P.O. Box 1000, New Paltz, NY 12561. Lists over 22,000 public relations outlets in nine different fields: daily newspapers, weekly newspapers, farm publications, televison stations, AM-FM radio stations, consumer magazines, business and financial papers, trade publications, and outlets in the black press and radio.

Cable TV Publicity Outlets Nationwide. $125. P.O. Box 327, Washington Depot, CT 06794. Lists over 660 contacts. Includes two completely up-dated and reprinted editions, printed semiannually.

Television Contacts. Larami Communication Association, Ltd., 151 E. 50th St., New York, NY 10022. A yearly directory on national, syndicated, and local programs' guest, product, and informational requirements. Local listings include affiliation, personnel, addresses, and programs. Monthly "change bulletin" up-dates programs, personnel, and editorial requirements. Daily up-dating service available for major markets.

Radio Contacts. Larami Communications. A yearly directory on radio programming with 2,500 major market station listings. Includes affiliates, personnel, format, local programs, guest, and information requirements. Network and syndicate listings include information on programs, contacts, and guest placements. Monthly "change bulletins" up-date information.

Public Relations Handbook. $53.50. Richard W. Darrow et. al., Dartnell, 4660 Ravenswood Ave., Chicago, IL 60640. Informative.

Selected Public Relations Periodicals

Jack O'Dwyer's Newsletter. 271 Madison Ave., New York, NY 10016. $90 per year.

PR Aids Party Line. 221 Park Ave. South, New York, NY 10003. Weekly. $90 per year.

PR Calendar. 245 E. 40th St., Apt. 6E, New York, NY 10016. Weekly. $100 per year.

Public Relations Journal. Public Relations Society of America, 845 Third Ave., New York, NY 10017. Monthly. $24 per year to nonmembers.

Public Relations News. 127 E. 80th St., New York, NY 10021. Weekly. $100 per year.

Public Relations Review. Communication Research Associates, Inc., Suite 500, 7100 Baltimore Blvd., College Park, MD 20740. Quarterly. $22 per year.

Publicist. 221 Park Ave. South, New York, NY 10003. Bi-monthly. $15 per year.

Bulldog. California Business News, 6420 Wilshire Blvd., Suite 711, Los Angeles, CA 90048. $92 per year.

Speechwriter's Newsletter. 407 S. Dearborn, Chicago, IL 60605. Weekly. $128 per year.

Social Science Monitor For Public Relations and Advertising Executives. Communication Research Associates, Inc., Suite 500, 7100 Baltimore Blvd., College Park, MD 20740. Monthly. $64 per year.

Communicator's Journal: The Magazine of Applied Communications. P.O. Box 602, Downtown Station, Omaha, NE 68101. $42 per year.

Communication Illustrated. P.O. Box 924, Bartlesville, OK 74005. Monthly. $96 per year.

Telecommunications

IN GENERAL

If you're an average American, chances are that by the time you're 72 years old, you will have spent 8,760 hours—*one entire year of your life*—talking on the telephone. There are plenty of other phone-users to talk *with*: Of all American households, 95 percent are equipped with at least one telephone. Of the 168 million telephones in the United States, 80 percent are controlled by the Bell System and 20 percent are controlled by independent telephone companies.

American business is a heavy user of telephones and other communications devices; telecommunications is where tens of thousands of dream jobs await management-minded job-seekers who are eager to understand new technology, provide service, and save their company money—a feat richly rewarded in the corporate world.

Telecommunications is the art and science of managing a company's communications sytems and the associated expenses. *Tele* is the Greek word for "far off," and telecommunications basically means "communications at a distance." The word has come to encompass all modern electronic methods of long-distance communication; not only telephones, but also data communications (the exchange of computer information via phone lines), videoconferencing (telephones with pictures), teletext (written messages transmitted to video terminals), telegram, telex, and facsimile (paper copies of documents transmitted over phone lines).

In his book *Telecommunications System Engineering*, Roger L. Freeman defines telecommunications as "the service of providing electrical communication at a distance." Brad Schutz, writing in *Graduating Engineer*, calls telecommunications "the generic term for whatever it takes to carry knowledge, information, sentiments or sensations across long distances, encompassing use of radio, television, telegraph, telephone and smoke signals."[1]

Telecommunications is one of industry's most poorly managed operating expenses. "Telephone bills are the biggest—and fastest growing—uncontrolled cost in American offices today," observes telecommunications publisher and author Harry Newton.[2] Improperly managed telecommunications systems cost U.S. industry $3–$4 billion a year. A good telecommunications manager can cut a company's telecommunications expenses by 15 to 20 percent and more. If a company with $100 million in sales has a $1 million phone bill, a good telecommunications manager might be able to save his firm $200,000 a year. Obviously, few other professionals can offer employers such a clear-cut return on their investment in the professional's salary. In addition, telecommunications professionals get involved with fiber optics, computers, office automation, and other state-of-the-art technology. And yet, there is "a shortage of skilled people in this field," according to Personnel Resources International, Inc., a New York consulting firm specializing in the recruitment of telecommunications professionals.

Why are qualified telecommunications people in such short supply?

One reason is that telecommunications is just now emerging as a legitimate professional area within the corporation, much the same as data processing emerged in the 1970s. Ten years ago, "telecommunications" simply meant checking the monthly phone bill and handling complaints from irate executives and support staff when the telephones didn't work. The unfortunate individual who performed these thankless tasks was often an office manager, administrative assistant, secretary, or junior data processing employee. Managing the telephone system was strictly a part-time job that went along with his or her other responsibilities. As phone bills grew, some companies saw that telephone and telegraph expenses were a cost that could be managed like other costs and that a properly managed telephone system could boost the company's bottom line. All Fortune 1,000 companies now recognize telecommunications as an important professional area. However, many smaller firms, as well as many old-time managers, still view the telecommunications manager as the "phone man"—a technician on the same level as the bookkeeper, shipping clerk, or night watchman. As a result, graduating engineering and business majors either avoided telecommunications because they were ignorant of its growing importance, or (more likely) they never knew it existed as a career option at all.

Other reasons for the shortage of telecommunications professionals include the scarcity of college-level training programs and the lack of clear-cut, entry-level positions in the field. A prelaw student goes to law school, earns a law degree, and goes to work as a lawyer for a law firm. However, in telecommunications, the career path is less well defined.

According to the *U.S. Industrial Outlook,* 1,130,000 workers were employed in the "telephone and telegraph services" industry in 1982. But this figure includes telephone operators, cable splicers, linepersons, repairpersons, engineers, and other occupations that don't concern us here. No one knows exactly how many telecommunications analysts and managers are employed by business, government, and industry, but estimates from several sources place the number between 50,000 and 100,000.

We believe that telecommunications is the "sleeping giant" of the corporate world. Under-publicized and little known to most job-seekers, it offers high pay, challenging careers, and a rare chance to contribute directly to a company's profitability early in your career. In this chapter, we'll tell you (1) how to prepare for a career in telecommunications, (2) how to learn more about the field, (3) how to find and evaluate prospective employers and the positions they offer, and (4) how to win the top spot in telecommunications—the director of telecommunications—where you can easily earn $1,500 a week and more.

WHAT IT TAKES

Before you plunge headlong into a search for a telecommunications career, you should decide whether your interest lies in technical or management areas. Do you want to design complex networks of phone lines, switches, and other equipment to transmit high-speed computer "conversations"? Or would you prefer working with people, providing them with the telephone service they need to conduct their business effectively?

"I think it's important for the individual to define where he or she is going to be happiest," says Joan Rodenberg of Rodenberg/Richardson, a New York recruiting and search firm that specializes in telecommunications. "There are some telecommunications jobs that are heavily engineering oriented, and for those kinds of people, a 'double E' (electrical engineering) degree is still a darn good idea. For the person who wants to go into management, a business degree is a better idea."

With its tie-ins to data processing, satellite communications, and other high-tech areas, telecommunications sounds like an engineer's industry. But it isn't. *You don't need a technical degree to succeed as a telecommunications professional.* (Most companies do prefer candidates with college degrees over those without, however.)

The aspiring telecommunications professional's main contribution to his or her employer will be to provide better communications services, while saving his or her company money in the process. To achieve this cost savings, you must have an understanding of the dollars-and-cents side of the technology. "Having an appreciation for financial analysis, accounting methods, and billing procedures is important," says Richard Donovan, Joan Rodenberg's partner at Rodenberg/Richardson. "You don't have to have a degree in accounting to do that, but as an entry-level person you must pick up those kinds of skills to be an important contributor."

Accounting and "double E" are two college majors that serve as excellent preparation for a career in telecommunications. A background in business and marketing also helps. And knowledge of computers is extremely useful, especially if you'll be involved in *data communications* (computer-talk) as well as *voice communications* (people-talk).

Naturally, the ideal training for a career in telecommunications would be a graduate or undergraduate degree program in the field. However, only in the last few years have colleges begun to offer such programs. Even now, less than two dozen accredited schools offer degrees in telecommunications (see box). What's worse, the academic emphasis in many of these programs doesn't address the needs of business, government, and industry.

Part of the problem stems from the disparity in how academia and the real world define telecommunications. When academia thinks of a curriculum for the study of "electronic communications at a distance," it emphasizes the more glamorous media—broadcast television, radio, and cable TV. At the New York University School of Continuing Education, for example, the program schedule includes such courses as "The New Communications Technology and the Entertainment Industry," "A Study of Careers at Cable TV Programming Services," and "Communications Satellites: Systems, Services, and Networks." Interesting as these courses may be, they are not relevant to telecommunications in business, which, according to telecommunications author Larry A. Arredondo, is "The science of effectively controlling telecommunications expenses and abuse, and turning the telephone system into a productive business tool."[3]

In other words, telecommunications is *not* a synonym for cable TV, broadcast television, radio, or any of the other electronic components of the entertainment industry. Telecommunications people handle the telephones and data links that let people or computers communicate. They may even get involved with automation in the office and factory. But they certainly don't package feature films or produce rock-and-roll videotapes for cable TV networks.

Although knowledge always helps, the lack of classroom courses in telecommunications won't be a stumbling block to finding a job. In the telecommunications field, most training is still *OTJ*—on the job. A large part of that job, as you may have guessed, will involve dealing with the telephone company. While the intricacies of grappling with the Bell System is also learned primarily on the job, we can give you some Bell basics right here:

The United States telecommunications network of 168 million telephones is primarily controlled by American Telephone & Telegraph (AT&T), better known as the Bell System or "Ma Bell." AT&T is the largest corporation in the world; its assets exceed those of General Motors, Ford, General Electric, Chrysler, and IBM combined. Founded on July 8, 1877, AT&T today employs over 1 million people, has an annual payroll of $21 billion, and an income of *$11,000 a minute.* Incidentally, if you've ever had a problem with your telephone, you're not alone; Bell System employees handle 33 million customer complaints and calls every day.

The Bell System is divided into five separate operating units:

1. *AT&T Long Lines*—Long Lines operates the interstate long-distance network that interconnects Bell with independent phone companies and links the United States to overseas telecommunications systems. When you place a long-distance call, you do it through the Long Lines network.
2. *Western Electric Company*—The manufacturing arm of the Bell System, Western Electric produces telephones, cables, switches, and related telephone equipment.
3. *Bell Labs*—AT&T's research center, Bell Labs is one of the largest research and development facilities in the world.
4. *AT&T International*—This operating unit markets AT&T products and services outside the United States.
5. *American Bell, Inc.*—A newly created subsidiary that competes against independent vendors of telephone equipment.

Until recently, the Bell System had a sixth component, the Bell Operating Companies. Because it owned controlling interests in 21 local operating companies and noncontrolling interests in two more, Bell had a virtual monopoly in the telephone industry. However, a 1981 agreement between the Justice Department and AT&T has forced Bell to divest itself of these local operating companies.

This agreement broke Bell's monopoly, which will stimulate competition in the telephone industry. What's more, it will create additional job opportunities for telecommunications professionals. James H. Morgan, an independent consultant, claims that, "Quite possibly, the additional number [of tele-communications managers] needed could equal the number of telecommunications managers around today." The reason: As AT&T divests itself of its local operating companies, users will have to deal with at least two companies—the local plus AT&T—instead of just one. "The user companies who previously handled telecommunications casually, as one of a half dozen duties shared by an administrative manager or financial manager, will be especially affected," continued Morgan. "No longer can this shared person ask the one AT&T rep to 'take care of this and that.' " As a result, user companies will have to hire more telecommunications professionals and devote more time to managing the telecommunications function.[4]

GETTING STARTED

As with many of our "dream job" industries, landing the first job can be the biggest hurdle to getting started in the field. In an emerging specialty such as telecommunications, job titles are hazy and departments may be loosely organized. It is therefore difficult to identify an obvious starting point.

"There is no natural progression into the position of Communications Manager," writes Larry Arredondo in *Telecommunications Management for Business & Government*. "Anyone can be singled out for it at any time." In the early days of telecommunications, this anyone was selected from other staff functions. Office managers, administrative assistants, and junior engineering types were most often singled out, often to their dismay.

As effective telecommunications management increased in importance, so did the professional qualifications required of the people chosen to fill the jobs. To give you a feeling for what employers look for in candidates, we've collected a few excerpts from help-wanted ads in a recent edition of *The Sunday New York Times* (2-6-83):

DIRECTOR OF COMMUNICATIONS
Major NYC medical center seeks individual to assume overall responsibility for installation and operation of new telephone system. Candidate must possess an in-depth knowledge of telephone system features, applications, and implementation, plus ability to interface effectively with all levels of staff. Minimum 5 years related background; hospital experience a plus.

PROGRAM ADMINISTRATOR/
TELECOMMUNICATIONS
Reporting to Director, responsible for continuing operation of telecommunications network including special studies, CACS functions and services, and interface with users, utilities, and vendor representatives. Bachelor's degree in electronic communications or related field or 3 years significant functional responsibility in telecommunications environment.

DIRECTOR OF TELECOMMUNICATIONS SYSTEMS
Directs implementation of 7000-line, 11-location dimension-based electronic telecommunications network. Responsible for continuing management programs including budgeting and billing, systems expansion, long and short-range telecommunications planning and strategy. Bachelor's degree in electronic communications or related field.

You'll notice that these positions call for a Bachelor's degree plus a few years experience. But how do fresh-out-of-college, entry-level people get their start? It's not easy. "We don't know of a clear way into the field," admits Joan Rodenberg.

One way to break in is to take on some telecommunications responsibility as part of your current job. For example, if you work in an office and the boss wants to up-grade the telephone system, volunteer for the job. You can then use this on-the-job training as leverage to move into telecommunications at a larger, more sophisticated firm.

A second method is to start in a sales or engineering position with a "vendor" company that manufactures telecommunications equipment. (Any company that markets telecommunications products is a *vendor*. Companies that buy these products and use telecommunications sytems to conduct their business are *users*. This chapter focuses on telecommunications at user organizations—banks, insurance companies, manufacturers, retailers, financial institutions, and other businesses that have large telecommunications departments.) Or, you might start your career with AT&T, an independent phone company, or even a telecommunications consulting firm. Any of these positions will provide the basic exposure you need to make yourself a desirable candidate for a telecommunications position with a user organization.

Some types of businesses, such as retailers, rotate entry-level people into telecommunications as part of basic training in store operations. After a time, they'll rotate you out again, but even this short stint can provide the experience that will help you get your "foot in the door" at other corporations.

YOUR FIRST BIG BREAK

Since computers are more sophisticated than telephones, your first job will probably involve some low-level assignments on the voice side of telecommunications. You may get hands-on experience working with the company's telephone system. Perhaps you'll handle moves and changes. When the marketing department moves from the 2nd floor to the 16th floor or when the advertising department needs five WATS lines, the neophyte telecommunications worker will handle the switching or changing of the telephone system. This frees upper-level managers to do financial analysis, long-range planning, system design and implementation, and other high-level work.

In larger telecommunications departments, even the beginner's assignments can be challenging. Apprenticeship, as defined by one communications training expert, provides "on the job training during which skills and knowledge accumulated by journeyworkers can be transmitted to new employees."[5] In telecommunications, no classroom can give you the practical training that work experience provides.

WHAT TO SHOOT FOR

Early in your telecommunications career you should ask yourself, "Where do I want to be?" The answer will determine your career path. Some people aspire to management, others prefer to be involved in system operation and implementation, and still others like hands-on activities. Some are planners, others are doers. Fortunately, says Joan Rodenberg, telecommunications salaries "are up there for doers, too. Not everybody belongs in management, and companies have begun to realize that they have to create a dual-ladder career track."

If you intend to make your career as a telecommunications professional with a user organization, a clear picture of the job functions and department structure will help you plan your career path. Let's take a look at what goes on in the telecommunications department of a large (fictitious) firm.

Kalco, Inc. is a Westinghouse-size manufacturing company with annual sales of $7 billion. For most companies, telecommunications costs run between 0.5 to 3 percent of sales. In companies with heavy telephone use, such as brokerage and commodities houses, telecommunications costs can amount to as much as 45 percent of operating expenses. At Kalco, the annual telecommunications budget is $140 million—2 percent of sales.

According to industry consultants, the average company employs one full-time telecommunications worker for every $1 million dollars spent on communications. Kalco follows this guideline and has 140 employees in its telecommunications department. This is a large department, but not the largest. One major New York bank has nearly 600 employees in its telecommunications department.

Budget is not the only factor that determines the size of the telecommunications department. The complexity of the telephone system, the extent that the company relies on telecommunications, the number of locations, and the scope of the department's responsibilities will all have a bearing on how many people are hired to handle the communications function.

At Kalco, entry-level people hold the title of *junior analyst*. In telecommunications, "analyst" is a catch-all term for every telecommunications professional who is not in management. Junior analysts are responsible for day-to-day maintenance and implementation of telephones, phone lines, and other system components. They do not have administrative or managerial responsibilities, such as budgeting or planning. Junior telecommunications analysts are paid well compared to beginners in advertising, cable TV, and many other industries, with salaries ranging from the high teens to about $30,000 a year.

The next step up the telecommunications ladder is the position of *senior analyst*. Not yet a manager, the senior analyst is involved in selecting new telecommunications systems and upgrading existing networks. This is no small responsibility. With telecommunications system installation costs estimated at about $1,000 a line, the new 2,000-line system for Kalco's recently opened West Coast office will be a $2 million investment. Senior analysts request, analyze, and evaluate proposals submitted by vendors. They then present their recommendations to senior management for approval. Senior analysts can earn salaries anywhere in the high $20,000 to $40,000 a year range.

When the senior analyst gets his or her promotion to the much sought-after title of manager, he or she will be involved in either the planning or implementation of systems. The *manager of telecommunications planning* surveys new technologies and is constantly looking for ways to improve service and cut operating costs. The *manager of telecommunications implementation* (or *manager of telecommunications operations)* installs and maintains the systems that the planning manager designs and recommends. There may be separate planning and operations managers for voice communications and for data communications. At this level, managers earn salaries in the low $30,000 to mid-$40,000 a year range.

Managers of planning and implementation or operations report to either the *manager of voice communications* or the *manager of data communications.* These are the spots they'll move into as they continue their climb up the telecommunications ladder. Managers of voice/data communications have total control over voice or data communications and are responsible for both long-term planning and day-to-day management of these areas. These high-level managers earn salaries upward from the mid- $40,000 a year range.

As technology moves the industry toward telecommunications networks that can transmit voice and data at the same time on the same equipment, the voice and data functions will be combined, and a single manager will handle both areas. Today, these functions are integrated only at some of the larger companies; smaller firms still have separate managers for voice and data communications.

At the top of the ladder is the *director of telecommunications.* The director oversees the entire 140-person department at Kalco, and has total responsibility for their huge $140 million budget; his $55,000 to $75,000 a year paycheck reflects this. The director's responsibilities, as outlined in the October 1, 1981 issue of *Telephone Angles,* includes the following tasks:

1. Preparing the annual telecommunications budget.
2. Examining and analyzing all communications bills.
3. Supervising the service, maintenance, and repair of equipment.
4. Analyzing the "traffic" (use) of the system.
5. Up dating all systems and equipment as needed.
6. Acting as liaison between vendors and users.
7. Working with company personnel to provide the telecommunications services they need.
8. Analyzing the telecommunications systems of new and prospective acquisitions, branches, and divisions.
9. Training company personnel to use the system.
10. Maintaining a complete inventory of all equipment.

The director of telecommunications is directly accountable to senior management. He has to control today's expenses while planning for future growth. And predicting the telecommunications needs 5 years from now is tricky business, because technology is changing so rapidly. Equipment introduced to the market this month will be obsolete in 3 years or less. Furthermore, the number of suppliers of systems and services is on the rise.

The telecommunications director must keep up with technical innovations. He must track changes in rates, tariffs, and regulations. He must blend an understanding of technology with financial and managerial skills. Also, he needs to be a "people person" who can work effectively with users, subordinates, coworkers, top management, vendors, and telephone company representatives.

Still interested in the job? We have some tips to help you get there. First, we'll start with your resume.

Because telecommunications professionals can achieve tangible, measurable results, it is important that your resume reflects your accomplishments. Did you cut your company's telephone bill by 12 percent? Say so. Did the system you installed increase productivity in the telephone marketing department? Let resume readers know that, too.

Resumes should be as specific as possible. "Be sure to include the type of equipment you worked with and, if you were a salesman, the products you sold and the type of customers you called on," advises Personnel Resources International in their pamphlet *Telecommunications Career Planning Guide.* "If you had a technical job, make it clear whether your function was hardware design, systems planning, installation and maintenance, etc. . . . keep the prospective employer's interest in mind when writing your resume."

Resumes can be organized either chronologically or functionally. Most telecommunications professionals use chronological resumes, which outline their experience position-by-position and include the periods each position was held. However, if your past jobs have all encompassed the same responsibilities, you might consider a functional resume, which breaks up your experience by function (proposal evaluation, changes and moves, system implementation, and so on) rather than by date. A combination resume could include a detailed functional breakdown followed by a short listing of past jobs in chronological order.

Resumes should be limited to information relevant to your

ability to handle the job you're seeking. By all means, mention published articles, memberships in trade associations, professional licenses, and industry awards, if you have them. On the other hand, hobbies, civic activities, and your height and weight don't mean much to prospective employers and should be omitted. "Professional or job-related activities are more important in the resume than being a Little League umpire," concludes the *Telecommunications Career Planning Guide* booklet.

The resume is the piece of paper that initiates any move you make. Two questions to ask when planning these moves are:

1. How often?
2. Where to?

The answer to the first question may surprise you. Traditionally, the corporate world has frowned on the job-hopper; it was not unusual for an executive to change companies only once or twice in a 25-year career.

But times change. Not only is job-hopping acceptable, but the tables have turned. The telecommunications professional who remains at a firm for decades is suspected of being somewhat narrow-minded in his view of how business should be conducted. Says Dick Donovan, "If you've been one place virtually your entire career, you begin to lose some perspective of how other organizations function." Donovan warns against staying at one place too long too early in your career. Telecommunications recruiters jokingly claim that people who stay at Bell Telephone too long come out with bell-shaped heads. Staying put can stagnate your career as you become permanently molded in the image of your only employer.

Joan Rodenberg comments on job-hopping at different stages in your telecommunications career:

"Get that first job in telecommunications under your belt. Change after a year or so. Then, plan to move every 2 to 3 years for a time to increase exposure and gain different types of experience."

"In the beginning, plan your career in 3-year chunks. After a while, slow down, or you'll get viewed as a job-hopper." (She notes that companies are more willing to accept job-hopping in telecommunications than they are in other areas.) "Continue your education, and go for a degree if you don't already have one. As your career progresses, become more selective when you make a move."

The answer to our second question—"Where to?"—is also surprising. When we began to research this field, we hoped to come up with a list, by industry, of what types of companies offer excellent career opportunities to their telecommunications staff and which are dead-ends. But no sweeping industry-by-industry generalizations are possible. Each company must be evaluated individually. Joan Rodenberg explains why:

"As a telecommunications professional, you're a journeyman. You can go to work for any variety of companies, because telecommunications is not locked in to a particular type of company, as is data processing. The telecommunications person can go from a manufacturer to a bank to an insurance company; the knowledge of the particular type of environment is *not* critical. People who work in the telecommunications department of a publishing company define themselves as telecommunications professionals, and not as publishers."

Telecommunications does, however, vary slightly from industry to industry. For example, financial institutions stress service because working telephone systems are vital to their ability to conduct business transactions, whereas manufacturers stress cost savings because their primary concern is profit margin. As far as employment opportunities are concerned, however, these differences are negligible. A basic knowledge of telecommunications is far more important than specific knowledge of an industry.

Prospective employers, then, must be evaluated on a case-by-case basis. Your key concern should be whether a company considers telecommunications to be vital to their successful operation and continued growth. Or do they see telecommunications workers as simply "phone men" who look over monthly phone bills and come running when the WATS line needs fixing? You can determine this by asking some pointed questions and listening carefully to the answers. Here are the questions to ask:

- "Will I report to a telecommunications manager?" (You want to report to a telecommunications professional, not an office manager or other nontelecommunications administrator. You should always report to someone whose job you aspire to.)
- "Is this person a seasoned telecommunications pro?" (You don't want to report to an old-fashioned "phone man" whose out-dated view of the telecommunications function will reduce your status in the corporation.)
- "Do you provide education and training in telecommunications?" (In-house or outside seminars and courses are important to your growth as a telecommunications professional, and they enhance your value to future employers. Outside seminars are expensive, and a company's willingness to pay for them is a sure sign that they respect the telecommunications function.)
- "What is your telecommunications budget? How many people are in the department?" (Remember, the telecommunications department should have one full-time employee for every $1 million spent on telecommunications. In an understaffed department, things will be so hectic that professional results can't be achieved. In an overstaffed department, you will not have enough meaningful work to keep you busy.)
- "How much has the telecommunications budget increased over the past few years? And if it hasn't, why?" (A stagnant budget indicates a stagnant department with little opportunity for growth.)
- "Do you expect staffing requirements to increase?" (Increases in staff is another sign that the telecommunications department is a healthy, growing one.)
- "Do you promote from within or do you fill management positions from outside?" (Beware of companies that do not promote their employees. You cannot build a career at such a firm.)
- "What is your attitude toward Bell versus other suppliers?" (Sophisticated companies know they can't be totally dependent on the Bell System.)

By planning a series of well-executed job changes with the right companies, you can quickly move from junior analyst to senior analyst to telecommunications manager. Add timing and a little luck, and you may head a telecommunications department sooner than you would rise to the top spot in many other fields.

WHEN YOU'VE MADE IT

In some respects, you've "made it" simply by having the foresight to choose a career in telecommunications. "Despite the recession, telecommunications is like the San Francisco Gold Rush," says Joan Rodenberg. "There's no way you can attach yourself to it with some reasonable degree of intelligence without making money and having a successful career."

Tom Sprecher, Director of Professional Management Group, another New York executive search firm specializing in telecommunications, agreed that telecommunications is one of the truly "hot" industries of the 1980s. "Communications is the name of the game for today's business world," said Sprecher. "We are talking more to each other, and sending and receiving more and more information."

As a result, a person isn't dead-ended when he or she reaches the director of telecommunications slot at the top of the telecommunications career ladder. On the contrary, changing technology and a constantly increasing need for cost control will make the job more and more challenging and vital to the company's success.

"The telecommunications professional who can make decisions, anticipate future growth needs, identify and carry out preventative maintenance, and provide the administrative staff with the phone service they need can be a hero—well paid, sought after, and entrusted with major decisions," said Sprecher. "Better yet, with the fast changing pace of technology—new generations of machines are heralded almost weekly—whatever the telecommunications pro does this year will need to be reevaluated next year—preferably by this same telecommunications pro working at a higher rate of pay. Such a challenging job will never end, but will always provide an avenue to contribute markedly to the competitive performance of the business."

Many companies reward the director of telecommunications with an annual bonus based on the amount of money he or she saved the corporation by effectively managing the telecommunications department. Remember Kalco, our fictitious manufacturer with a communications budget of $140 million? If Kalco's director of telecommunications managed to cut costs by 15 percent—a reasonable goal achieved at many firms— he'd have saved his company $21 million a year. And that kind of contribution will not go unrewarded come bonus time.

A LOOK TO THE FUTURE

Telecommunications, computers, and office automation are slowly blending into the single discipline of "electronic information." At many firms, for example, the telecommunications manager is responsible for converting the company to the much-discussed "paperless office," in which electronic workstations equipped with computer keyboards and video screens replace typewriters, paper, pencils, pens, and file cabinets. A study by SRI International predicts that the number of automated work stations will surpass the existing number of electronic typewriters by the end of the decade. Integrating telecommunications with office automation requires more computer know-how than traditional voice communications, and "the telecom job market is hot for college grads . . . who are trained in engineering or computer systems," according to the cover story of the March, 1983, issue of *Career World*.

On the telephone side of telecommunications, a new "cellular technology" has greatly increased the effectiveness of mobile telephones. *Time* magazine predicts this will grow into a $10 billion a year industry by 1990.[6] Telephones have traditionally been leased to customers by AT&T, but now Bell, along with GTE, ITT, and about 100 other companies, is selling phones outright. In 1983, 10 million Americans will have bought their own phones.[7]

In addition to voice and data, users can now send pictures

over phone lines. As we mentioned earlier, AT&T offers teleconferencing systems that allow managers in distant offices to "meet" electronically by transmitting their images as well as their voices.

Teletext and videotext are two more innovations that will change the nature of the telecommunications industry. Teletext is a one-way broadcast of pages of text to a viewer's computer screen or TV set. Videotext is an "interactive" two-way system that allows viewers to respond to information displayed on their screens via a keypad or other control device. Used in coordination with cable TV systems, videotext will let subscribers vote, shop, bank, and take courses over their TV sets. In business, similar systems are known as "electronic mail." Instead of writing a memo on paper and waiting one week for the reply to come back through the mailroom, you can type the memo on your work-station keyboard and transmit it over the phone lines. Your correspondent will instantly receive the electronic text on her terminal, and she can reply within minutes. These same systems can serve as "electronic file cabinets" by storing memos, letters, and other information on magnetic disks or tapes.

Hair-thin fiber optic cables, which allow voices and computer data to be transmitted as beams of laser light, are fast replacing less-efficient copper cables in many telecommunications networks. These fine-glass fibers carry far more messages and take less space than heavy metal cables. This technology will greatly increase the capacity of the U.S. telecommunications network, a system that already handles more than 800 million local and long-distance calls a day.

As we move forward into the "Computer Age," data communications may eclipse voice communications in the telecommunications function. Communications writer Brad Schutz explains how this affects the corporate telecommunications department:"While the telephone lines engaged by these companies mostly carry voice, rather than data communications, it is clear to their top management that data communications—next to the flow of money—functions as a modern organization's lifeblood . . . Realizing this, top management in many companies has begun to demand computing expertise in people selected to be telecommunications managers."[8] And a recent article in the newsletter *Telephone Angles* gives additional reasons why computer buffs make good telecommunications managers: "EDP (electronic data processing) people have the analytical skills needed for receiving and analyzing the huge volume of data which is basic to the telecommunications function," the article explains, and "the technological trend in telecommunications is towards computer-driven hardware which an EDP department is, of course, familiar with.[9]

An increased emphasis in technical knowledge does *not* make traditional managerial skills obsolete. The written job description for a "Corporate Manager of Voice/Data Communications" at a Fortune 150 corporation states that the candidate must have "the ability to communicate in person and in writing, and to 'sell' management on effective telecommunications for current and future needs." In telecommunications, managerial and communications skills do not take a back seat to scientific knowledge.

What's in store for the future of telecommunications? Jay Jacobsen, President of Personnel Resources Recruiters, reports that the telecommunications industry is doing "substantially better" than the general business environment. Salary levels continue to increase. And specialized jobs have been created by the growth in cellular radio, fiber optics, common carriers (see "A Glossary of Telecommunications Terms"), satellite operations, and computers. AT&T's reorganization will create even more positions. And the defense sector will continue to have a strong demand for qualified telecommunications personnel.[10]

In 1982, American organizations and individuals spent $50 billion on telecommunications. William B. Saxbe, former U.S Attorney General, calls the field "the fastest-moving and most promising area of development in the United States."[11] And James Martin, in his book *Telematic Society*,[12] sees no limit to the industry's potential for growth:

"Whatever the limits to growth in other fields, there are no limits near in telecommunications and electronic technology," writes Martin. "There are no limits near in the consumption of information, the growth of culture, or the development of the human mind . . .

"The users of telecommunications . . . will change work patterns, leisure time, education, health care, and industry. The news media, the processes of government, and the workings of democracy could be fundamentally improved. The entire texture of society will be changed by telecommunications and related products. The new technology should give a new hope to today's college generation who must mold it and use it."

Colleges and Corporations That Offer Training Programs in Telecommunications[13]

Colleges and Universities

George Washington University, Washington, D.C. 20052, (202) 676-6040.

Golden Gate University, San Francisco, CA 94105, (415) 442-7000.

Michigan State University, East Lansing, MI 48824, (517) 355-8332.

New York University, School of Continuing Education, Telecommunications Program, 331 Shimkin Hall, New York, NY 10003, (212) 598-3591.

North Carolina State University, Raleigh, NC 27650, (919) 737-2434.

Ohio University, Athens, OH 45701, (614) 594-5174.

Southern Methodist University, Dallas, TX 75275, (214) 692-2058.

Syracuse University, Department of Electrical and Computer Engineering, Syracuse, NY 13210, (315) 423-3031.

Texas A&M, College Station, TX 77843, (713) 845-1031.

University of Colorado/Boulder, Boulder, CO 80309, (303) 492-6301.

University of Houston, Houston, TX 77004, (713) 749-2948.

University of Kansas, Lawrence, KS 66045, (913) 964-3911.

University of Southern Mississippi, Hattiesburg, MS 39401, (601) 266-7111.

University of Southwestern Louisiana, Lafayette, LA 70504, (318) 264-6457.

Georgia Institute of Technology, School of Information and Computer Science, Atlanta, GA 30332, (404) 894-3152.

Wabash Valley College, 2200 College Dr., Mt. Carmel, IL 62863, (618) 262-8641.

The Pennsylvania State University, Continuing Education Department, P.O. Box 1830, Wilkes Barre, PA 18708, (717) 675-2171.

Northeastern University Institute for Advanced Professional Studies, 1 Gateway Center, Newton, MA 02158, (617) 964-1412.

University of California Extension, 2223 Fulton St., Berkeley, CA 94720, (415) 642-4151.

Corporations

Bell System, Customer Education Center, 15 W. 6th St., 7th floor, Cincinnati, OH 45202, (800) 543-0401 (513-352-7419 in Ohio).

Illinois Bell Customer Education Center, 1 East Wacker Dr., 39th floor, Chicago, IL 60601, (312) 645-7528.

MCI Education Center, 1301 Ave. of the Americas, New York, NY 10019, (212) 582-6520.

Note: Seminars sponsored by Bell or MCI tend to be expensive— between $400 and $1,000 for a few days of training.

Other Career Opportunities in Telecommunications

In this chapter, we've focused on the telecommunications management function in the user organization—a company that uses telecommunications as a business tool. Although user organizations offer high pay and challenging careers, they account for only 10 percent or so of the more than 1 million telecommunications jobs. Here, then, is a quick rundown of what else is available in the field.

As we mentioned, there are 1,600 telephone companies that function independently of the Bell System. Independents operate 33 million phones—about 20 percent of the U.S. telecommunications network. The six largest independents—GTE, United Telecom, Continental Telephone, Central Telephone, Mid-Continent Telephone, and Rochester Telephone—account for 90 percent of independent telephone company revenues and control approximately 12 percent of all U.S. telephones.

The independent phone companies offer a wide variety of technical, administrative, and managerial positions. These include service representatives, telephone operators, cable splicers, telephone installers, equipment technicians, outside plant engineers, and many others. The independents are always on the lookout for qualified people with degrees in engineering, accounting, business administration, math, science, data processing, and marketing.

If phone companies don't appeal to you, maybe you would enjoy working for a vendor. Vendors manufacture and market telephones, cables, switches, modems, multiplexers, and a variety of other telecommunications products. They need technical people—computer scientists, analysts, electrical engineers, and technologists—to create these products. An entry-level engineer can expect a starting salary in the mid- to upper $20,000 a year range. The vendors also need marketing and sales specialists to sell their products to the users. An entry-level sales rep will earn between $21,000 and $32,800 a year, while an experienced marketing executive is worth $45,700 to $55,600 and up. (Salary figures for sales and marketing people are taken from the 1983 *Telecommunications Industry Salary Survey* published by Personnel Resources International, Inc.)

Finally, experienced telecommunications professionals have a third option. They can become independent consultants. Telecommunications consultants, says Dick Donovan, can earn from $300 to "upwards of $1,000 a day, depending on how esoteric their skills are." But esoteric skills do take time to develop. "I don't think you leave a company 5 years out and become a consultant automatically," observes Donovan. "The more successful consultants have 15 to 25 years invested in their field and are very well established. And, they have an extensive network of contacts."

A Glossary of Telecommunications Terms

Central office. The telephone company office where your telephone lines are attached to switching equipment that switches those lines.

Cross talk. An unwanted signal from one transmission circuit that interferes with another circuit.

Data communications. The transfer of information processed by computers from one computer to another. Such data is transmitted over telephone lines and via microwaves with the aid of special equipment.

Earth station. Equipment on the ground used to transmit and receive satellite signals. An earth station contains three components: an antenna, a receiver, and an amplifier.

Electronic telephone. A telephone containing electronic circuitry that provides additional features and improved performance.

Facsimile. Reproduction of a printed document transmitted by telephone line or radio signal.

Federal Communications Commission (FCC). The Washington, D.C. commission that regulates all electrical and radio communications.

Interconnect. A company that sells, rents, or leases telephone equipment competing with Bell System equipment.

Key systems. A small telephone-switching system for commercial installations. Key systems telephones are equipped with buttons to allow users to select from multiple telephone lines.

Mean-Time-Between-Failure (MTBF). A manufacturer's estimate of the average time that will pass before a failure occurs in a piece of equipment. MTBF is a measure of product reliability; the greater the MTBF, the more reliable the product.

Modem. Short for MOdulator-DEModulator. Telephone lines are built to carry voice as *analog* signals. But computers process information in *digital* form. Modems convert digital signals to analog signals and back again so that computer information can be transmitted over telephone lines.

Multiplexer. Multiplexers let you send many computer transmissions over a single telephone line. By doing so, they save on line costs.

PABX. Short for Private Automatic Branch Exchange. A private corporate telephone system linked to the public network.

Specialized common carrier. Private long-distance phone companies that compete directly with AT&T. MCI, ITT, and Southern Pacific are common carriers.

Subscriber. An individual or organization that subscribes to telephone service.

Telemetry. The transmission of information from remotely located devices.

Teletext. A one-way broadcast of pages of printed text to television sets and computer terminals. Already in use on some cable TV channels.

Telex. A message sent over telegraphic circuits and printed up on a teleprinter (Telex machine).

Trunk. The telephone communication path between you and the phone company's central switching office.

TWX. A Western Union system allowing printed messages to be sent and received via teleprinters.

Value added carrier. A company that leases its facilities from another company (such as a specialized common carrier or AT&T), and then adds some function or service to the original facility.

Videotext. A two-way "interactive" system. Videotext subscribers receive pages of printed text on their TV or computer screens, and can communicate with the system via keypads hooked up to the set. Videotext allows subscribers to use their TVs for such activities as shopping, voting, and taking home study courses.

WATS (Wide Area Telecommunications Service). Long-distance telephone service provided by the Bell System to reduce the phone bills of frequent long-distance callers. WATS cuts costs, but *it is not free,* as some people mistakenly believe.

Professional Associations Involved in Telecommunications

Ad Hoc Committee for Competitive Telecommunications, 415 2nd St., N.E., Suite 301, Washington, D.C. 20002, (202) 543-0777. An association for common carriers.

Association of Data Communications Users, P.O. Box 984, New York, NY 10019.

Association of Long Distance Telephone Companies, % Victor Toth, 2719 Soapstone Dr., Reston, VA 22091, (703) 476-5515. Equipment manufacturers, users, and providers of long-distance telecommunications services.

IEEE Communications Society, Institute of Electrical and Electronics Engineers, 345 E. 47th St., New York, NY 10017, (212) 644-7867.

International Communications Association, 9550 Forest Lane, Suite 319, Dallas, TX 75243, (214) 233-3889. For telecommunications managers in corporations and other organizations.

National Telephone Cooperative Association, 2626 Pennsylvania Ave., N.W., Washington, D.C. 20037, (202) 745-7300.

National Communications Association, 485 Fifth Ave., Suite 311, New York, NY 10017, (212) 682-2627. An information source in communications systems.

North American Telephone Association, 511 2nd Street, N.E., Washington, D.C. 20002, (202) 547-4450. Association of interconnect companies.

Society of Telecommunications Consultants, 1 Rockefeller Plaza, Suite 1912, New York, NY 10020, (212) 582-3909. For individuals involved in the marketing, manufacture, or distribution of telecommunications products or services.

Tele-Communications Association, 424 S. Pima Ave., West Covina, CA 91790, (213) 919-2621. Members are organizations that use telecommunications systems.

Telecommunications Marketing/Sales Association, 565 Fifth Ave., Suite 820, New York, NY 10017, (212) 682-0774.

United States Independent Telephone Association, 1801 K St., N.W., Washington, D.C. 20006, (202) 872-1200. Association of independent telephone companies.

Sources of Information on Telecommunications

Books

Telecommunications: An Interdisciplinary Survey, Leonard Lewin, Ed., $45. Artech House, Inc., 610 Washington St., Dedham, MA 02026, 1979, 728 pp.

Telecommunications Management for Business & Government by Larry A. Arredondo, $30. The Telecom Library, 205 W. 19th St., New York, NY 10011, 1981, 280 pp.

Professional Management via Telecommunications by Harry Newton, $7.50. Telecom Library, 1980, 48 pp.

The Telematic Society—A Challenge for Tomorrow by James Martin, $15. Englewood Cliffs, NJ: Prentice-Hall, 1981, 244 pp.

Co$t-Effective Telecommunications Management—Turning Telephone Costs into Profits by Bob Kaufman, $24.95. New York, NY: Telecom Library,1982, 288 pp.

The Encyclopedia of Telephone Cost Reduction Techniques by Alan Herbert Jordan, $99. *Telephone Angles,* P.O. Box 633, West Hartford, CT 06107, 246 pp.

Communications and the Future: Prospects and Problems, Howard F. Didsbury, Jr., Ed. World Future Society, 4916 St. Elmo Ave., Bethesda, MD 20814-5089, $14.50 paperback.

The Biggest Company on Earth: A Profile of AT&T by Sonny Kleinfield, $8.25. New York, NY: Holt, Rinehart, and Winston, 1982, 322 pp.

Data Communications: A User's Guide by Kenneth Sherman, Englewood Cliffs, NJ: Reston Publishing Co., 1981, 341 pp.

Magazines and Newsletters

Communications News, Harcourt Brace Jovanovich, 124 S. First St., Geneva, IL 60134, (312) 232-1400. Monthly.

Phone Calls, NTCA, 2626 Pennsylvania Ave., N.W., Washington, D.C. 20037, (202) 342-8200.

Telecommunications, 601 Washington St., Dedham, MA 02026, (617) 326-8220. Monthly.

Telephone Angles, P.O. Box 633, West Hartford, CT 06107, (203) 247-6355. Monthly.

Telephone Engineer & Management, 124 S. First St., Geneva, IL 60134, (312) 232-1400. Semimonthly.

Telephony, 55 E. Jackson Blvd., Chicago, IL 60604, (312) 922-2435.

Personnel Agencies/Executive Recruiters Specializing in Telecommunications

Associated Recruiters, 870 Market St., Suite 1128, San Francisco, CA 94102, (415) 781-5914.

Personnel Resources International, Inc., 342 Madison Ave., Room 937, New York, NY 10173, (212) 682-2030.

Professional Management Group, 211 E. 43rd St., New York, NY 10017, (212) 557-1585.

Tele/Data, Inc., P.O. Box 2304, Glenbrook, CT 06906, (203) 348-4916.

Rodenberg/Richardson, Inc., 521 Fifth Ave., Suite 1715, New York, NY 10017, (212) 986-4983.

Professional Management Group, 211 E. 43rd St., New York, NY 10017, (212) 557-1585.

William McCulloch Associates, Inc., 20 E. 46th St., New York, NY 10017, (212) 490-3334.

Leading U.S. Telecommunications Equipment Manufacturers

Western Electric Co., Inc., P.O. Box 25000, Greensboro, NC 27420.

ITT World Communications, Inc., 67 Broad St., New York, NY 10004, (212) 797-3300.

Siemens Corp., 186 Wood Ave. South, Iselin, NJ 08830, (201) 321-3400.

GTE Telenet, Inc., 1 Stamford Forum, Stamford, CT 06904, (203) 357-2855.

NEC Telephone, Inc., 532 Broadhollow Rd., Melville, NY 11747, (516) 752-9700.

Northern Telecom, 344 New Albany Rd., Moorestown, NJ 08057, (609) 234-5700.

Motorola, Inc., Satellite Earth Terminals, 82301 E. McDowell Rd., Scottsdale, AZ 85251, (602) 949-2814.

General Electric Corp., Data Communications Products Department, GE Dr., Waynesboro, VA 22980, (703) 949-1188.

Plessey Microsystems, 19546 Clubhouse Rd., Gaithersburg, MD 20760, (301) 948-2791.

Ford Aerospace & Communications Corp., 20th floor, 300 Renaissance Center, P.O. Box 43342, Detroit, MI 48243, (313) 568-7708.

Racal/Milgo, 8600 N.W. 41st St., Miami, FL 33166, (305) 592-8600.

Fujitsu America, Inc., Component Division, 910 Sherwood Dr., Lake Bluff, IL 60044, (312) 295-2610.

Harris Corp., P.O. Box 1700, Melbourne, FL 32901, (305) 724-3660.

Rockwell International, Collins Telecommunications Products Division, 855 35th St., N.E., Cedar Rapids, IA 52406.

Hitachi America, Ltd., 2696 Peachtree Sq., Doraville, GA 30360, (404) 458-6921.

M/A-Com, Inc., Northwest Industrial Park, Burlington, MA 01803, (617) 272-3000.

OKI Electronics of America, Inc., 4031 N.E. 12th Terr., P.O. Box 24260, Fort Lauderdale, FL 33334, (305) 563-6234.

General Dynamics Communications Co., 12101 Woodcrest Executive Dr., St. Louis, MO 63141, (314) 434-6900.

Training and Development

IN GENERAL

"I'm in the field of training and development."

"What's that?"

Everyone in training and development has probably had this conversation at least once in his or her career, for the field is just now beginning to gain national attention. The media is discovering though that this area of human resources is booming, even while the economy is slack; the field is luring educators, psychologists, social workers, and MBAs at a growing rate.

Business "training" is designed to teach employees how to do their job, to learn new skills. "Development" is designed to help employees who are already trained to further develop and enhance their existing job skills. For example, teaching a newly promoted supervisor how to delegate authority is *training*. Helping an experienced manager learn how to better prepare a departmental budget is *development*.

Public and private employers already spend more than $30 billion a year for employee training and development (an amount equal to roughly one-half the cost of all higher education in America).

In 1979, the federal government alone spent 33.3 million hours training its 2 million civilian employees. Consolidated Edison of New York spent $400,000 training its 26,000 employees in 1970. In 1980, with only 24,000 employees, Con Edison reported $5.5 million spent for formal employee training.

The Bell System spends almost $2 billion annually to conduct 12,000 courses for up to 30,000 employees at 1,300 training sites. A few years ago, Xerox opened a $75 million training and management center in Leesburg, Virginia, where it trains 12,000 employees a year.

Lockheed, Bell, Holiday Inn, TWA, IBM, Bank of America, and General Electric are among the many companies providing in-house courses that may be used for college credit. Additional companies pick up the tuition for workers who attend college. Citibank, for instance, spends $1 million annually on tuition reimbursement.

The Bureau of National Affairs found that out of 75 large companies (1,000 or more employees) and 39 small companies, 75 percent had in-house supervisor-training programs. More than one-half of these companies also provided training through outside seminars, professional or trade association meetings, and self-training courses.

Training and development is fast becoming a haven for teachers in their mid-30s who are looking for a career change that will bring better salaries, more challenging classroom experiences, and more job stability. But teachers form only one part of the training and development field. To see the field in its true perspective, you should become familiar with the American Society for Training and Development (ASTD), an association that practically dominates the industry.

According to an ASTD brochure:

> ASTD is an organization through which Training professionals from business, industry, and education exchange knowledge and ideas in mutual dedication to the fullest exploration of human resources.

> The New York Metropolitan Chapter of this national organization consists of some 2,000 members including trainers, managers, supervisors, employment and human resource personnel who are involved in improving both productivity and the quality of work life for employees in organizations.

To paraphrase a popular TV commercial, training and development must "earn its wings every day." Old-timers in business tend to look down on the idea because it does not contribute directly to bottom-line profits. Thus, training managers must often struggle to gain managerial approval for courses with the persistence of college professors fighting to institute a new elective.

Those who are sold on training see it as an aid in the campaign for greater national productivity. They strive to increase training budgets, even in the face of a down economy. One senior economist put it this way: "Improving the quality of the work force is the principal route to increased national productivity, particularly in the coming decade, when capital will become scarce and the technology of many other nations will be comparable to ours."

ASTD is the largest combined group of training, career development, and organizational development professionals in the world. It also includes members whose primary focus is other human resource areas (such as compensation and benefits). ASTD was founded in 1945, when it was known as the American Society of Training Directors. It was given a major push forward by the human potential movement of the 1960s and the more recent concern over "productivity." In 1972, ASTD had only 8,853 members. Today, it has more than 28,000 members and is growing rapidly.

Each ASTD chapter holds monthly meetings and workshops. Some issue newsletters, form committees, offer programs, and offer help to those seeking employment. The New York Metropolitan chapter of ASTD offers a package of materials for those entering the field. Within each chapter are special interest groups that offer programs for each level of professional.

In addition, there are also lots of consultants. Most spend their time currying favor with top management at Fortune 500 companies, offering them advice and training programs in everything from problem solving and crisis management to technical writing and interviewing skills. Training managers often need to go outside their company to hire a "vendor" who can provide expertise that is simply unavailable within the organization.

Yet, for every training consultant, there is a highly talented, and probably well-paid, person within the organization who occupies a position in a training department. Since the functions for each of these positions can differ radically from organization to organization, let's look at a few typical job descriptions:

> Sales training supervisor. Design and implement sales training programs for top consumer product corp. Minimal travel required. To $45 thousand.
>
> (from *The New York Times*)

> Data processing trainer. NYC and LI Banks seek qualified individual to teach basic programming. Must have knowledge of OS and JCL. Especially suitable for users with strong training interests and for trainers who seek closer affinity with users. Salary $25,00-$28,000.
>
> (from *ASTD Newsletter*)

> Training Director. $38-44,000. Banking. Wall Street. Financial Institution experience in training at management and supervisory levels. Develop programs.
>
> (from *The New York Times*)

> *Senior Field Training Specialists.* The specialist will be responsible for management of projects at field locations, such as plant start-ups and productivity improvement projects, training of management personnel in the field, and working with the management development staff in program development, coordination and training.
> The successful candidate will have strong consulting skills, with proven abilities in assessing and meeting client's need. A Bachelor's degree is required; four plus years of training and/or consulting is desired. Effective oral and written communication skills and potential to assume project management responsibility is necessary.
>
> (In-house job description)

These positions all require some experience in the field. However, entry-level trainers can use these job descriptions as guides for their own growth within the field. Though entry-level jobs may pay as poorly as college teaching jobs ($15,000 to $25,000 a year), they provide the background necessary to make the jump into the $25,000 to $35,000 a year range within a few years. Unlike teaching, advancement in training is based on merit rather than on longevity.

Steve Wahl, Training Director of Pepsico, said in a *Training and Development Journal* interview that people who want to start out in training should go for an advanced degree. He went on to predict that degrees in organizational psychology will be highly valuable, and that other "hot" areas for the future will include computer-assisted instruction, interactive video, and out-placement.

Organizations (Besides ASTD) Involved in Training and Development, Management, and Personnel

American Personnel and Guidance Association
30 Park Dr.
Berea, OH 44017
(216) 234-2080

American Vocational Association
2020 N. 14th St.
Arlington, VA 22201
(703) 522-6121

Bureau of Business and Technology
331 Madison Ave.
New York, NY
(212) 490-3895

National Association for Management
146 N. Gow
Wichita, Kansas
(316) 686-3776

National Society for Performance and Instruction
??-1 Vermeer Dr.
South Amboy, NJ 08879
(201) 727-9160

NY Society of Association Executives
60 East 42nd St.
New York, NY 10017
(212) 564-8889

International Association of Personnel Women
150 W. 52nd St.
New York, NY 10019
(212) 246-0532

Management Development Forum
Bernard Small
No. American Philips
100 E. 42nd St.
New York, NY
(212) 697-3600

Many teachers attempt to break into training and development but find the transition difficult. Training and teaching are not synonymous, especially if the would-be trainer has been steeped in liberal arts and has had little exposure to the business mentality. Also, the profit motive can be as foreign to teachers as the Dead Sea Scrolls. The teachers who persist in their business education often find the corporate world far more dignified, hospitable, and stimulating than the world of college teaching.

WHAT IT TAKES

Academic credentials, true enough, are a good first step toward entering the field. In fact, according to ASTD, 89 percent of the members have Bachelor's degrees, 41 percent have Master's, and 13 percent have Ph.D.'s. Any academic fraternity would be proud of those statistics.

Training and development is still a rarity as a college major, but more and more colleges and universities are introducing courses in the field. New York University, which does offer a Training and Development (T&D) certificate, regularly advertises such courses as "Training and Development Functions and Techniques," "Principles of Management and Organization," "Starting a Career in Human Resources Management," and "Human Resources Planning and Development."

Such courses provide students with a smattering of management, a dollop of personnel administration, a drop of pedagogical theory, and an introduction to training's place in most organizations. It is there, no surprise, to help make people more productive so that they can get out there and make more profit.

So, you may be wondering how training differs from college teaching (which also increases human productivity). Simply put, training never deteriorates—or shouldn't—into aimless philosophizing; it never rambles because there just isn't time. It usually has measurable objectives. Most college professors and high school teachers would cringe at the idea of being asked precisely how their students were going to change after being in their class.

Training aims at building skills, which is best accomplished when the teacher functions as a facilitator rather than a lecturer. Trainers who only "lecture" don't last long. Adults, you see, learn by doing. They require—get ready for the first of many T&D buzzwords—"hands-on" experience. In other words, they need to work with tangible exercises and role play rather than merely take notes on theory.

Training also implies an awareness of, agreement with, and empathy for the profit motive. Managers and support staff are busy people, and they often resent having to take training classes. They need to be motivated, but not in the same way as the typical college or high school student. Businesspeople need to see how training will increase their skills to do a job faster, easier, and better. They need to see a bottom line. Thus, there's no way that you can convince them that every bit of knowledge is good for them. Shakespeare and modern art, for instance, won't contribute to gaining a profit. Therefore, training must take practicality, thoroughness, accuracy, and conciseness to their furthest degree. A writing consultant may be brought in to hone writing skills that 12 years—or 16 years—of formal education failed to perfect. You can see why a teacher—or indeed, anyone—would have difficulty in making a rapid transition into this demanding field.

The average age of ASTD members is 41, and 75 percent of the members are internal practitioners employed by an organization in a human resource development capacity.

Several other statistics help us form the picture of a T&D practitioner: 66 percent are female; 95 percent are white; the average salary is $25,000 a year; and 53 percent have annual incomes between $25,000 and $50,000.

So, who is best-suited for success in this field? They're people who are highly educated and highly motivated, and who have made their peace with the world of profit. They have good presentation skills, good interpersonal and writing skills, and they are good at working with people.

Since clothes make the man—or woman—we should complete this section with a few comments on appropriate clothing. As in other occupations, training and development people dress well. The men prefer suits to slacks and sports jackets. Topsiders, cardigans, and turtlenecks are saved for the weekend. The women go in for short hair and suits or at least a blazer and skirt. A jacket, for women, spells power, boldness, and seriousness. Women with long hair are often not taken seriously. As one $35,000 a year woman in the training field comments: "Women with long hair may look great, but from a practical point of view, how could they travel? They'd have to wash their hair every night. At least, a woman with long hair would have to get used to wearing it up. I've never met a powerful woman with long hair—even Jane Fonda cut her hair! Mary Cunningham may be the exception that proves the rule."

Women in the training and development field, as in many others businesses, don't wear pants. They do wear tasteful jewelry such as pins and pearls. They avoid clanking arrays of bracelets or flashy religious ornaments. They also avoid high heels—they're too seductive, too "nighttime."

The important thing for both men and women is to choose good, soft fabrics that don't wrinkle easily. Polyester is *out*. Men should stick to gray or navy. Women should use compatible colors, emphasizing shades that complement their hair and eye color.

Manuals, Periodicals, and Other References of Value to Trainers

Manuals and Other References

The ASTD Training and Development Handbook by Robert Craig. $27.50/members; $34.50/nonmembers. ASTD, Suite 300, 600 Maryland Ave., S.W., Washington, D.C. 20024, (202) 484-2390.

The Training Director's Handbook. $29.50. Bureau of Business Practice, Waterford, CT 06386, (203) 442-4365.

Mid-Life Career Change—A Concept In Search of Reality by Solomon Arbeiter. $5.50. The College Board, 888 Seventh Ave., New York, NY 10019, (212) 582-6210.

ASTD Buyer's Guide and Consultant Directory. Published annually by ASTD. Free to members. Under $10 to nonmembers, (202) 484-2390.

Human Resources Development (The New Trainer's Guide) by Donaldson Scannell. $10.95. Addison-Wesley, Inc., Jacob Way, Reading, MA 01867, (617) 944-3700.

Periodicals

Training and Development Journal, published by ASTD.

Training Magazine, 731 Hennepin Ave., Minneapolis, MN 55403, (612) 333-0471.

Training World, Woodbury Communications, 80 N. Broadway, Hicksville, NY 11801.

Harvard Business Review, Soldier's Field Rd., Boston, MA 02163, (617) 495-6800.

Training News, 176 Federal St , Boston, MA 02110, (617) 542-0146.

Personnel Administrator, 30 Park Dr., Berea, OII 44017, (216) 826-4790.

Psychology Today, 1 Park Ave., New York, NY 10016, (212) 725-3900.

What's Happening in Training, 401 N. Broad St., Philadelphia, PA 10108.

Business Week, 1221 Ave., of the Americas, New York, NY 10020, (212) 997-1221.

The Wall Street Journal, 22 Cortlandt St., New York, NY (212) 285-5000.

The New York Times (Business Section), 229 W. 43rd St., New York, NY 10036, (212) 556-1234.

GETTING STARTED

Everyone finds his way into training in a different way. Here is an example of one person who entered the field after she outgrew her teaching position:

> "I was a teacher and educational coordinator for the Head Start program," says one management development consultant. "I came to New York and went to grad school in Academic Methodology. It was '73 and zillions of teachers were being laid off. Meanwhile, I realized that I wanted—I craved—adult feedback, to work with adults. I even worked as a secretary for a while. Eventually, I found my way to a workshop at Training House.
>
> "After taking a workshop with them, I managed to convince them to hire me. But when they moved to New Jersey, I decided to stay in New York.
>
> "I started doing more networking. Eventually I found a job in Human Resources at Equitable Life—that's how I got into supervisory training. I conceived of a program, wrote it, and did statistical validation. Eventually I became versed in about 25 different programs. Now, I'm on my own. For me, success in this field is simply influencing the growth of the people I teach. As long as I make enough money to maintain my lifestyle, I'm happy."

Very few people become trainers right out of college. It is still an area that attracts people who have experimented with other careers first. Here is how a training officer at a large bank found her way into the field:

> "I spent 10 years globetrotting with my husband. Wherever we went, I filled teaching gaps, from nursery school to college. Eventually I took the job of head of a nursery school, but, before long, I started to feel bored. So, I started taking business courses at night. Again, I looked around for work. I found a position doing public relations for a software company. Suddenly, I became aware that I wanted to make some money. I tried selling insurance, but it was a disaster. So, I started a full-time job search. I rewrote my resumé every week. I read about the personnel field. Finally, I got a copy of the *Training Handbook*. Read it from cover-to-cover. I realized that I had done this stuff before. I then starting sending my resumés to T&D people.

"It's difficult to enter this field directly from college. You need some technical skills or teaching experience. Also maturity.

"To get into a training position, it isn't enough to want to be a trainer; you have to have the skills. There was a job open at Bank of New York. I took it. It was exactly 2 years after I had made up my mind to enter the field. It took me a while to adjust to the corporate life. Teachers sometimes have trouble adjusting to being a facilitator instead of being the all-knowing expert who lectures all the time.

"Now that I've been doing this awhile, I find it much more satisfying than teaching. Interviews with parents were much harder than firing someone."

This trainer had some suggestions for people thinking about getting involved within training at a corporation.

"First of all: lay low until you get the lay of the land. Don't make too much noise or try to change things all at once. Things move slowly. You have to learn how groups function. Listen to people, observe how things are done, how people dress, how they phrase things. Understand the difference between your personal point of view and what is good for the whole organization.

"Remember that, as a trainer, you're visible throughout your organization. That can be a big plus if you handle yourself well.

"Most important, remember that training is not the most important thing in life for most managers. They usually view training as an interruption of their day-to-day work. It's only through your professionalism that you can change Neanderthal attitudes toward the value of training and its place within the corporate structure. The first few weeks I was on the job, I was put through teller training. It was a terrific orientation: I really understood the pressure on those people.

"In a shaky economy, it's vital that you take a bottom-line view of training. The word at organizations is productivity, not enrichment or human potential. In other words, if you don't prove that a course is worth the bother, you may not get a chance to teach it again for a long, long time."

As with many training administrators, our interviewee recommends that entry-level trainers take courses in the human resource field. For supervisory training, she recommends DDI (Development Dimensions, International), a Pittsburgh-based company specializing in teaching supervisory training.[1] For those interested in pursuing the area of career development, there are excellent courses offered at Blessing-White, a top human resource consulting firm in Princeton, New Jersey.

Her idea of success? "To gain versatility; to develop as well as present programs; to focus on an area you're good at, and eventually, be a consultant. Then you can aim at becoming a training director."

What else can you do to get started? The American Society for Training and Development (ASTD) has several suggestions: First, join ASTD and become active in the chapter. This means that you should get on a committee and begin meeting and working with people. You'll gain visibility and prospective employers will see your name in the newsletter.

Check out the chapter placement service. You can use this service of the ASTD to get your resumé out and about. Keep your resumé confined to one page. Emphasize those skills and experience that would be valuable in a training position. (Put them near the top of the page.) But don't just say what you were responsible for on your last job. Give some results. For instance, "We increased the number of enrollees by 45 percent in the first year. . . ."

Meet People. Enlarge your circle of acquaintances by attending monthly meetings and taking workshops. Go out of your way to introduce yourself to people. That is how you'll build a network and be remembered when an opening arises. But do it subtly and indirectly. Don't ask for jobs or offer resumés.

Keep reading. There's a great amount of literature in this field. Keep current by getting into the habit of reading newspapers as well as several of the weekly or monthly training magazines. You should also attend lectures and take courses.

25 Popular Topics in Training and Development

The following areas are among the most popular topics and issues in training and development. If they interest you, you may have come to the right field:

Improving Productivity and Performance
Strategic Planning
Writing Skills
Presentation Skills
Stress Management
Assertiveness Training
Instructional Design
Out-placement
Needs Assessment
Organizational Development
Management by Objectives
Behavior Modeling
Supervisory Training
Negotiating Skills
Management Development
Assessment Centers
Quality Circles
Designing Training Materials
Group Dynamics
Career Pathing
Equal Employment Opportunity
Affirmative Action
Conflict Resolution
Time Management
Computer-Aided Instruction

GETTING AHEAD IN TRAINING AND DEVELOPMENT (T & D)

For the training and development specialist, the first break is often a first job.

As with many people in training, Wesley Masters started out in another field. He took a Master's degree in Business Administration at Pace College in New York, and decided to look into personnel. He applied for a position at Mutual of New York, and found that there was an opening in recruiting and affirmative action. He got the job.

For about 1 year, Wes wrote policy papers, revised manuals, and gave a lot of thought to where he could move. At Mutual of

New York, the Human Resources Department consists of four areas: Employee and Affirmative Action, and Training and Development work closely together, and so do Salary Administration and Benefits. Since Mutual of New York encourages its personnel managers to become generalists, Wes was given the opportunity to break into training and development.

He was told to brush up his platform and writing skills. He was sent to the American Management Association's Train-The-Trainer program where he was taught how to use audio-visual equipment, as well as articulation and delivery. He took a Communispond course to shore up his newly acquired presentation skills, and was soon ready to deliver his first training program.

His first training and development program was a "canned" seminar, one that had already been developed by Xerox Learning Systems. Essentially, Wes prepared to teach it by studying a trainer's manual, getting together several handouts, and by thinking of study questions. As it turned out, the class was about 50 percent lecture, so Wes put his new presentation skills to work at once.

Now that he's in training and development, he's started to become familiar with a variety of other training programs. He's learned how to evaluate and to negotiate with consultants. And he keeps taking new seminars to keep his skills current.

What about the future? Wes, like many training specialists, recognizes that he would eventually like to get more involved with the design of training than its delivery. He would like to develop needs assessments, and learn more about the best ways to follow up successful training programs. "Keep your options open," advises Mr. Masters. "You can carve out your own niche once you get your feet in the door at a human resources department."

One consultant tells of breaking into training consulting by being asked by a local college to teach a class in presentation skills at a local manufacturing company. Although the consultant received a flat rate—less than one-quarter of the price that the college charged the client—she soon gained enough information about how to approach training directors and how to negotiate fees to start her own small consulting business.

After gaining a first client, most consultants go after bigger and better clients, eventually shooting for clients who are in the Fortune 500. Those clients are usually generous with fees and provide the most professional environment for training.

In a small organization, where it is the exception and not the rule, training is often slapdash. An instructor may be brought in to teach in much the same way a substitute teacher is hired for a junior high school. There may be no real preparation for him and no motivation for the trainees to listen or learn. Furthermore, in many training situations, the rooms, the blackboards, the flipcharts, the chairs and even the room temperature all conspire to raise the level of apathy.

However, when you work with an organization that has a commitment to training, you may step into a teaching situation akin to an academic "Fantasy Island." The students are well mannered and eager to learn, the flipcharts are new, and the blackboards are large and already washed. Coffee and danish pastry may be served as a pre–training snack, and the chairs and tables will probably be arranged exactly as you've specified. To a trainer, such things can spell the difference between enjoying the seminar and watching it fall apart.

As you progress through a career in Training and Development, you'll want to stay visible. This is especially important for consultants, which is why many of them try to keep a steady stream of books or articles flowing. Articles in a trade magazine help to give consultants visibility in that particular industry. They also provide them with handy reprints for mailing to other prospects. Books, of course, lend an aura of expertise and experience to all who publish: They make an impressive calling card when a consultant sits down face-to-face with his prospects.

Herb Cohen, former training director, became an overnight success with his book *How To Negotiate Anything*. Before long, banks such as Chase Manhattan and Manufacturer's Hanover Trust Company were inviting Cohen to give pep talks to their top managers. His fee is now upward of $2,000 a day.

Dorothy Sarnoff, who practically has a lock on the presentation skills field, has gained great visibility by working with such political figures as Menachem Begin and Adlai Stevenson as well as top corporate managers. Her firm is part of Ogilvy and Mather, and Ms. Sarnoff is a frequent guest on *The Today Show*. But she was training people long before the field of training was a field.

Less known, but still quite visible, Richard Stern is perhaps one of the most successful "training brokers" in the field. He uses his many contacts to match consultants with organizations that require training. For this service, Stern takes 25 percent of the fee charged to the organization. Most of Stern's consultants earn about $1,000 a day when on assignment. Stern has become visible through his years of participation in the American Society of Training and Development and his ability to relate well to training directors, consultants, and people in technical industries.

As with other people at the top of their profession, these people have achieved versatility and visibility. Sarnoff and Cohen use the media to their advantage, while Dick Stern combines a knowledge of the industry with superb telephone technique and innumerable contacts. They have made it. People call them, instead of the other way around. They are able to fill their time, far in advance, with high-paying consultancy work.

You can never really stop learning about training and development. The field changes quickly, and while emphasis may be placed on one set of skills this year, the entire field may be different next year.

The only way to maintain a position in training and development, therefore, is to grow along with the field. That means becoming familiar with the whole range of resources, from technical training, through human resources planning, to organizational development. It means keeping up with significant current research in fields such as management and organizational theory, psychology, and sociology, and knowing your own area well, whether it's technical writing, stress management, or program design. It also means keeping up with current programs and consultants, so that you're as familiar with what's available and what it costs as you are with the relative merits of your local supermarkets or coffee shops.

Make the most of your first job. Find a mentor and let him or her teach you. Gain an understanding of the concept of needs assessment, since training never exists in a vacuum. Gain confidence in your use of visual aids such as the chalkboard, flipcharts, overhead projectors, and 35-millimeter projectors.

Consultants who wish to stay on top cannot afford to become lax. They must continue to market their services, by telephone, advertising, publicity or direct mail. Some training and development companies even make use of advertisements on postcards distributed in a "pack" by *Training Magazine.* (For information on training action postcards, call 612-333-0471 or write "Training Action Postcards," 731 Hennepin Ave., Minneapolis, MN 55403.)

Consultants in this field are always looking to add names to their mailing lists. They also use source books to learn more about American organizations. ASTD puts out a reference book titled *Who's Who In Training*, that gives the name, title, and address of every one of its members. It will provide you with names of people whom you may approach for information or perhaps even a job interview. This book also gives you a sense of which companies are actively committed to training and which have relatively small training divisions.

The ASTD membership list covers 61 percent of the Fortune 500, and new members join the organization at the rate of 500 to 800 every month. Many are job seekers. To stay ahead of the crowd, check out the job listings in the ASTD newsletter in your locality, and keep up with the job listing in *Training, Training and Development Journal*, and the Business Section of *The New York Times.*

Now you know what training and development is all about. It's still a small field, at least in its tight-knit relationships and job grapevine. The whole field is great for word-of-mouth. Reputations can be built quickly. The 1980s promises to be a decade of unprecedented growth in training and development, and it's the place to be for people who are bright, alert, and able to relate well to others.

Training and Development: A Reading List

The following books are considered to be among the most important in the training and development field.

The Supervisor As An Instructor: A Guide for Classroom Training by Martin M. Broadwell, 3rd ed., Reading, MA: Addison-Wesley Publishing Co., 1978.

Training and Development Handbook: A Guide To Human Resource Development Robert L. Craig, Ed., 2nd ed., New York, NY: Mc-Graw-Hill Book Co., 1976.

A Practical Guide For Supervisory Training and Development by Donald L. Kirkpatrick, Reading, PA: Addison-Wesley Publishing Co, 1971.

Evaluating Training Programs by Donald L. Kirkpatrick, A Collection of Articles from the *Journal of the American Society for Training and Development,* Madison, WI: ASTD, 1975.

The Adult Learner: A Neglected Species by Malcolm S. Knowles, 2nd ed. Houston, TX: Gulf Publishing Co., 1978.

The Consulting Process in Action by Gordon L. Lippitt and Ronald Lippitt, La Jolla, CA: University Associates Press, 1978.

Management Development and Training Handbook Gordon Lippitt and Bernard Taylor, Eds., New York, NY: McGraw-Hill Book Co., 1975.

Goal Analysis by Robert F. Mager, Belmont, MA: Fearon Publishers, 1972.

Preparing Instructional Objectives by Robert F. Mager, 2nd ed., Belmont, MA: Fearon Publishers, 1975.

Developing Human Resources by Leonard Nadler, Houston, TX: Gulf Publishing Co., 1970.

Training By Objectives: An Economic Approach to Training by George S. Odiorne, New York, NY: Macmillan Publishing Co., 1970.

Training and Development: A Few Terms

One of the most difficult things about the training and development area is its language, which blends academic, managerial and behavioral psychology buzzwords. Here are a few terms to be familiar with:

Assessment Centers. An information-gathering method by observation of behavior in standardized performance situations at a common location.

Behavior Modification. Behavioral change through manipulation control and conditioning (i.e. rewards).

Career Planning. To prevent conflict between the organization's and the individual's job goals through systematic and consciously controlled approaches.

Consultant (Training). Any outside individual or firm who is paid primarily for the delivery of professional training advice and/or service.

Data Processing Training. Skill training for data processing personnel to include such things as keypunch and data-entry training, machine operation training, programming training, and systems analysis training.

Job Enrichment. The process of redesigning work in order to build in or emphasize those things that motivate people to work effectively.

Manpower Planning. Having the right numbers and the right kinds of people, at the right places and at the right time, doing things that result in maximum long-term benefits for both the organization and the individuals.

MBO (Management by Objectives). A system under which the manager and subordinate agree on job goals.

Needs Assessment. A survey conducted to uncover the training programs that are requested or desired by an organization.

OD (Organizational Development). A systematic effort to help people work more effectively to achieve organizational goals.

OSHA. Occupational Safety and Health Act.

Performance Appraisal. The review of performance evaluation data to plan performance improvement activities.

Team Building. Individual or team standards of excellence are set and team barriers to their achievement are analyzed in group or team sessions.

TA (Transactional Analysis). A system of defining and analyzing what goes on when people communicate and interact.

Publishing Companies That Publish Training-Related Materials

Harcourt, Brace, & Jovanovich
757 Third Ave.
New York, NY
(212) 888-4444

John Wiley & Sons
605 Third Ave.
New York, NY 10017
(212) 850-6000

Business Research Publications
817 Broadway
New York, NY
(212) 673-4700

Holt, Rinehart and Winston
383 Madison Ave.
New York, NY 10017
(212) 421-4136

Folett Publishing Co.
1010 W. Washington Blvd.
Chicago, IL 60607
(312) 666-5858

David Sage Publications
711 Third Ave.
New York, NY
(212) 986-9394

McGraw-Hill
1221 Ave. of the Americas
New York, NY 10020
(212) 997-1221

Research Press
2612 N. Mattis
Champaign, IL 61820
(217) 352-3272

Addison-Wesley
Jacob Way
Reading, MA 01867
(617) 944-3700

---

48 Companies That Care About Training and Development

The following organizations are among those that employ a number of training and develoment specialists. They are leaders in their fields and all display company-wide commitment to human resources.

IBM
Old Orchard Rd.
Armonk, NY 10504
(914) 765-1900

Sperry Corp.
1290 Ave. of the Americas
New York, NY 10104
(212) 484-4860

Rolm Corp.
4900 Old Ironsides Dr.
Santa Clara, CA 95050
(408) 496-0550

Bank of America
Bankamerica Center
San Francisco, CA 94104
(415) 622-3456

Schering Plough Corp.
Galloping Hill Rd.
Kenilworth, NJ 07033

Citicorp
399 Park Ave.
New York, NY 10043
(212) 559-0349

Richardson-Merrill
10 Westport Rd.
Wilton, CT 06897
(203) 762-2222

American Express
American Express Plaza
New York, NY 10004
(212) 480-2000

American Telephone & Telegraph
195 Broadway
New York, NY 10007
(212) 393-9800

Arthur Andersen & Co.
1345 Ave. of the Americas
New York, NY 10019
(212) 708-4000

Bristol-Myers
345 Park Ave.
New York, NY 10022
(212) 644-2100

Aetna Insurance Co.
151 Farmington Ave.
Hartford, CT 06156
(203) 273-0123

Digital Equipment Corp.
1 Federal St.
Springfield, MA 01109

Home Box Office
1271 Ave. of the Americas
New York, NY 10020

American Stock Exchange
86 Trinity Pl.
New York, NY 10006

Olin Corp.
460 Park Ave.
New York, NY
(212) 486-7200

Allen Bradley Co.
1201 Second St.
Milwaukee, WI 53204

Scott Paper Co.
Scott Plaza
Philadelphia, PA 19113

Smithkline
1500 Spring Garden St.
Philadelphia, PA 19101
(215) 854-5154

Polaroid
750 Main St.
Cambridge, MA 02139
(617) 577-2537

Coca-Cola USA
310 North Ave. N.W.
Atlanta, GA 30313
(404) 898-2121

Transamerica Interway
255 Fifth Ave.
New York, NY 10036

C&P Telephone
801 Roeder Rd.
Silver Spring, MD 20910
(201) 565-8520

Coopers & Lybrand
80 Park Plaza
Newark, NJ 07102
(201) 643-3301

Chemical Bank
277 Park Ave.
New York, NY
(212) 310-6161

Chase Manhattan Bank
1 Chase Manhattan Plaza
New York, NY 10081
(212) 552-2222

Xerox Corp.
800 Long Ridge Road
Stamford, CT 06904
(203) 329-8711

International Paper Co.
77 W. 45th St.
New York, NY 10036
(212) 536-6000

Merck Sharp & Dohme
126 E. Lincoln
Rahway, NJ 07065
(201) 574-4000

Warner Communications
75 Rockefeller Plaza
New York, NY 10020
(212) 484-8000

General Electric
3135 Easton Tpke.
Fairfield, CT 06431
(203) 373-2211

Philip Morris
100 Park Ave.
New York, NY 10017
(212) 679-1800

Connecticut General
Cottage Grove Rd.
Hartford, CT 06152
(203) 726-6000

Control Data Corp.
8100 34th Ave. South
Minneapolis, MN 55420
(612) 853-8100

Eastman Kodak
343 State St.
Rochester, NY 14650
(716) 724-4000

Metropolitan Life Insurance
1 Madison Ave.
New York, NY 10010
(212) 578-2211

Equitable Life Assurance
1285 Ave. of the Americas
New York, NY 10019
(212) 554-1234

General Foods
250 North St.
White Plains, NY 10625
(914) 683-2500

Johnson & Johnson
501 George St.
New Brunswick, NJ 08903
(201) 524-0400

Texas Instruments
13500 North Central Expressway
Dallas, TX 75265
(214) 238-4855

GTE
1 Stamford Forum
Stamford, CT 06904
(203) 357-2000

Hewlett-Packard
1501 Page Mill Rd.
Palo Alto, CA 94304
(415) 856-1501

Honeywell, Inc.
Honeywell Plaza
Minneapolis, MN 55408
(612) 870-5200

Rockwell International
600 Grant St.
Pittsburgh, PA 15219
(412) 565-2000

Mutual of New York
1740 Broadway
New York, NY 10019
(212) 708-2000

Prudential Life Insurance Co.
745 Broad St.
Newark, NJ 07101
(201) 877-6000

Westinghouse Electric
Gateway Center
Pittsburgh, PA 15222
(412) 255-3800

Chessebrough-Ponds
33 Benedict Pl.
Greenwich, CT 06830
(203) 661-2000

A Selected List of Personnel Agencies That Sometime Deal with Training-Related Jobs

Abbott Smith
P.O. Box 459
Millbrook, NY 12545
(914) 677-5051

Einstein Associates
380 Lexington Ave.
New York, NY 10017

Ford and Ford
850 Providence Hwy.
Dedham, MA 02026
(617) 329-5600

Fox Morris
1211 Ave. of the Americas
Suite 900
New York, NY 10036
(212) 840-6930

Kenmore, Inc.
555 Fifth Ave.
New York, NY
(212) 599-6161

Marbrook Personnel Agency
295 Madison Ave.
New York, NY 10017

Peak Consultants
353 Lexington Ave.
New York, NY 10016
(212) 889-3580

Snelling and Snelling
155 E. 55th St.
New York, NY 10022
(212) 759-5900

The Jones Group
111 Main St.
Hasbrouck Heights, NJ
(201) 288-5400

Womankind Executive Resources
310 E. 51st St.
New York, NY
(212) 758-3004

Training Conferences: 1984

People in training and development just love to confer with one another. During 1984, there will be a number of conferences at which training people will gather. Here are a few you might wish to explore further:

Association	When/Where
American Management Associations (AMA) (HR Conference) 135 W. 50th St. New York, NY 10010 Contact: June Baldino (212) 586-8100	March 19-21 New Westin Hotel Copley Place Boston, MA

American Society for Healthcare
   Education and Training (ASHET)
840 N. Lake Shore Dr.
Chicago, IL 60611
Contact: V. Brandon Melton
(312) 280-6111

June 3–7
Detroit Plaza
Detroit, MI

American Society for Training and
   Development (ASTD)
600 Maryland Ave. S.W.
Washington, D.C. 20024
Contact: Director of Conferences
(202) 484-2390

May 20–25
Dallas Convention Center
Dallas, TX

American Society for Personnel
   Administration (ASPA)
30 Park Dr.
Berea, OH 44017
Contact: Jan Csokmay
(212) 466-8137

June 27–29
Chicago, IL
Contact: Rubin Berry
(312) 782-3870

Association for Educational
   Communications and
   Technology (AECT)
1126 16th St. N.W.
Washington, D.C. 20036
Contact: Lois Freeland
(202) 466-4780

January 18–23
Dallas Convention Center
Dallas, TX

Travel

IN GENERAL

Have you ever stopped to consider how many of our favorite childhood stories feature travel to far-off lands? Dorothy's Oz and Alice's Wonderland provide backdrops to exciting adventures, colorful characters, and intriguing customs. Robert Louis Stevenson's *Treasure Island* offers the tropical allure and romance that Caribbean travel brochures can only faintly suggest. Peter Pan, in James Barrie's play, leads us to Never-Never Land, with its image of sunlit, eternal youth and happiness that every travel destination can only hope to portray.

Is it any wonder, then, that the travel industry holds fascination for many job-seekers and career-changers? Just as the poor fantasize about abounding riches, people who have done little traveling dream of what it must be like to see the Eifel Tower at dawn, to wade into the pristine, warm waves of the Caribbean, or to watch giraffes and elephants roam freely on the plains of Kenya.

Fantasies aside, the travel business is like most other businesses: Modest pay, an interesting array of colleagues and clients, lots of routine desk work, and the need to combine a head for details with managerial and interpersonal finesse. It would be impossible to describe all the types of employment in the travel business, which includes everything from airline ticket agent to cruise ship director, from pilot to skycap. We will therefore concentrate on a key figure in this glamorous and growing field: The travel agent.

Before we get into strategies for entering and succeeding in the world of travel, let's briefly survey the industry as a whole.

In 1980, there were approximately 52,000 people in the United States working as travel agents. Most worked for one of the more than 19,200 travel agencies throughout the 50 states. Branch offices accounted for only about 22 percent of these agencies. Almost 70 percent are single office locations. In other words, it's an entrepreneur's occupation.

In 1981, American travel agencies helped clients book more than $31 billion in travel revenues (compared with $19 billion in 1978). Today, 68 percent of the travel agencies are automated; by the end of 1982, almost 80 percent are expected to be computerized or to have signed up for automation. In travel, computerization is the wave of the present as well as the wave of the future.

In 1981, the average annual gross sales for a travel agency was $1,613,000. Agencies with bookings of more than $1 million account for 80 percent of the total amount booked through agencies. In other words, a few agencies are doing the largest volume. Of course, travel agents receive only a small percentage of the cost of each trip they sell—from 10 to 13 percent, depending on the nature of the transportation, wholesaler, hotel, and so on.

Most travel agents are paid employees, and the pay, in general, is low. Experience, sales ability, and the size and location of the agency determine the salary of a travel agent. Average salaries of a travel agent ranged from $9,500 to $18,000 a year in 1980. Salaried agents at large agencies may have standard benefits—pension plans, insurance coverage, paid vacations—that self-employed agents must provide for themselves.

Despite the hassles of running your own agency, it is probably the best bet for those who have initiative and who dream of autonomy, potentially high income, and freedom to travel. This chapter will point us in that enviable direction.

The notion of helping people with travel plans dates back to Queen Isabella's support of Christopher Columbus, but the field got its first real boost in the middle of the last century.

In 1841, a man named Thomas Cook talked some British

railway officials into running a special train to a sight-seeing spot. The railroad later agreed to run regular excursion trains if Cook filled them with passengers. That was the beginning of Thomas Cook and Sons, British travel agents, and an historic name worldwide. "Cook's tour"—an expression used by many who never heard of Thomas Cook the travel agent—has become synonymous with the phrase "grand tour": The type of first-class travel adventure that might be undertaken by an upper-class, recently graduated young man wishing to become "worldly."

Travel agents are not the only people who help ease one's passage. There are many jobs that will allow you to bask, however faintly, in the glow of travel. Airlines employ thousands of people who sell tickets, answer questions, help you on the plane, and find your baggage when it is lost. Steamship companies rely on stewards, pursers, cruise directors, bartenders, chefs, and entertainers as much as they do on captains and first mates. Railroads depend on ticket agents, porters, conductors and maintenance crews as well as on engineers. To sort out the possibilities, it helps to know where the travel industry is headed in the next few years.

One agent comments: "Cruises are coming back. Let's face it: airports are a disaster. If the flight isn't late, your luggage is. People want the hassle-free, detail-free experience of a cruise." Other agents point to the continued growth of "GIT's"—group inclusive tours—but warn that people who sponsor these trips (tour operators or wholesalers) will have to be clever to be able to keep up with fluctuations in the dollar and other currencies.

In general, travel agenting is expected to grow faster than other occupations, according to industry sources, even though the field is wide open to the problems inherent in economic fluctuations. There will probably be more charter flights in the future, as groups band together to bring down the cost of travel. The deregulation of the airline industry has paved the way for new opportunities and new headaches. Airlines are wooing travel agents with a barrage of "fam" trips (familiarization trips) to help keep agents abreast of new routes and new services. These familiarization trips are generally low cost, and some are free. One week, all expenses paid to Lisbon,

Madeira, and the Algarve could, on a "fam" trip, cost as little as $400 per agent.

There is definitely a trend toward more corporate accounts handled by travel agencies. Business travel has grown faster than pleasure travel. Conventions and meetings provide agents with high volume for booking many people at once. Of course, prices keep rising, causing business as well as pleasure travelers to reassess their plans. In 1982, the average cost of one night in an American hotel room was $55.90, according to Pannell, Kerr, Foster, a hotel accounting and consulting firm. That represents an 11 percent increase from the 1981 average of $50.35 a night. Of course, this doesn't reflect the cost of even moderate hotels in large cities.

It takes a special person to succeed as a travel agent, because you need to be aware of the trends and geography; you need to be an accountant, a promotion expert, and a ticket writer. The next section will discuss precisely what you will need to launch yourself in the field.

WHAT IT TAKES

Becoming a travel agent does not necessarily entail getting a college degree, but it doesn't hurt. A number of college courses would help prepare you for the challenges of working in the field:

- *Foreign languages*—You'll be booking trips to many foreign countries, so it's a great advantage to know at least the rudiments of French, Italian, Spanish, and German. Languages not only give you a taste of a country's culture, history, and customs, but they may also help give you more international clientele.
- *Speech*—Interpersonal communications is important because you're dealing with the public. Clients share a lot of intimate information with their travel agents, so you have to know how to make them feel comfortable. A good speaking voice and an ability to empathize with people will allow you to help your clients articulate their travel needs.

- *History*—A knowledge of history helps a travel agent to understand the landmarks of a society's development. Tidbits of history can also help agents to avoid booking a client into a location at a bad time. For example, France is noisy on Bastille Day, and shopping in London on Boxing Day is impossible because the city is shut down.
- *Archaeology*—A smattering of archaeology will help you serve travelers who literally want to dig into a nation's cultural past. Booking clients in Luxor or sending them to the ruins of Turkey or Pompeii calls for a modicum of knowledge as to what makes these areas special.
- *Religion*—It's essential to have more than just a passing knowledge of the religions of the world. Observing religious customs in Rome or Jerusalem or Tokyo is important. This knowledge also involves understanding what constitutes proper dress at the Vatican, proper etiquette at a mosque in Istanbul, or dietary laws in Tel Aviv.
- *Computer studies*—Travel agencies are becoming computerized at a rapid pace. Therefore, a course in computers will help you get oriented to the types of computers used in agencies. The most common computer, SABRE, is designed to issue tickets quickly.

Naturally, knowledge about almost any topic can help make you a more well-rounded travel agent. In our age of specialization, travelers now band together to explore their joint interests in wine, film, theater, rafting, antiques, or mountain climbing. The better informed you are as a travel agent, the more helpful you'll be in recommending particular destinations, hotels, and means of transportation.

And that's where some problems begin.

There are a lot of travel agents who have never roamed more than a few miles from their front door. Often, in a blind rush to enter the travel field, people forget to confront their own attitudes toward traveling. If you aren't comfortable away from home, how can you legitimately talk to your clients about back-packing on the Appalachian Trail or the food in Dubrovnik?

There are a number of travel schools—Frommer's, Sobelsohn's, Travel Institute's, ASTA's come to mind—but don't rely on these schools to give you a traveler's instinct. Veteran travel agents sometimes complain about the preparedness of the graduates of these schools. Their chief complaint is that the recent graduates lack the logical frame of mind and the travel savvy necessary to develop into fine agents. (Still, you can take the ASTA correspondence course, consisting of 15 lessons, a bibliography, and a final examination, which, if passed, certifies you as competent in the field.)

Here's how one travel agent characterized a graduate of a travel school who recently applied to her for a job: "This gal had paid more than $7,000 for her training! Imagine! No computer knowledge. Didn't even know what an OAG was [the OAG, Official Airline Guide, is a comprehensive time-table of all airline flights]. They taught her how to look at a map, answer a telephone. It was really a course in how to be a receptionist for a travel agency! She was ripped off. All she had to show for it was an official-looking diploma with several stamps and seals on it."

So, then, what is needed to succeed? A good sense of geography, for one thing. If it takes you more than a few seconds to locate Panama, Peking, or Paris, you may need a refresher course in geography. Also, you need the ability to listen to an airline representative quote five different fares for the same flight, and then know which is the best one for your client. And *best* isn't always *cheapest*. You may be able to save a client a few dollars on a trip from New York City to Los Angeles by first routing him to Boston. But time and convenience may also matter. Is your client is a paraplegic or someone who hates flying? Such a client is unlikely to want to change planes no matter how much money is involved.

It's become a cliché to say that you have to "like people" to be a travel agent, but you really do have to have an understanding of human foibles. You have to be the type of person who enjoys giving service. That sometimes means having a client remind you that she hates sitting near bathrooms on the plane or that she needs an aisle seat, a kosher meal, and a seat for her beagle. It means giving people instructions on what number tanning lotion to bring, telling them how warm the water is in Barbados, or trying not to giggle when a 90-year-old gentleman tries to find a polite way to say that he'll be traveling with his 19-year-old girlfriend.

Agents deal with *everyone:* Businesspeople on tight schedules, families, senior citizens, spouses cheating on their mates, and musicians booking first-class seats for their basses or saxophones. In addition to being babysitter, trip planner, and ticket booker, the travel agent must remind international travelers about passports, visas, certificates of vaccination, and recent exchange rates.

It will take a year or so just to learn the basics, conquer the mysteries of the Official Airline Guide, make friends with the sales reps at all the airlines, and have a sampling of reactions to your sales style. Pretty soon, though, your telephone conversations will take on the lilt of an experienced pro. "Hi . . . I made the reservation . . . This is what I have you on. . . . By the way, the round trip air fare is . . . You're on American flight number 602, leaving Atlanta at 9:03 A.M., arriving Dallas, 12:30 P.M. Remember that this fare is only good for week departures."

GETTING STARTED

Ask five agents how they got started, and each will tell you a different story. A few have attended travel schools, but many others started in the business by working with the airlines as reservation or ticket agents. Let's take a brief look at how this type of job helps you get oriented to travel.

Mostly, reservation and ticket agents deal with the public, usually from large central offices. They answer customer telephone inquiries on such subjects as arrivals, departures, fares, schedules, and the cities served by their airline. When weather conditions are bad and operations are interrupted, agents also serve as the main buffer between the airlines and their customers—at all hours. Their main function, however, is to book customer reservations. After finding out where a customer wants to go, when, and from which airport, agents check to find out if space is available. Each agent has access to a computer terminal and, by typing in instructions on the keyboard, can quickly obtain the necessary information on flight schedules and seat availability.

Ticket agents generally work a 40-hour week, but their schedules are sometimes irregular, since airlines operate flights at all hours. Agents with the least seniority often work nights and weekends. Holidays may also be hectic.

Reservations agents receive about a month of classroom instruction. They are taught company policy, government regulations that cover ticketing procedures, and other matters related to the airline. They learn to read schedules, calculate fares, and plan passenger itineraries—all of which are very helpful if the ticket agent later wishes to join a travel agency. They are also taught to use the computers to obtain information on schedules, seat availability, and to secure space for passengers.

The problem is that advancement opportunities for ticket agents are limited. However, entry-level jobs proliferate. In 1980, the airlines employed about 49,000 reservation agents and 37,000 ticket agents. If you've got a high school diploma, a good speaking voice, and some previous experience in dealing with the public, you're a good candidate for the job.

Being a reservation or ticket agent for a major airline is excellent preparation for work at a travel agency. It should be highlighted on your resumé. In a brief, descriptive paragraph following your job title and place of employment, you should succinctly summarize the skills you acquired, such as reading reference books, writing itineraries, figuring out logical geographical routing, and advising on access to airports, hotels, and motels.

For people who wish to take the sales route to being the owner of a travel agency, a different strategy is called for. You need an outgoing personality and the ability to introduce yourself to strangers. You need a good memory, the type that remembers the idiosyncracies of clients and their spouses. Your mind, in a sense, should be like a computer: Processing the particulars of each person's trip while devising new means for getting your business card into the hands of new prospects. If you hear of a group that's planning a trip, your mind will immediately focus on how you might have arranged the same trip. You, as a sales rep, are always interested in the many ways in which clients and travel agents begin their relationships.

No matter which route you take—sales, travel school, or the ticket desk at an airline—you must decide which path will allow you rapid growth. Unlike so many fields, travel does not have "hot" shops that any newcomer should strive to join. It makes little difference whether your first job is at Thomas Cook or your local neighborhood agency, since your real job is to learn everything you can learn. Therefore, seek an agency that is willing to show you the ropes, and not just have you write tickets and answer ringing telephones all day. There are a lot of skills you'll need before you can, one day, open your own agency; you need to find someone willing to share the managerial side of the business with you.

For example, the most important financial task of any travel agency owner is meeting air reports (the cash settlement of each airline ticket sold by an agent during a proscribed period). Since airline tickets must be paid for every 7 days (funds are automatically withdrawn from the agency's bank account), a travel agent must maintain a good cash flow. He cannot afford to "carry" a client for very long because he is responsible for the payment of every ticket sold. As a newcomer, you should look for an employer who will show you how to do an air report, and who is willing to share with you tips on how to keep your financial house in order.

Why is it that college graduates accept the low pay of a travel career, willingly answer telephones all day, and never say "boo"? Because agencies can tempt you with the lure of an occasional free trip. If you've never left your home state, a trip to the Caribbean or Russia or Bogota can look pretty good. However, you will not get to go anywhere your first year, since the governing bodies of travel agencies insist that a person put in a minimum of 1 year before his or her name can be added to the "list" of full-time agents.

If you are interested in becoming a travel agent so that you can take exotic trips, fine. But if that is your only reason, you've got the wrong attitude, particularly if you eventually want to own your own agency. An agent has to familiarize himself with various destinations so that he can sell those destinations to his clients. That's why they call travel agent trips "familiarization" trips instead of "vacations." When you travel free or at little cost, you are usually the guest of an airline, a wholesaler, a tourist board, or a cruise line. That means there is a *quid pro quo*. You get to travel and they get to give you a commercial about their hotels, their ships, their airline, or their cities. So, you may arrive in sunny Barcelona, but instead of taking in the museums or the shops or walking on the famous "Ramblas," you may be stuck in a hotel listening to blurbs about the glories of a hotel, its roominess, its access to tourist sights, and so on. There may be a free lunch, but you may have to sit through an hour-long presentation by a local travel agent "welcoming" you to town.

If you're in travel just to travel, you'll probably sit there bored and angry. But, if you're in travel because you recognize it is a pleasant *business*, you'll realize that business comes before pleasure. You may be dying for a dip in the Caribbean instead of whisking through hotel rooms and studying brochures, but as a professional, you'll know that the information gained will be useful for the rest of your life as a travel agent. You can't afford to simply "tune out."

The best attitude to have as you get started is one that emphasizes professionalism. You have to look beyond the low pay, the free trips, and the writing of tickets. You have to resist the urge to gab on and on with clients about the wonders of Paris or Brussels or Helsinki. Travel agents know that travel is a gabby business, but your job is to sell travel and not daydream about far-away places.

One more thing you should know before getting started. A lot of clients are abusive. You would think that people about to travel would be so filled with anticipation that they would be in a cooperative and "up" mood. Unfortunately, such is not the case. People compete for the best flights, the best tours, and the best accommodations with a sense of territoriality that would scare an anthropologist. One female agent speculated that so many women enter travel because, "Frankly, women will accept more abuse than men!" The point is that you should not accept any abuse from a client. Do your best, but don't feel that you must take personal responsibility if your client is bumped from a flight, or the flight is cancelled, or it rains all week in Guadalajara. You can only control so much, and then you have to toss the ball to the fates and the elements.

YOUR FIRST BIG BREAK

You've found your way into an agency, and that is your first big break. You're probably working in an urban center, where the best business opportunities exist. Or, you could be working in the suburbs, booking trips for neighbors as well as strangers. About one-half of all travel agencies are in cities, about one-third are in suburban areas, and about one-fifth are in small towns and rural areas.

Chances are you're in a small office. Roughly one-quarter of all travel agents are self-employed. Generally, these people gained experience and recognition in an established agency before going into business for themselves.

In small towns, one agency usually has the whole town sewn up (although competition is growing, and some medium-size towns have three or four travel agencies). Often, in this type of setting, everyone is on salary. But, there also are outside agents—independent salespeople, usually paid on a commission rather than a salary basis.

In major urban centers, it is not uncommon to work in an agency that uses outside agents. After all, a travel agency owner has little to lose by allowing a salesperson to work for his agency on commission. If you do find yourself at an agency that gives space to outside agents, see if you can become their buddy. If they're earning their living on their commissions, they must be doing something right. Treat them as mentors, and they may pass along valuable sales tips to you.

Once you've arrived at an agency, you should become a veritable sponge, soaking up all the information you can about ticketing, reference books, client idiosyncracies, and the vagaries of each airline, wholesaler, and hotel. This may seem like a tall order, but pretty soon you'll have a working knowledge of

New York, Washington, San Francisco, and Miami. Before much longer, you'll be familiar with the hotels of the Caribbean and Bermuda. Later on, you'll know the names of hotels in Europe and their American representatives and which airlines offer the best service or serve the best food between New York and Zurich, Athens, or Stockholm. It also helps to read the travel brochures that come into the office. Soon you'll know the details about tour leaders like Lindblad, Maupintour, or Four Winds. Your job is to become knowledgeable, to be the indispensable person when it comes to knowing all there is to know about particular destinations. Even experienced travel agents, however, may have no more than passing knowledge of hotels or airlines servicing destinations such as Johannesburg, Manila, or Bangkok, so don't feel that you have to be a walking encyclopedia.

Not every employer will encourage you in your pursuit of knowledge. Since most agencies are small, they tend to concentrate on day-to-day business. In other words, you may be hired to fill a slot; to write tickets, answer the telephone, or file correspondence. It's up to you to make the agency your own little university.

The best type of training is on-the-job training, but you must fight getting into a rut. After a while, you'll learn about air reports, sell a variety of destinations, get practice in using the OAG, and perhaps even get your agency to pay for your training on the SABRE computer. While you're salaried, you can learn, make mistakes, and gain ideas on how you would run your own shop.

The big break for a person hoping to land a spot as an outside agent is the moment he convinces an agency owner to give him a telephone and a desk. He may work out an arrangement to be paid a percentage of the commissions he brings in. In other words, if an outside agent sells $10,000 worth of business, the agency might, typically, receive 10 percent or $1,000. The outside agent who brought in the business might receive a minimum of 25 percent of $1,000 or $250. His commission will probably be commensurate with his volume.

Now, selling $10,000 a week is *very* difficult. It means that you're selling $500,000 worth of travel a year. Frankly, if you're selling that much travel you should be working for yourself and keeping all of the commissions. So, what you're doing at this point is serving an apprenticeship and building your client list. Therefore, don't expect to make too much money your first year.

You can make the most of this break by setting and meeting sales goals. You should also push your employer to give you up to 50 percent of the commissions if you really start to produce volume business. Then, your $10,000-a-week volume would be worth $500 to you. In addition, the agency should be picking up the tab for some of your secretarial and postage needs. Eventually, if you're productive enough, you should ask them to pick up postage and letterhead expenses for promotional mailings, help with making reservations, and give assistance in billing.

You should completely familiarize yourself with the structure of commissions, since agency earnings come mainly from commissions paid them by transportation carriers and tour operators with whom the agency books clients. Commissions vary widely. Agents may get 10 percent for domestic transportation bookings, 10 percent for domestic hotel reservations, 8 to 11 percent for international travel, 5 to 10 percent for foreign hotel reservations, an average of 10 percent for car rentals, and 10 to 11 percent for complete tour packages.

If you know a lot of people who love to go on cruises, you can do very well indeed. You can book a tour on the Queen Elizabeth II, a trip that may cost as much as $10,000, and pick up a $1,000 commission with one telephone call. (But don't count on this happening every day.) Since cruises do not involve connecting flights, itineraries, or the hassles of airports, they are the easiest, most paper-free way of making commissions; all agents love to book them.

WHAT TO SHOOT FOR

In travel, you're probably shooting to own your own travel agency. It's only by owning your own agency that you can collect 100 percent of the commissions on each sale you make.

Then, if you do manage to sell $500,000 worth of trips per year, you'll emerge with $50,000 or so in commissions. Of course, you'll have overhead, but that's all tax deductible.

Once you've made up your mind that you want your own agency, you should filter all of your new knowledge through that prism. When you hear of an agency going out of business, find out why. When you see students or businesspeople traveling in groups, try to discover who's handling the business. Also, you'll think of ways to promote your agency. In short, see what works and what doesn't—while you're still on salary.

As we have hinted, you should be shooting for corporate business, and you'll do best serving an industry you empathize with. Bon Bon Travel, a medium-size New York agency, specializes in handling entertainers and film crews. They understand the special needs of these people and are therefore able to make their traveling smooth and worry-free. Some agencies specialize in businesspeople who attend conferences. Others like to book sports figures, politicians, or import/export executives. The more you know about the goals of the people your firm services, the better you can serve them.

One problem that you'll face as you climb the ladder is that *everyone* knows *someone* who is a travel agent. Families have been torn asunder because one relative gave his business to his sister's daughter while another relative felt loyalty to his uncle's brother. In business, you have to care about the business of strangers, not relatives. One agent put it very well: "In travel, don't count on your friends to give you business or your relatives to bring you business; count on your *head* to bring you business and keep the business."

As you grow and gain confidence, keep your eye open for special opportunities. If Disney's new theme park is about to open, you might put a special tour together. If the tour is successful, you may well be able to put a second one together. Suddenly, the effort will pay off. People will come to you because they've heard that you're the person who can best accommodate groups at the Disney park. There's nothing wrong with specializing in a particular industry, type of tour, or section of the world.

While you're learning your trade, you'll get to know agents

at other firms. This is the time to start finding out who might be interested in forming their own agency. You can be qualifying people as you meet them as to who would make a compatible and productive partner. Bon Bon Travel started when two middle-aged women, both go-getters, decided that they could make more money by pooling their clients and founding their own agency.

As with most new businesses, travel agencies make very little money their first year. This is not just because the first year of any new business is a "shakedown cruise." Agencies cannot issue plane tickets until they gain formal approval from the various conferences that govern travel. Conferences are organizations of airlines, shiplines, or railroads. The International Air Transport Association, for example, is the conference of international airlines. To gain conference approval, an agency must be in operation, must be financially sound, and must employ at least one experienced travel agent.

Conference approval can take 3 to 6 months to obtain, so most self-employed agents make very little profit in their first year. Their income is generally limited to commissions from hotels and tour operators and to nominal fees for making complicated arrangements. For those considering starting their own agency, a working capital of between $37,000 and $50,000 will be needed to carry the agency through the first year.

There are no federal licensing requirements for travel agents. However, Rhode Island, Ohio, and Hawaii now have licensing requirements. In California, travel agents not approved by a conference are required to have a license.

WHEN YOU'VE MADE IT

"You'll know when you've made it to the top, because you won't feel any pressure from your bank," says one New York agent, smiling sweetly.

Another says: "You've made it when you have cash flow and good personnel—nothing else matters."

Obviously, other things occasionally do matter.

You first have to operate from a location you like. Some agents choose locations near clients they wish to reach. Others try to avoid a certain type of customer—street business.

"Street people who wander in and want to pick your brain for an hour before deciding whether to spend $69 to go to Jacksonville on People's Express—these kind of people you can live without," says a Philadelphia agent. Any agency that operates at street level has to expect browsers, shoppers, time wasters, and brochure collectors. You'll know you've made it in travel when you can spot them and get rid of them politely, but fast. Most of your good clients won't come off the street. They'll be referred to you by your satisfied customers.

Naturally, the first year is the hardest. That's the year for meeting Air Traffic Conference (ATC) and International Air Transport Association (IATA) requirements, getting appointed, gaining accreditation, putting up a bond (usually $10,000 for beginners), and meeting air reports before all your clients have paid you for their tickets. Since you must pay your air reports each week, every day that you extend credit to your clients costs you money.

Your volume is also a measure of your success. The minimum amount of volume you are required to have, by ATC edict, is $100,000. The average for travel agents is about $250,000 annually. You'll actually earn about 10 percent of that figure unless you do a lot of groups or conventions. If you do handle large groups, you can negotiate your own commissions with hotels, airlines, and even restaurants.

In travel, there are so many things to learn that it is only at great risk that we summarize a few of them. Every agent can give you a dozen stories of how things went wrong or trips they would like to forget. Here, however, are a few words of wisdom from several agents who have been in business for many years:

- "If you make a mistake, be the first one to tell your client." Take responsibility for any mistake you make. Admit that you booked someone on the wrong flight or airline or forgot to send the voucher (confirmation of paid reservations). If you let the client discover a mistake before you tell him about it, you've probably lost the account forever. However, if you are honest and can think of some way to salvage the trip, you may win your client back.

- "Don't let your ego get between you and your client." You're in a service business. The minute you stop being polite or start letting people know that they're bothering you or wasting your time, you can expect to lose a client.
- "When they tell you book them on Monday the third, make sure that Monday *is* the *third*." Travel is a Murphy's Law type of business. If something can go wrong, it probably will. You have to develop a fine talent for anticipating possible errors.
- "Make it easy for clients to come back to you." By knowing a client's idiosyncracies as well as what's available, you can make it easy for someone to reach out to you. If you remember that Ms. X hates sitting in the bulkhead and that Mr. Y likes cabins with portholes, you'll endear yourself to them. Similarly, when someone asks you about a special price, whether it's to Bhutan or Bogota, your job is to come up with the information. If you ask, "Where's Bogota?" or say, "Why would you want to go there?" you may be burning out. And that may mean it's time for you to take a vacation.

Starting a Travel Agency:
Here are a few things you'll need

Reference books	*Calendars*
Telephone	*Stamps, letterhead, envelopes*
Bond (based on the volume	*Desks*
your agency does annually)	*Postage scale*
Fire and theft insurance	*Plates from each airline*
Brochure racks	*Ticket stock*
Files	*Atlas*

After being appointed by ATC and IATA, each airline will make its own decision as to whether or not to issue a ticketing plate to represent them in ticket sales.

Major American Airlines

Air Florida
P. O. Box 592337
Miami, FL 33159
(305) 592-8550

Air New England
Logan International Airport
Boston, MA 02128
(617) 569-5650

American Airlines
P. O. Box 61616
Dallas/Ft. Worth Airport
Dallas, TX 75261
(214) 355-1234

Capitol International Airways
P. O. Box 325
Smyrna, TN 37167
(615) 459-2561

Delta Air Lines
Hartsfield Atlanta
International Airport
Atlanta, GA 30320
(404) 346-6011

Eastern Airline
International Airport
Miami, FL 33148
(305) 873-2211

Hawaiian Airlines
P. O. Box 30008
Honolulu, HI 96820
(808) 525-5511

National Airlines
P. O. Box 592055 AMF
Miami, FL 33159
(305) 874-4111

Northwest Orient
Minneapolis/St. Paul
   International Airport
St. Paul, MN 55111
(612) 726-2111

Ozark Airlines
P. O. Box 10007
International Airport
St. Louis, MO 63145
(314) 895-6600

Pan American World Airlines
Pan Am Building
New York, NY 10017
(212) 880-1234

Piedmont Airlines
Smith-Reynolds Airport
Winston-Salem, NC 27102

Republic Airlines
7500 Airline Dr.
Minneapolis, MN 55450
(612) 726-7411

Trans World Airlines
605 Third Ave.
New York, NY 10016
(212) 557-3000

United Airlines
P. O. Box 66100
Chicago, IL 60666
(312) 952-4000

US Air
Washington National Airport
Washington, D.C. 20001
(202) 783-4500

Western Airlines
P. O. Box 92005
World Way Postal Center
Los Angeles, CA 90009
(213) 646-2345

World Airways
Oakland International Airport
Oakland, CA 94614
(415) 577-2000

America's Top Car Rental Companies

Avis Rent-A-Car System
1114 Ave. of the Americas
New York, NY 10036
(212) 398-2900

Budget Rent-A-Car
35 E. Wacker Dr.
Chicago, IL 60601
(312) 580-5000

The Hertz Corp.
660 Madison Ave.
New York, NY 10021
(212) 980-2121

National Car Rental
5501 Green Valley Dr.
Minneapolis, MN 55431
(612) 830-2121

Schools for Travel Agents

The Sobelsohn School, 1540 Broadway, New York, NY 10036, (212) 575-1500. The Sobelsohn School offers a popular course to help people prepare for a career in travel. Subjects covered include:

How Travel is Sold
"Wholesalers" and Tour Operators
Opportunities in Travel—Airlines, Hotels, Steamships, and Cruise Line
     Companies, etc.
Terminology
Domestic Air Transportation and Fares
Routing, Scheduling, and Ticketing
"Worldwide" (International) Air Transportation and Fares
Hotel/Motel/Resort Accommodations Reservations Procedures—Do-
     mestic and Foreign
Rail and Bus Transportation
"Sightseeing" Trips
The Professional Representation of Hotels
Hotel/Motel Management
Procedures and Opportunities
World Wide Steamship Transportation and Cruises
Sea/Air/Sales/Promotion
Packages and Tours
Sales of Related Services
Automation and Data Processing.

The Sobelsohn School Travel Course consists of 15 sessions on consecutive Saturday mornings. Primary emphasis is on a practical approach to help you deal with real situations. All materials needed, as well as "field trips," are included in the tuition of $325. Free advisory placement assistance is available to all who enroll.

Travel Institute, Inc. has three locations:

910 Bergen Ave.
Jersey City, NJ 07055
(201) 420-7855

657 Main Ave.
Passaic, NJ 07055
(201) 773-0190

15 Park Row
New York, NY 10007
(212) 349-3331

Here are the topics covered in their travel course:

UNIT 1
Aircraft Identification
Airline Route Systems
Flight and Maintenance
    Schedules
Government Agencies
Industry Associations

UNIT 2
United States Geography
United States Time Zones
24 Hour Clock (Military Time)
International Time Zones
Worldwide Geography
Elapsed Flying Time

UNIT 3
Code Designators
  City/Airport Codes
    Carrier Codes
    Class of Service Codes
    Type of Trip Codes

UNIT 4
Official Airline Guide
    North American Edition
Official Airline Guide
    Worldwide Edition
Flight Itineraries

UNIT 5
Travel Industry Career
    Opportunities
        Airline Job Descriptions
        Travel Employee Benefits
        Travel Employee
        Responsibilities
Travel Agency Operations
    Types of Travel Agencies
    Travel Agents—Employees

UNIT 6
Steamship Travel
    Cruises
    Crossings
Official Steamship Guide
(OAG) Worldwide Cruise and
    Shipline Guide
Deck Plans

UNIT 7
Railroad Travel
    AMTRAK
    Types of Trains
    Accommodations
    Time-tables

Travel Institute graduates receive a Certificate of Completion upon graduation. Placement assistance is offered to graduates.

American Society of Travel Agents (ASTA), located in Washington, D.C. (202) 965-7520, offers a Travel Correspondence Course as well as a course given at headquarters. The goal of the intensive course offered at headquarters is to equip future travel agents with the basic skills and knowledge needed by public contact employees in travel agencies.

Here's what the ASTA course offers:

Topic	Hours
Selling and customer contact skills.	$5^3/_4$
Air Transportation (scheduling, ticketing, fare construction, air reports, etc.).	$24^1/_2$
Steamship/cruises (scheduling, rates, deck plans, etc.).	$4^1/_2$
Hotels and resorts (guides, rates, payment, vouchers, etc).	$2^1/_4$
Geography, as it applies to tourism.	$2^1/_2$
Car rental (rates, reservations).	1

Tours (foreign, domestic, independent, escorted).   3½

Classes meet 2 nights per week, Tuesday and Thursday from 7:00 to 9:30 P.M. for 12 weeks (24 class sessions). Actual instruction time is approximately 54 hours. Outside assignments should take an average of 4 hours per week. To qualify, applicants must hold a high school diploma (or equivalent) and have a strong command of the English language.

A Reader's Guide to Travel

General Interest Magazines

Frequent Flyer
888 Seventh Ave.
New York, NY 10019
(212) 977-8300

National Geographic
17th and M Sts.
Washington, D.C. 20036
(202) 857-7000

Signature
880 Third Ave.
New York, NY 10022
(212) 888-9450

The Sunday New York Times
  (Travel Section)
229 W. 43rd St.
New York, NY 10036
(212) 556-1234

Travel/Holiday
Travel Magazine, Inc.
51 Atlantic Ave.
Floral Park, NY 11001
(516) 352-9700

Travel & Leisure
1350 Ave. of the Americas
New York, NY 10019
(212) 399-2500

Travel: Trade Periodicals

Business Travel
Travel Trade Publications
605 Third Ave.
New York, NY 10016

Travel Industry Monthly
342 Madison Ave.
New York, NY
(212) 661-0656

Travel Trade: The Business Paper of
  The Travel Industry
Travel Trade Publishing Company
6 E. 46th St.
New York, NY 10017
(212) 883-1110

ASTA Travel News
488 Madison Ave.
Room 1110
New York, NY 10022
(212) 826-9464

Thomas Cook Business Traveler
352 Nassau St.
Princeton, NJ 08540

The Travel Agent
2 W. 46th St.
New York, NY 10036
(212) 575-9000

Travel

229

Travel Weekly
Ziff-Davis Co.
1 Park Ave.
New York, NY 10016
(212) 725-3600

Travel Guide
1085 Raritan Rd.
Clark, NJ 07066
(212) 964-3480

Travel Illustrated
2 Park Ave.
New York, NY 10016
(212) 340-9883

Travel Industry Personnel Directory
2 W. 46th St.
New York, NY 10036
(212) 575-9000

Travel Marketing
2 W. 46th St.
New York, NY 10036
(212) 575-9000

Travel North America
1 Park Ave.
New York, NY 10016
(212) 725-3600

*Travel & Tourism Executive
  Newsletter*
53 Church
Stonington, CT
(203) 535-3866

Travel Digest Magazine
342 Madison Ave.
New York, NY 10017
(212) 986-5700

Travelscene Magazine
888 Seventh Ave.
New York, NY 10019
(212) 977- 8337

Travel Management Daily
88 Seventh Ave.
New York, NY 10106
(212) 977-8312

Pacific Travel News
274 Brennan St.
San Francisco, CA 94107
(415) 397-0070

Travel Age East (West, Southeast)
888 Seventh Ave.
New York, NY 10019
(212) 977-8300

Travelage Midamerica
Official Airline Guides, Inc.
Suite 2416
Prudential Plaza
Chicago, IL 60601
(312) 861-0432

Travel Associations

American Society of Travel Agents
4400 MacArthur Blvd. N.W.
Washington, D.C. 20007
(202) 965-7520

Association of Retail Travel Agents
8 Maple St.
Croton-on-Hudson, NY 10520
(914) 271-9000

Institute of Certified Travel Agents
148 Linden St.
Wellesley, MA 02181
(617) 237-0280

Travel Industry Association of America
1899 L St., N.W.
Washington, D.C. 20036
(202) 293-1433

WEXITA (Women Executive's International Tourism Association)
1790 Broadway
Suite 711
New York, NY 10019
(212) 265-7650

Ships That Pass in the Night:
America's Popular Cruise Lines

Holland American Cruises
2 Penn Plaza
New York, NY 10001
(212) 290-0100

Cunard Lines
555 Fifth Ave.
New York, NY
(212) 880-7500

Hellenic Mediterranean Line
200 Park Ave.
New York, NY 10017
(212) 697-4220

Lindblad
8 Wright St.
Westport, CT 06880
(203) 226-8531

Costa
733 Third Ave.
New York, NY 10017
(212) 682-7520

Royal Caribbean Cruise Lines
903 South America Way
Miami, FL 33132
(305) 379-2601

Norwegian Caribbean Lines
1 Biscayne Tower
Miami, FL 33131
(305) 358-6670

United States Cruise Lines
2200 Sixth Ave.
Seattle, WA 98121
(206) 624-1926

Carnival Cruise Lines
3915 Biscayne Blvd.
Miami, FL 33137

Paquet Cruises, Inc.
1370 Ave. of the Americas
New York, NY 10019
(212) 757-9050

Royal Viking
1 Embarcadero Center
San Francisco, CA 94111
(415) 366-2223

Bahama Cruise Lines
61 Broadway
New York, NY 10006
(212) 785-1090

Princess Cruises
2029 Century Park East
Los Angeles, CA 90067
(213) 553-1770

Sitmar Cruises
80100 Santa Monica Blvd.
Los Angeles, CA 90067
(213) 553-1666

Home Lines Cruises, Inc.
1 World Trade Center
New York, NY
(212) 432-1414

Travel: Major Reference Books

Official Steamship Guide International. Published by Thomas Guides, Inc., Publishers, 111 Cherry St., New Canaan, CT 06840, (203) 966-9784. Contains travel information on passenger vessels throughout the world, including ferry and freighter traffic.

The Cruise and Shipline Guide. Official Airline Guides, Publishers. Gives cruise information and ship profiles, maps of sea routes, port diagrams.

OAG (Official Airline Guide). Information about direct flights, connecting flights, departure and arrival time, type of aircraft, meal service, stops en route, connecting times at airports. Fares are not updated. You still have to call airlines for fares.

Office Hotel and Resort Guide (OHRG). A guide to the hotels and resorts of the United States, Europe, and the rest of the world. Updated several times a year.

Hotel and Travel Index. 1 Park Ave., New York, NY 10016, (212) 725-3833. Published four times a year. Lists predominently American hotels and those in the Caribbean.

OAG Travel Planner. 40 Gramercy Park North, New York, NY 10010, (212) 473-4688. Published four times a year. Tells nearest airport to cities; how to get from airport to city. Alphabetical by city. Gives locations of all colleges and military installations.

JAX FAX Travel Marketing. Listing of discounts, charters, tours. Put out once a month by *Travel Marketing* magazine.

Footnotes

ADVERTISING

1. S. Watson Dunn and Arnold M. Barban, *Advertising: Its Role in Modern Marketing* (Hinsdale, IL: The Dryden Press, 1978), p. 319.
2. Oliver H. Darling, "Beware of the Creative Fog," *Magazine Age*, June, 1981.
3. For his work on Federal Express, MCI, Volvo, and other national accounts, Amil Gargano was elected to the Art Director's Hall of Fame.
4. "Job Hunting," *Advertising Age*, Section 2, February 23, 1981, p. S–6.
5. Mary Alice Kellogg, "Rules of the Recruitment Game," *Adweek*, July 26, 1982, p. S.S. 20.
6. "Job Hunting," *Advertising Age*, Section 2, February 23, 1981, p. S–4.
7. "Job Hunting," *Advertising Age*, Section 2, February 23, 1981, p. S–4.
8. Check Leo Rosten's *The Joys of Yiddish* for a definition.
9. David Ogilvy, *Confessions of an Advertising Man* (New York, NY: Atheneum, 1980), p. 142.
10. From *Adweek 1982 Agency Directory*, Eastern Edition.
11. Mary Alice Kellogg, "Rules of the Recruitment Game—for Buyers and Sellers," *Adweek*, 1982 Salary Survey, July 26, 1982, p. S.S.16.

BIOTECHNOLOGY

1. Tamar Lewin, "The Patent Race in Gene-Splicing," *The New York Times*, August 29, 1982, p. 4F.
2. *High Technology*, Special Advertising Supplement on Illinois, May/June, 1982, p. 19.
3. "1983 Employment Outlook," *Chemical & Engineering News*, Vol. 60, No. 42, October 18, 1982, pp. 37–61.
4. Nicholas Basta, "Down-the-Road Comer: A Career in Biotechnology," *Graduating Engineer*, September, 1982, pp. 33–37.
5. "I Know You're a Chemist, But What Do You Do?," *American Chemical Society Student Affiliate Newsletter*, Vol. 15, No. 1, Fall, 1982, pp. 6–15.
6. Ted Howard and Jeremy Rifkin, *Who Should Play God?* (New York, NY: Dell, 1977), p. 191.
7. Eugene Raudsepp, "Company Image is Top Concern of Engineering Grads," *New Equipment Digest*, December, 1982, pp. 12–12A.
8. Irene R. Miller, "CPI Mapping Big Plans for Genetic Engineering," *Chemical Engineering*, November 3, 1980, pp. 40–43.

CABLE TV

1. Marianne Costantinou, "Cable TV: Room on the Ground Floor," *The New York Times*.
2. *MCNT Newsletter*, December, 1981.
3. Thomas E. Wheeler, "The Cable Explosion," *The Washington Post*, September 16, 1982, Job Supplement.
4. *MCNT Newsletter*, April/May, 1982.
5. Tony Schwartz, "Cable TV Programmers Find Problems Amid Fast Growth," *The New York Times*, September 28, 1982, pp. Al and C22.

6. B. G. Yovovich, " 'Age of Cable' Dawning on Impatient World," *Advertising Age,* April 26, 1982, pp. M11–12.

COMPUTERS

1. From an article in *Executive Fitness Newsletter,* August 21, 1982, Vol. 13, No. 17.
2. Alexander L. Taylor III, "How Programmers Get Rich," *Time,* December 13, 1982, p. 56.
3. William D. Marbach, "A Byte—And a Bonanza," *Newsweek,* October 4, 1982, p. 75.

CONSULTING

1. By "Bertie Ramsbottom." Reprinted with the permission of the author, Ralph Windle. © Ralph Windle.

PUBLIC RELATIONS

1. Everything in a newspaper, magazine, radio broadcast or TV show that is *not* advertising (e.g. paid messages) is considered "editorial."
2. The Public Relations Society of America's brochure, *Public Relations Sequences and Courses in United States Colleges and Universities (1979),* lists many courses on public relations given through schools of journalism.
3. *East Side TV Shopper,* January 8–14, 1983.

TELECOMMUNICATIONS

1. Brad Schutz, "Data Communications: Out of This World," *Graduating Engineer,* February, 1983, pp. 35–57.
2. Doran Howitt, "Smart Talk on the Phone," *Inc.,* September, 1982, pp. 61–68.
3. Larry A. Arredondo, *Telecommunications Management for Business & Government* (New York, NY: Telecom Library Inc., 1980), p. 2.
4. "Rare Breed," *Telephone Angles,* September, 1982, Vol. 5, No. 9.
5. Stephen H. Confer, "Apprenticeship: An Old Training Idea Whose Time May Have Come Again," *Telephony,* April 19, 1982, pp. 34–44.
6. John Greenwald, "New Bells Are Ringing," *Time,* October 25, 1982, p. 67.
7. Alexander L. Taylor III, "Dial 'M' for Money," *Time,* January 31, 1983, pp. 52–53.
8. Brad Schutz, "Data Communications: Out of This World," *Graduating Engineer,* February, 1983, pp. 35–37.
9. "Communications Management," *Telephone Angles,* October 1, 1981, Vol. 2, No. 10.
10. "Questions and Answers," *Telephone Angles,* January, 1982, Vol. 4, No. 1.
11. From *Telefuture,* a pamphlet published by the North American Telephone Association, Washington, D.C.
12. James Martin, *Telematic Society: A Challenge for Tomorrow* (Englewood Cliffs, NJ: Prentice-Hall, Inc., 1981).
13. Sources: *Telecommunications Management for Business & Government* by Larry A. Arredondo (New York, NY: Telecom Library); Jane M. Clemmensen, "Telecommunications Curricula," *Telecommunications,* September, 1982, p. 99; and Gene C. Edwards, "Technical Training to Meet Changing Industry Needs," *Telephone Engineer & Management Directory,* 1982/83, pp. 551–552.

TRAINING AND DEVELOPMENT

1. For more information, write DDI, Development Dimensions Plaza, 1225 Washington Pike, P.O. Box 13379, Pittsburgh, PA 15243 (412) 257-0600.

Index

ABOUT THE AUTHORS

Robert W. Bly is an independent copywriter/consultant specializing in industrial advertising and promotion. He is the author of *A Dictionary of Computer Words*.

Gary Blake is director of The Communication Workshop, a New York City communications consulting firm helping management improve business and technical writing skills. His clients include major insurance companies, manufacturers, and financial institutions. Mr. Blake is the author of *The Status Book*.

Together, Robert W. Bly and Gary Blake have written *How To Promote Your Own Business* (New American Library) and *Technical Writing: Structure, Standards, and Style* (McGraw-Hill).